AF471211

ROAD TO 2012

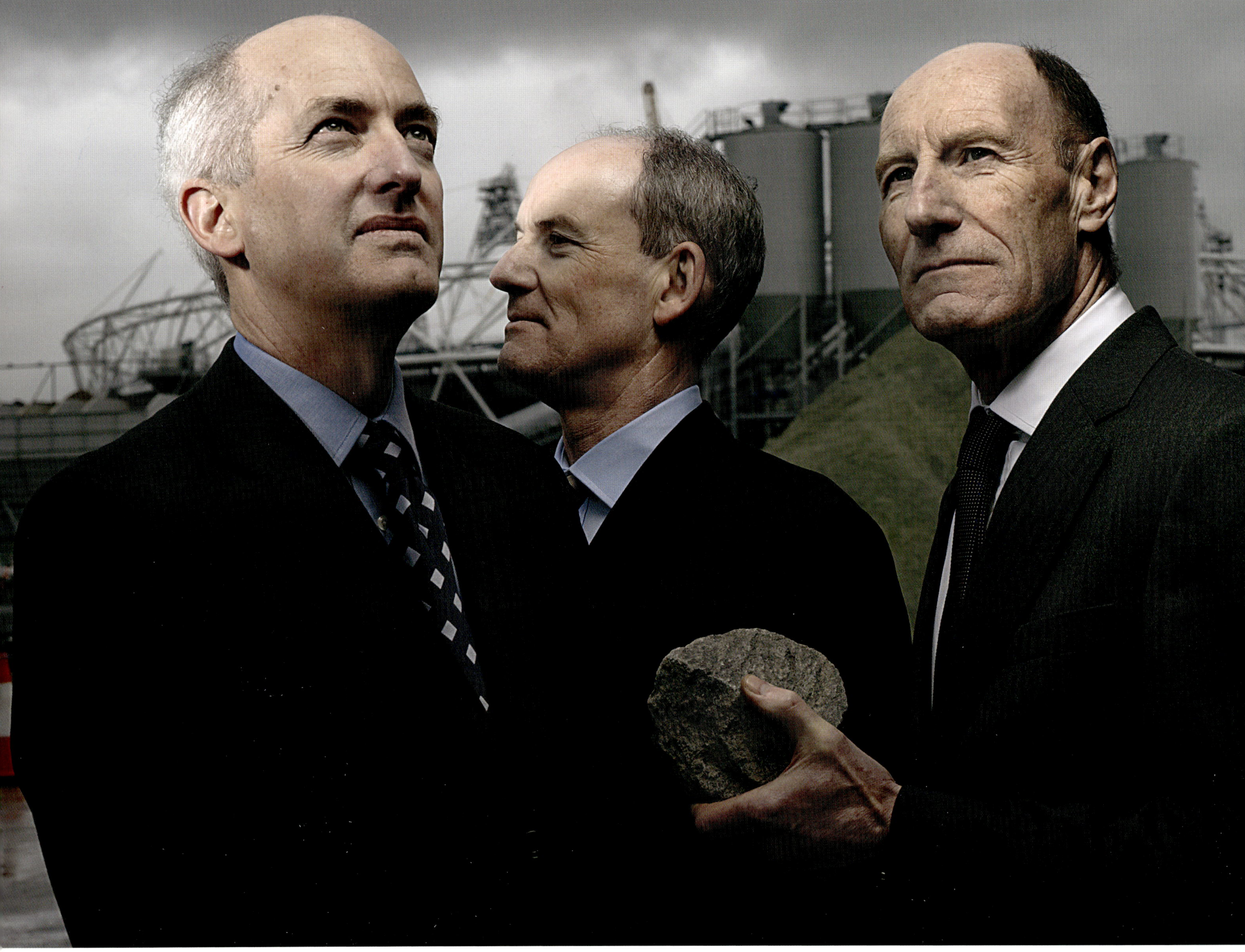

ROAD TO 2012

WITH AN INTRODUCTION BY SEBASTIAN COE KBE

NATIONAL PORTRAIT GALLERY, LONDON

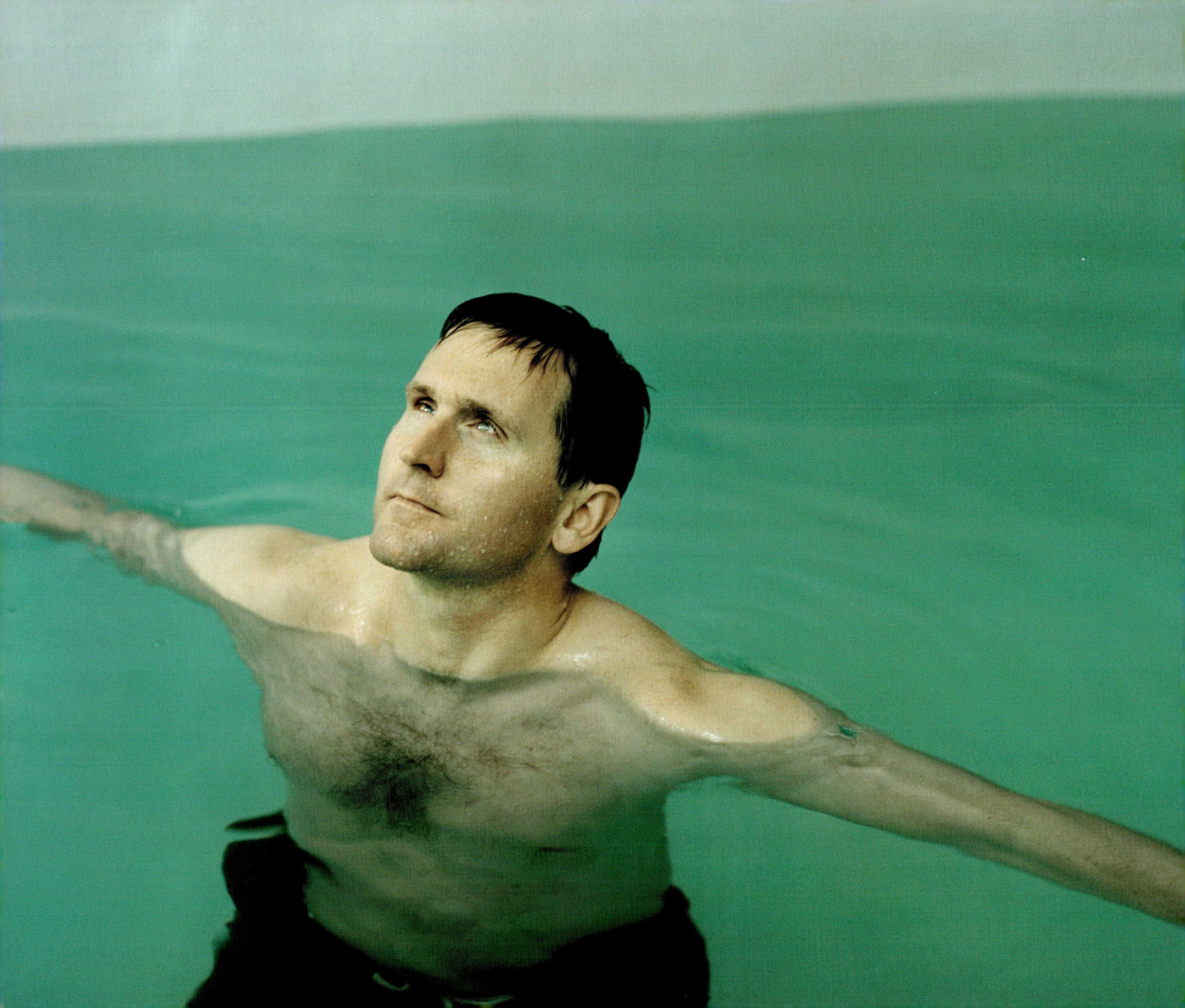

CONTENTS

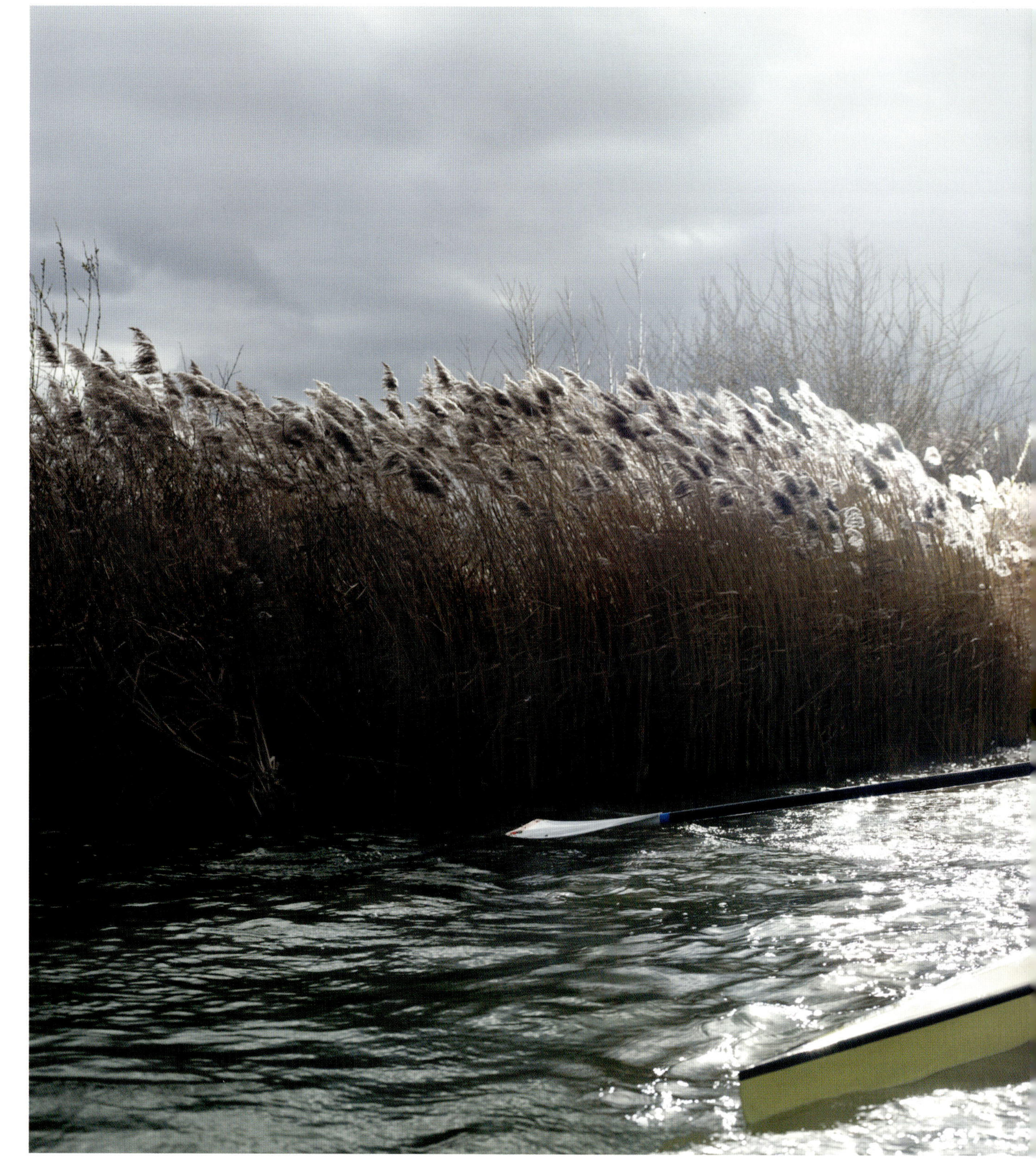

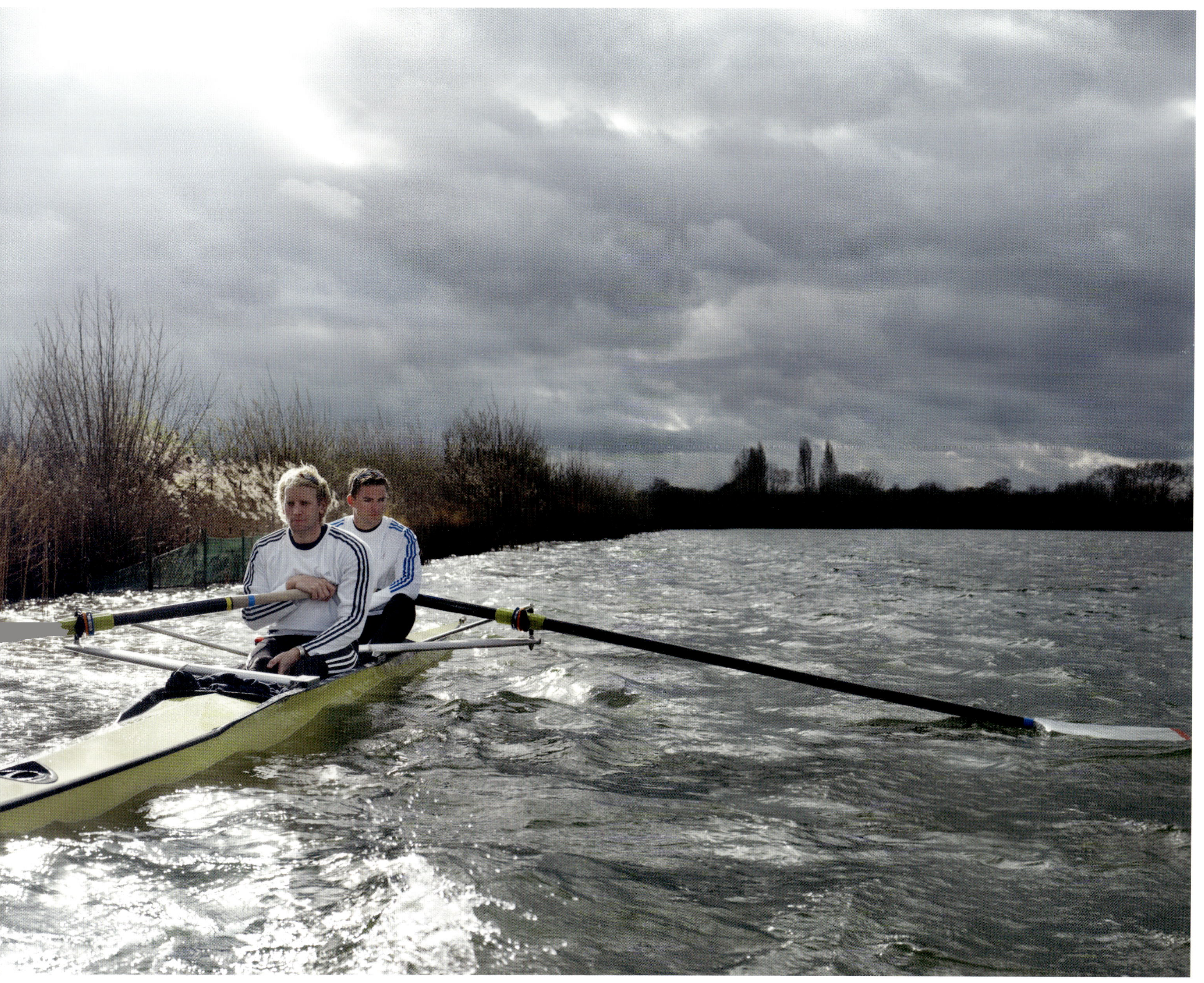

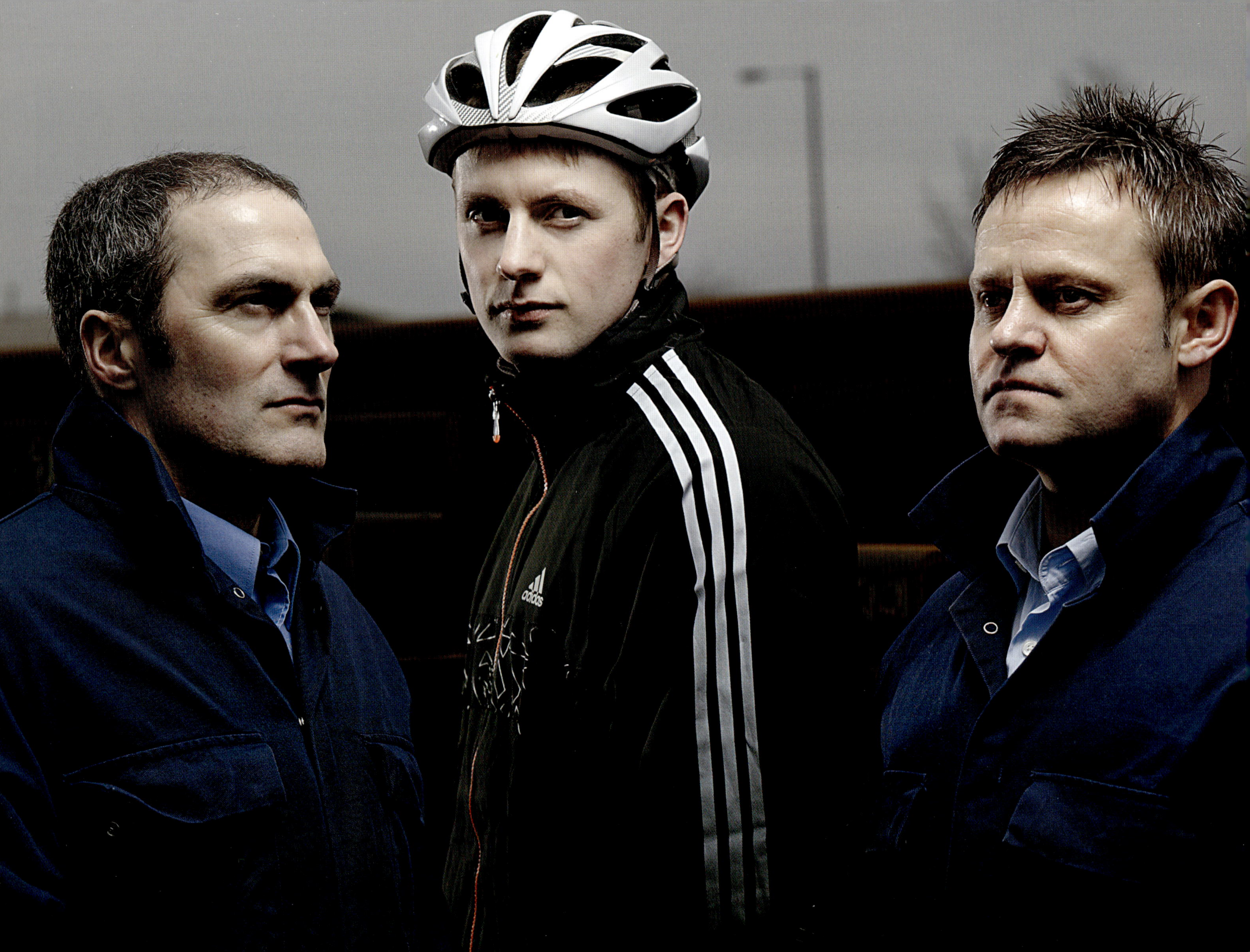
adidas

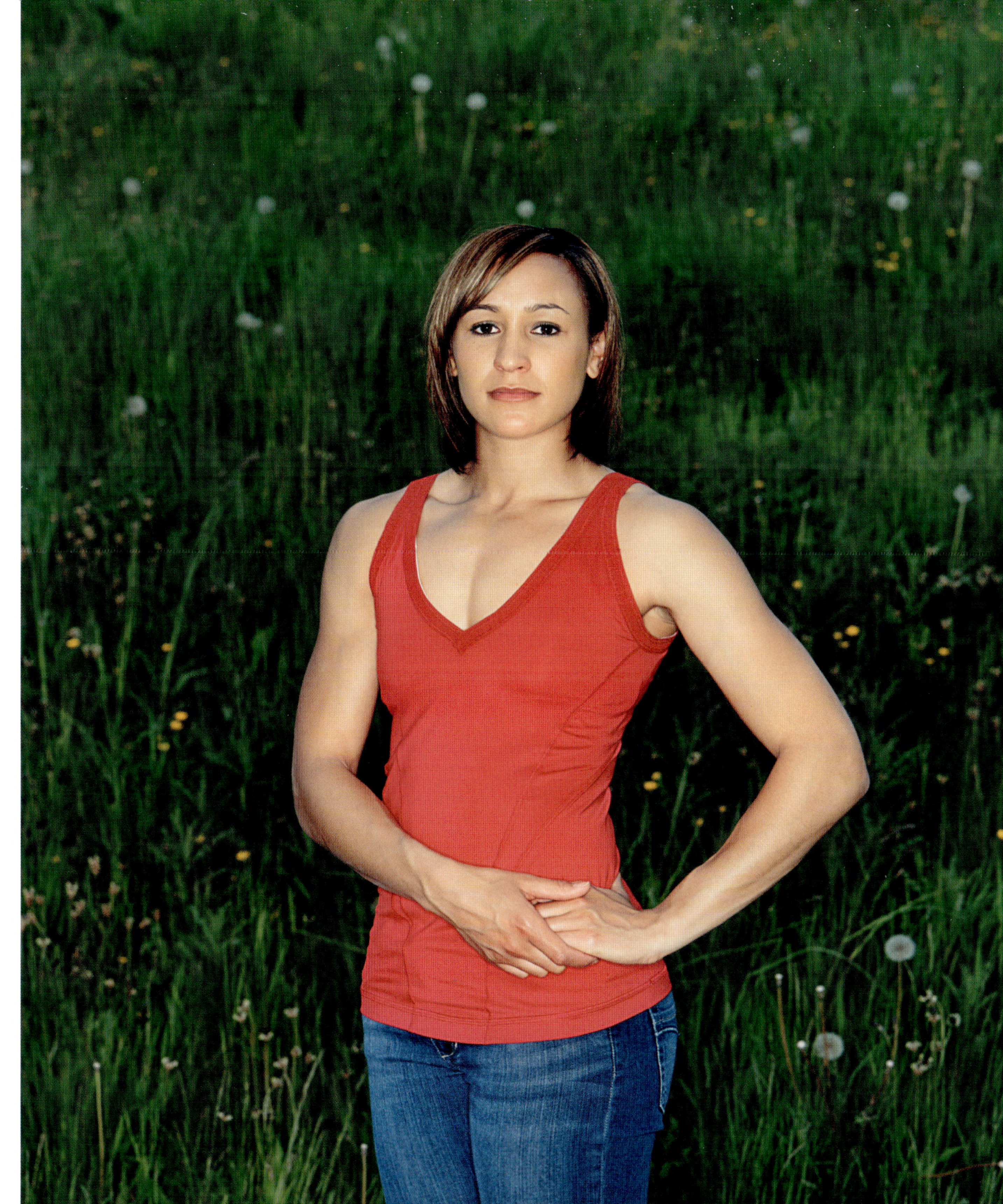

DIRECTOR'S FOREWORD

Art and sport have a long-standing relationship going back to ancient Greece. Although intense physical skill and competitiveness may sit somewhat uneasily with artistic finesse and intellectual complexity, Pierre de Coubertin, as leader of the modern Olympic movement, aimed to create a more holistic view of sport and the arts. He wanted to celebrate the best international co-operation for the creative arts as well as for the competitive sports. For London 2012 it was an essential part of the bid: to promote an excellent and diverse cultural programme, open to all.

For the National Portrait Gallery, the *Road to 2012* project is an essential element of the Olympic and Paralympic Games. Its aim is to celebrate exceptional British sportspeople, and some of the crucial figures working behind the scenes – from coaches and managers to soil engineers, architects and the producers of the key ceremonies. These are outstanding photographic portraits that convey the determination, skill and mental prowess of those working at the highest level of international sport. The project became a reality through the generous support of BT, and the close involvement of the London Organising Committee of the Olympic and Paralympic Games (LOCOG).

The Gallery has a history of commissioning new portraits, but a project on this scale, involving eight photographers, over a hundred sitters and displays across three summer seasons, is very special. Our thinking always included a community programme in east London, a city-centre tour, this publication and a special section of the Gallery's website featuring stories and interviews alongside the images themselves. When the Games are over these portraits and materials will become part of the legacy: a special part of the Gallery's Collection.

I am hugely grateful to photographers Anderson & Low, Jillian Edelstein, Katherine Green, Brian Griffin, Emma Hardy, Nadav Kander, Finlay MacKay and Bettina von Zwehl, who have shown exceptional commitment to creating these portraits, often in considerably constrained circumstances. I thank all the sitters, and their families, agents and supporters who have helped throughout the project. I am particularly grateful to Anne Braybon for her outstanding management of the commissions, and for the leadership work of Pim Baxter and Liz Smith, with the close support of Naomi Conway, Jane Chambers and Helen Whiteoak, as well as Austin Barlow, Rob Carr-Archer, Angharad Davies, Laura Down, Andrea Easey, Neil Evans, Ian Gardner, Matthew Lewis, Ruth Müller-Wirth, Terence Pepper, Lucy Ribeiro, Sarah Ruddick, Christopher Tinker, Sarah Tinsley, Denise Vogelsang, Ulrike Wachsmann and the many others at the Gallery who have made the project possible. I also offer my thanks to writer Richard McClure and designers Smith & Gilmour for their excellent work on this publication.

The partnership with BT has involved many colleagues, and I am particularly grateful to Suzi Williams, Group Marketing and Brand Director, as well as Suzy Christopher, David Mercer and Lee Hamill. I should also like to thank Bill Morris, Fran Hegyi, Will Hutchinson, Laia Gasch and Paul Woodmansey at LOCOG, as well as other colleagues who have supported the project.

The *Road to 2012* project may have been ambitious and complex, but it exemplifies the strength of photographic portraiture in Britain and offers a special legacy for future generations.

Sandy Nairne

SANDY NAIRNE
DIRECTOR, NATIONAL PORTRAIT GALLERY

SPONSOR'S FOREWORD

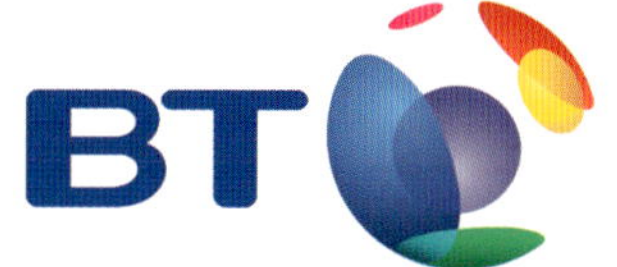

National Portrait Gallery + BT ROAD TO 2012

BT is very proud to be the official communications services partner of the London 2012 Olympic and Paralympic Games. We're responsible for providing the communications services to all the Games-time venues, and we'll help to communicate the sporting action to a global audience.

However, London 2012 is about more than sport: it's also about celebrating the people who will collectively make the Games happen. To this end, we're proud to be supporting the Cultural Olympiad as a Premier Partner of the London 2012 Festival.

Our partnership with the National Portrait Gallery is a major part of our cultural involvement. We began our journey with the Gallery back in 2009, setting out to create one hundred new photographic portraits that would tell the stories of the people behind the London 2012 Olympic Games from the bid phase, via the construction of the venues right through to the delivery of the Games this summer, as well as the stories of the athletes aiming for a place in the British Olympic and Paralympic teams. The first exhibition of portraits, *Road to 2012: Setting Out*, went on display over the summer of 2010, and was followed by *Road to 2012: Changing Pace* in 2011. This year's exhibition at the Gallery, *Road to 2012: Aiming High*, will be a fantastic finale to our partnership, bringing together portraits from previous years as well as unveiling new photographs. Some of the portraits have also been on the road this year, touring as a free outdoor exhibition to some of Britain's busiest cities. Thirty printed panels of photographs went on display in Cardiff before moving to Edinburgh and then to Birmingham. Importantly, the National Portrait Gallery/BT *Road to 2012* project will be a lasting record of the story of the London 2012 Games for generations to come, and we're proud to have played our part in creating this cultural legacy.

SIR MICHAEL RAKE
CHAIRMAN, BT GROUP PLC

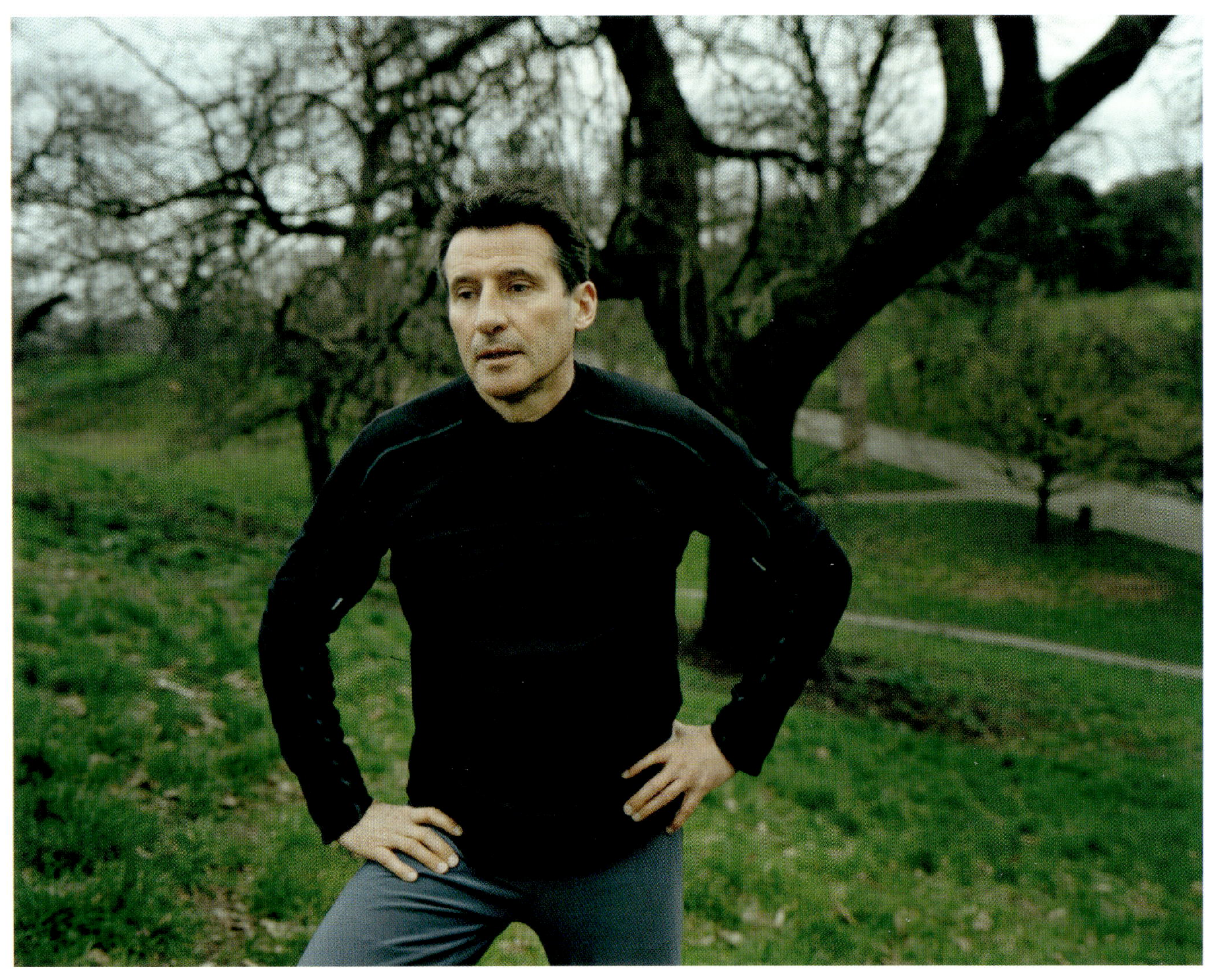

Sebastian Coe, by Emma Hardy

INTRODUCTION

The city of London has a proud Olympic history, having first hosted the Games in 1908, the fourth of the modern era, and later the so-called 'Austerity Games' of 1948, which were held in the wake of the Second World War and included the very first Paralympics. I am enormously proud to have been part of the team that has brought the Games back to London for an unequalled third time in 2012. Since 2005, when London's successful bid to host the Olympic and Paralympic Games was announced, a huge number of dedicated, motivated experts have been working tirelessly to fulfil that dream, and it gives me great pleasure to see the invaluable contributions of so many people recorded in this book.

In the 1908 Olympic Games, 2,008 athletes competed; in 2012, 10,500 athletes will take part. The scale of the London 2012 Games is unprecedented, as is the National Portrait Gallery/BT *Road to 2012* project, which documents both the athletes taking part and the people working behind the scenes to stage the Games. The undisputed stars of the Olympic and Paralympic Games are the world-class athletes who will compete in front of a global audience of four billion people this year, but *Road to 2012* is a unique three-year project that also recognises the untold stories and contributions of the people behind an event of this extraordinary magnitude. It tells the story of the 2012 Games through the people who have made them happen, from those behind the bid, who marshalled political support, to those responsible for the smooth running of London's transport network during the Games.

The Olympic and Paralympic Games experience extends to the hugely varied Cultural Olympiad programme, which culminates in 2012 and has facilitated and encouraged creative and artistic participation in events across the UK. The *Road to 2012* project brings together fine-art photography and sport, and I am extremely grateful to the high-profile, internationally renowned photographers who have accepted the National Portrait Gallery's commission to capture the inclusive spirit of the 2012 Olympic and Paralympic Games so perfectly for the displays, the national display tour and for this book.

I firmly believe that the 2012 Games will have a positive, long-term effect on the lives of people in London and across the UK, by means of regeneration and a legacy of world-class sports facilities that will continue to inspire sporting participation long after the closing ceremonies. BT's support of, and commitment to, the *Road to 2012* project over the last three years reflects this forward-thinking, long-term investment in a project that, thanks to the National Portrait Gallery, will provide a valuable resource for future generations.

SEBASTIAN COE KBE
LOCOG CHAIR
LONDON, MARCH 2012

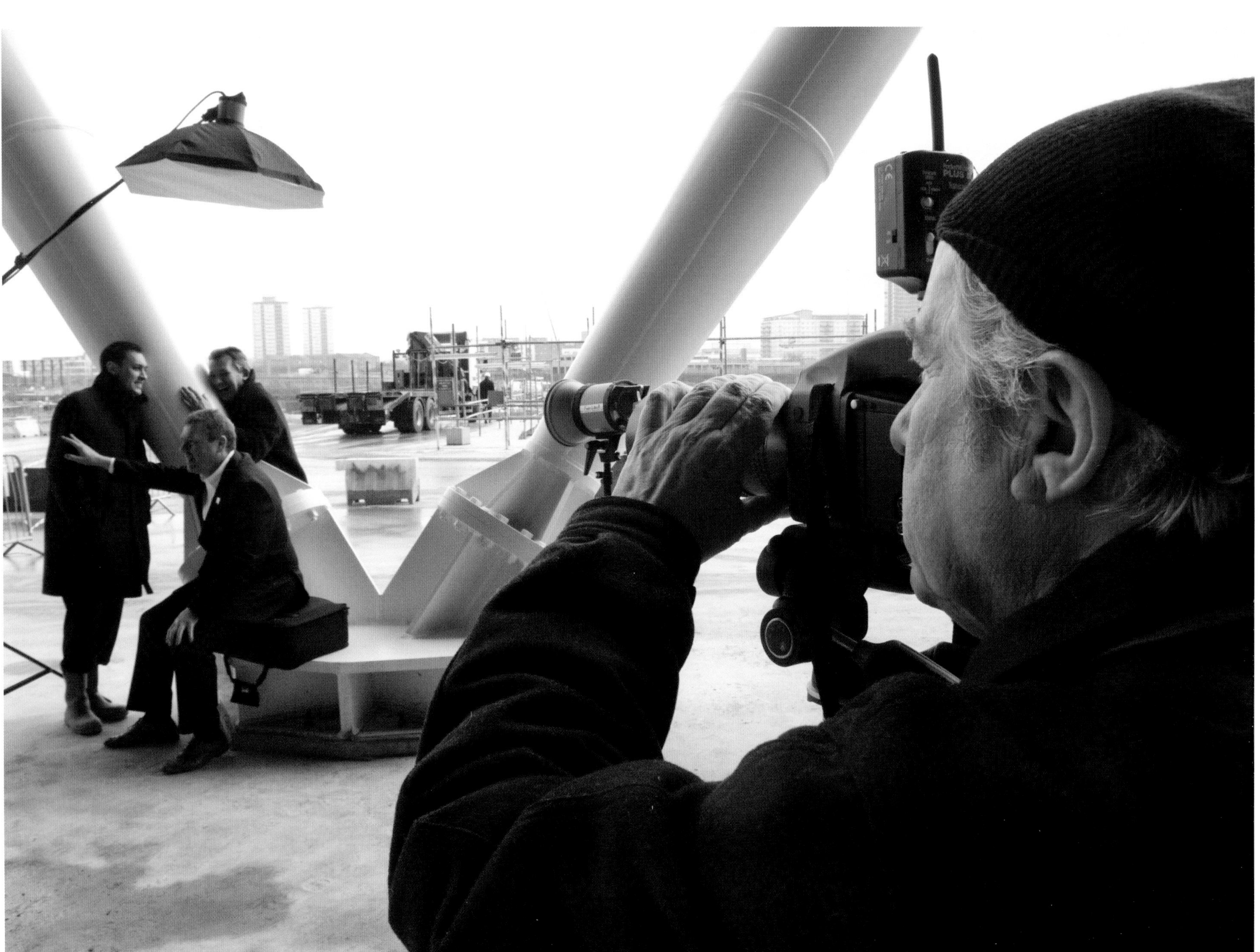

THE PROJECT

The thinking began on 6 July 2005, the day that Jacques Rogge, president of the International Olympic Committee, announced that London had won the honour of hosting the 2012 Olympic and Paralympic Games. As Sebastian Coe, the bid leader, celebrated with members of the winning London team at the IOC session in Singapore, the jubilant scenes were echoed in Trafalgar Square, where thousands of people had gathered to watch events unfold on a live screen. On hearing the decision, the crowd's exuberant response was audible in the National Portrait Gallery.

The success over long-term favourite Paris in the nail-biting final ballot meant that the Olympics would be coming back to Britain for the first time since 1948, making London the only city to host the modern Games on three occasions. It was, in the words of then Prime Minister Tony Blair, 'a momentous day' for the country.

Within weeks, preparations were in full swing. By October, the London Organising Committee of the Olympic Games and Paralympic Games (LOCOG) was sitting for its first board meeting, chaired by Coe. Soon afterwards, the National Portrait Gallery began drawing up plans to provide a unique and lasting record of the build-up to the Games.

In October 2009, to mark one thousand days until the opening ceremony, Coe and fellow Olympic gold medallist Dame Kelly Holmes were present at the Gallery for the announcement of the National Portrait Gallery/BT *Road to 2012* project. Conceived as part of the Cultural Olympiad, *Road to 2012* was launched as a three-year partnership between the Gallery and BT, the official communications services partner for London 2012, to create more than a hundred specially commissioned photographic portraits that would serve as a record of the London Olympic and Paralympic Games. It was to be the largest photographic commission that the National Portrait Gallery has ever undertaken.

'From the start, we decided to take a broad view,' says Sandy Nairne, Director of the National Portrait Gallery. 'As well as celebrating sport at the highest level, the project would portray some of the myriad roles crucial to staging the Games, in areas such as transport, engineering, design, construction, food, marketing, ceremonies, music and art.'

The title of *Road to 2012*, agreed early in the planning stages, determined the structure of the project, with the commission divided into distinct phases of work entitled *Setting Out*, *Changing Pace* and *Aiming High*. 'We conceived the project as a chronology that the audience would follow,' says commissions manager Anne Braybon. 'It was a journey along a road, with a beginning, a middle and an end.'

BT came on board as the sponsor partner in 2009. 'BT has been totally committed and enthusiastic about the project from the outset,' says Pim Baxter, Director of Development at the National Portrait Gallery. 'It has been a very productive and creative relationship.'

For each phase of *Road to 2012*, two photographers were commissioned to depict the parallel journeys of the athletes and the facilitators. The brief was simple: a compelling portrait made on location. The project team would select the sitters then work with the photographers to find a place that was relevant to the sitter's role in 2012. It was a brief that would eventually send the photographers the length and breadth of the country, from Aberdeenshire to Devon, taking in moors, beaches, forests, suburban streets, pubs, museums, state-of-the-art training facilities and the ever-changing backdrop of the Olympic Park.

Inspirational personal stories played a critical part in the selection of sitters. 'We looked for individual narratives that contributed to our overarching theme – the extraordinary, collective achievement that London 2012 represents,' says Braybon. 'We wanted to capture the imagination of a broad audience.'

Those narratives included a number of remarkable family relationships. Among the chosen sitters were Anna Sharkey and her brother Michael, both of whom have a congenital eye condition that causes partial sightedness, and are members of the Paralympic goalball squad. Commonwealth 1500m champion Lisa Dobriskey was selected to be photographed alongside her father Mike, an expert in

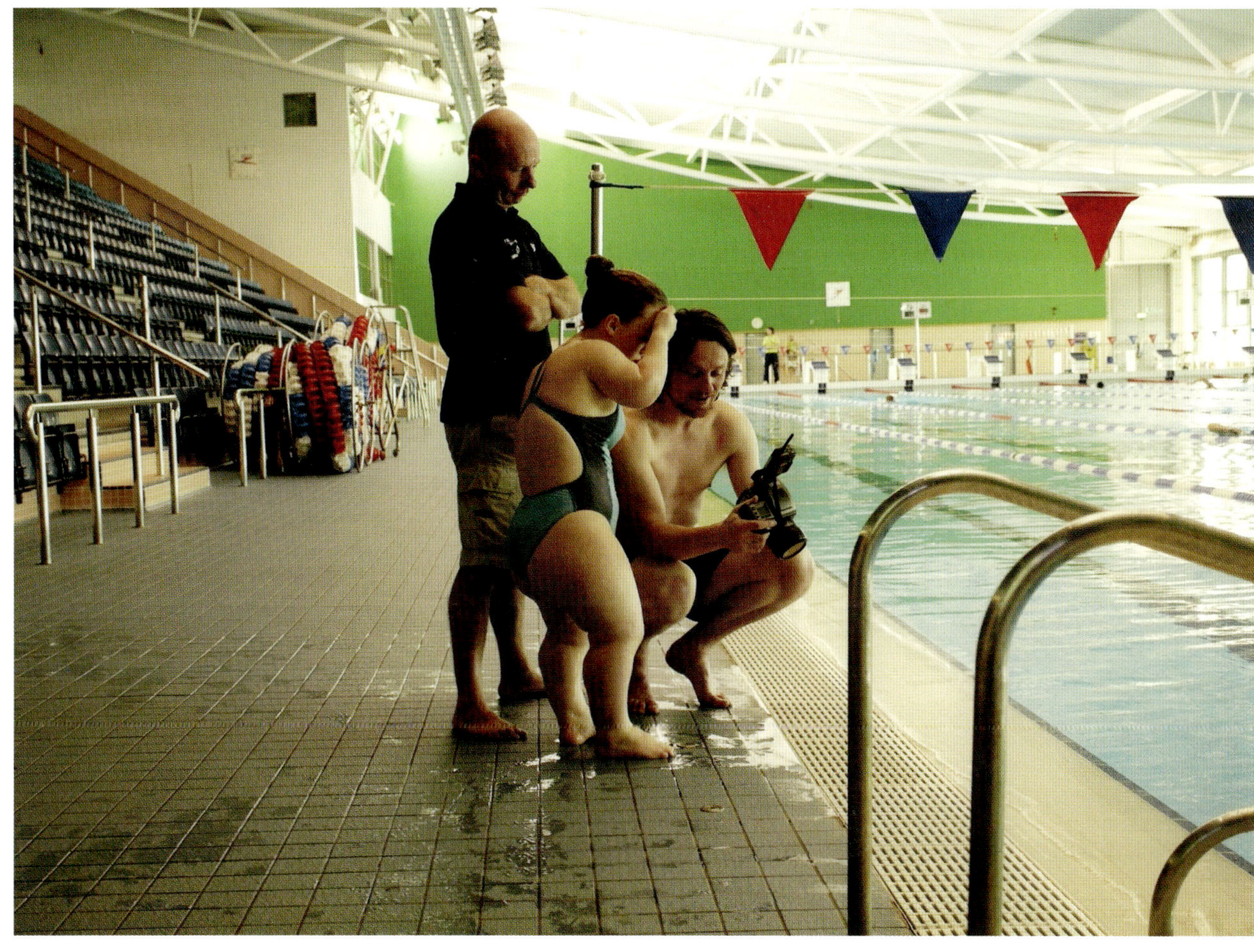

PAGE 14
Brian Griffin on location with Team Stadium
RIGHT
Finlay MacKay on location with Eleanor Simmonds and Billy Pye

soil analysis, who happened to be working for the Olympic Park decontamination team cleaning up the site.

At times, the sitters' circumstances took dramatic twists and turns as the project progressed. A year after Dobriskey was photographed with her father in one of *Road to 2012*'s earliest portraits, the athlete was diagnosed with an injury that put her selection for Team GB in jeopardy. Likewise, boxer Khalid Yafai was considered a medal hope when he was photographed at his Birmingham club, only for the young flyweight to be defeated in a 'box-off' at the end of 2011, costing him a place in the 2012 squad. 'We always knew that some of our sitters might ultimately not be selected for the team,' says Braybon. 'But that, too, is part of the story.'

On other occasions, the selection process changed course as a result of personal recommendations. Danny Boyle, the Oscar-winning artistic director of the London 2012 Opening Ceremony, insisted on being

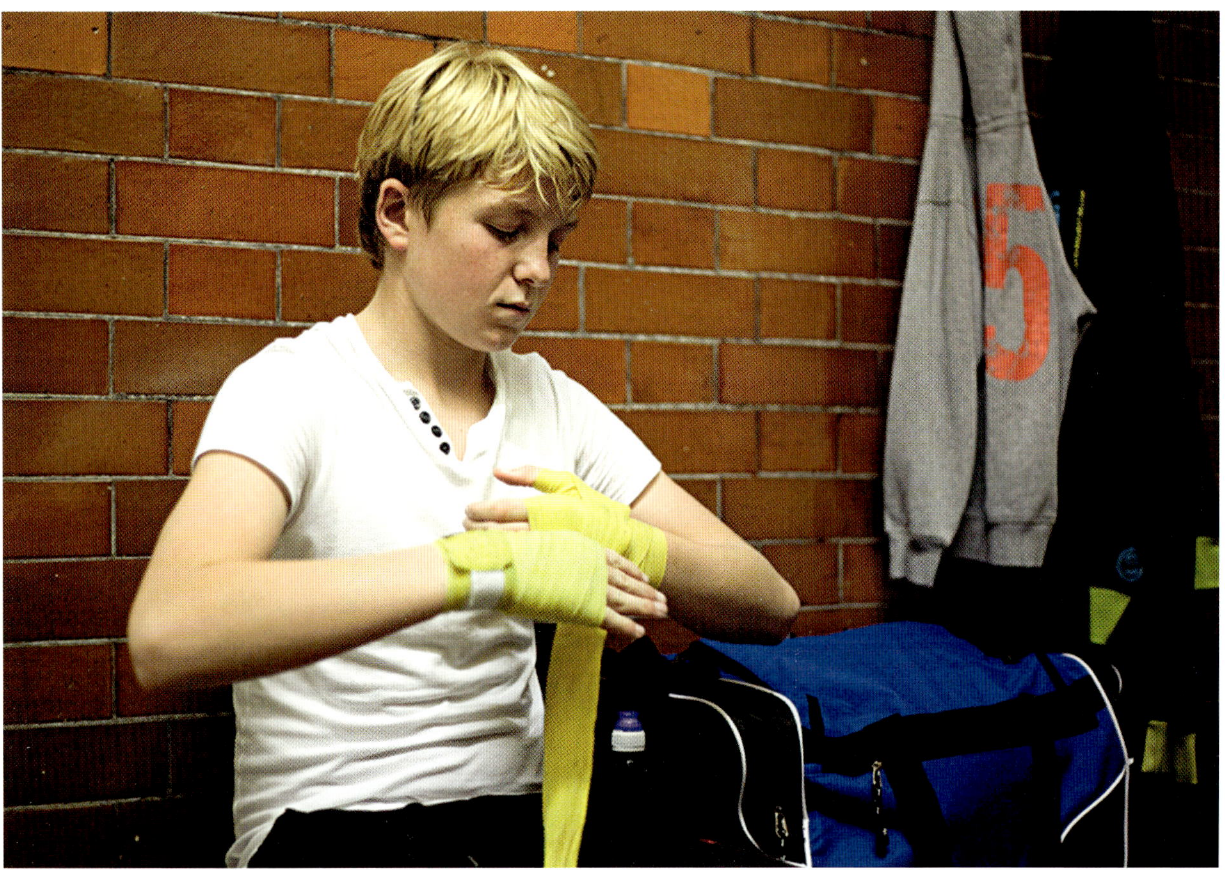

ABOVE
Michael at Repton Boxing Club, by Katherine Green
OPPOSITE, LEFT TO RIGHT
An Allegory of Prudence, by Titian
Brian Griffin on location with the Young Ambassadors

photographed with longtime members of his creative team Mark Tildesley and Suttirat Larlarb, whom he considered vital to his vision. 'We challenged this at first,' recalls Braybon, 'but Danny was very clear that he wanted to be heard. After speaking to Mark and Suttirat, I understood why. They were key to the creative thinking around the ceremony.'

The addition of local voices to the overall national narrative expressed by the commissioned portraits was important to to *Road to 2012*. The Gallery's Participation and Learning department invited creative responses from students at the University of London, Goldsmiths College and the University of East London, and commissioned locally based photographer Katherine Green to document a range of thriving grass-roots sports clubs in the vicinity of the Olympic Park. 'Central to the project from the outset was an ambitious plan to capture the stories and opinions of those living through this period of dramatic local change,' says Liz Smith, Director of Participation and Learning. 'These have brought texture and vibrancy to the overall project.'

As part of this initiative, specially created digital content, including a blog and video interviews with the photographers and sitters, allowed visitors to track the commissioning process and contribute to the project's creative archive by uploading their own photographs to the website.

Road to 2012 also presented an exciting opportunity to bring together a variety of approaches to portraiture and a longlist of photographers with widely differing aesthetics and experience was drawn up. Final decisions on which photographers to commission were taken as the project took shape, with the team assessing the body of work that had been created at each stage before commissioning the next year's photographers. 'We were looking for a tension of opposites,' explains Braybon. 'Each year, we took stock of where we were, and responded to what had already been created.'

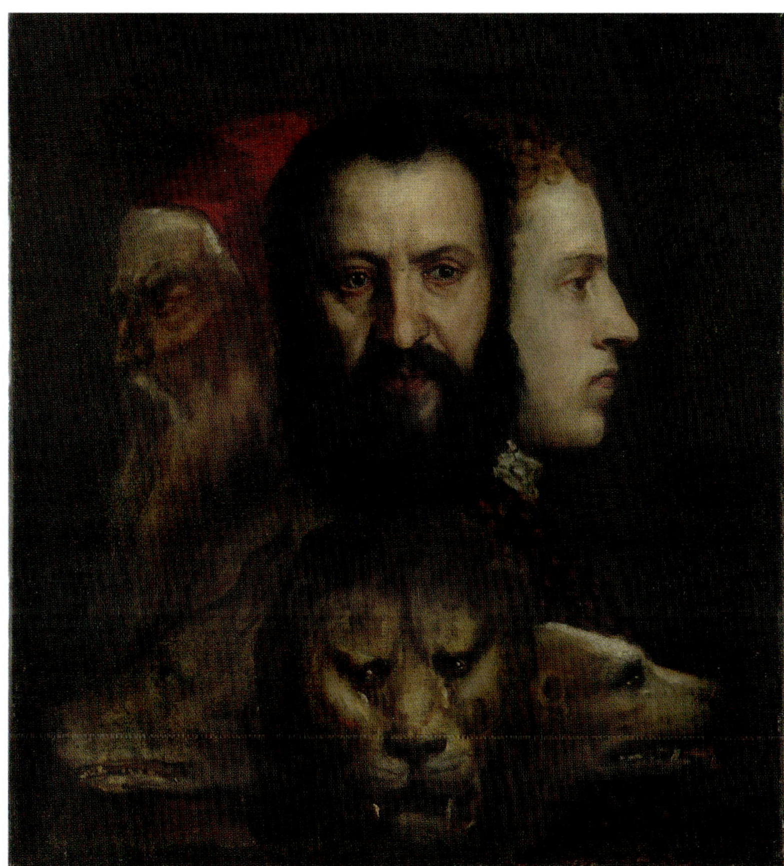

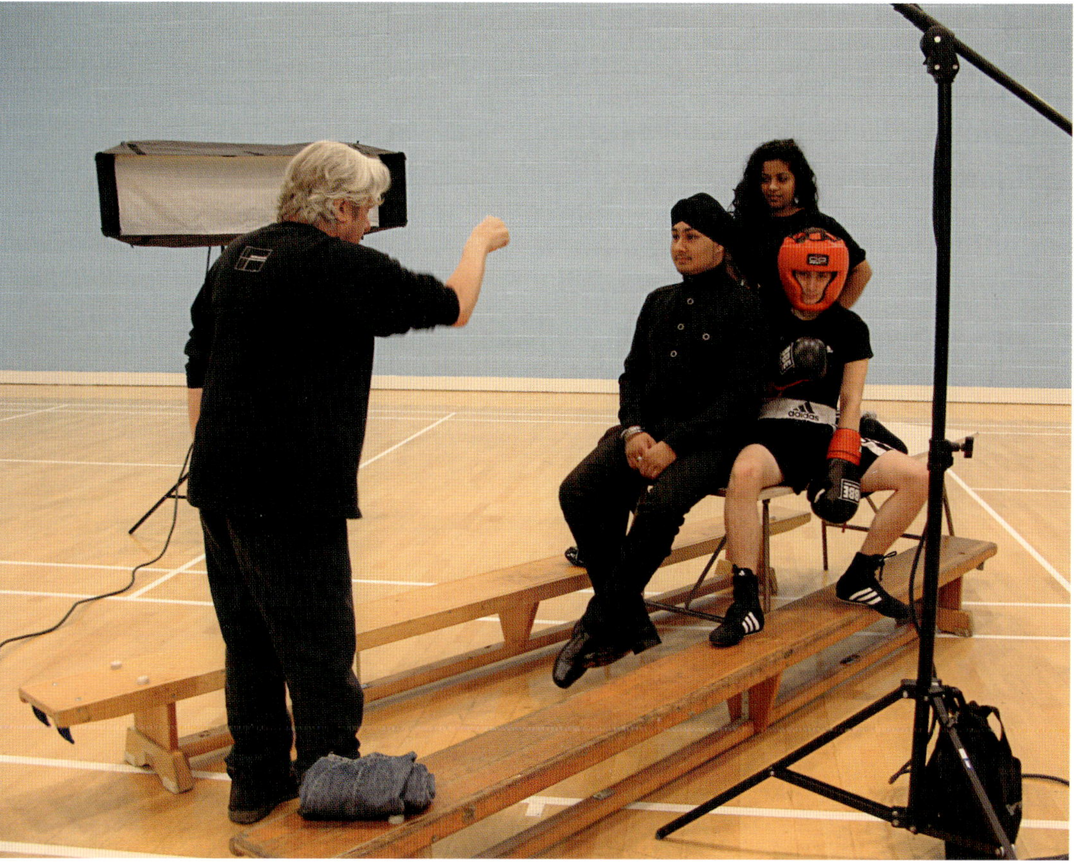

SETTING OUT

For the first phase of *Road to 2012*, *Setting Out*, Brian Griffin was selected to launch the project with group portraits of the visionary figures who conceived and won the bid for London, as well as those responsible for designing, building and delivering the Olympic Park infrastructure. 'Brian is hugely respected by his peers for the imagination and technical virtuosity he brings to complex portraits,' says Braybon. 'His forte lies in the heroic poses he observes on a building site and the body language of the boardroom.'

Griffin's experience and patience were critical in working through the production challenges. Dealing with time constraints and inclement weather were familiar problems, but the imperatives of the athletes' training, competition and lockdown schedules were unique to *Road to 2012*, as were Olympic Park building timetables and the tight security surrounding access to the site, where Griffin shot many of his portraits. Restricted at first to viewing the Park from inside a minibus, he had to submit his preferred locations to the relevant authorities for approval before the areas were taped off, hard hats removed and the portrait-making process could begin.

The opening image for any portrait series lays the foundation for the creative thinking that follows. Griffin, who draws on a broad range of visual culture, took inspiration from Titian's *An Allegory of Prudence* for his first photograph of four young people from east London selected to travel to Singapore as part of the London bid team. 'Brian brought these Young Ambassadors together as "four heads on one body", and they were all relieved to

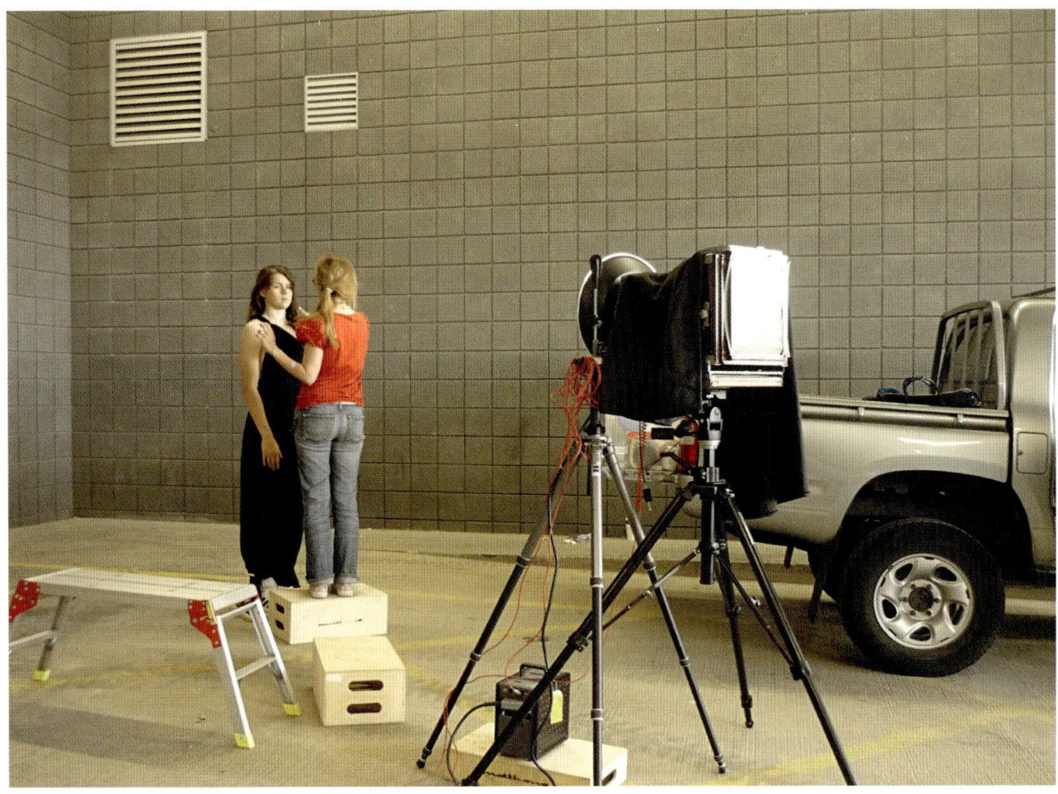

LEFT
Bettina von Zwehl on location with Savannah Marshall
OPPOSITE
Finlay MacKay on locaton with Aaron Cook and family

understand the idea behind the awkward and uncomfortable pose,' says Braybon. 'Brian's strength lies in his acute observation and ability to find and use a gesture he can build on. When young boxer Alex Loukos leant out of the group as if to spar with the camera, the portrait started coming together.'

For the second part of *Setting Out*, artist-photographer Bettina von Zwehl portrayed athletes at different stages of their career in settings where they live or train. Unlike Griffin, von Zwehl had never been handed such an exacting brief, but her test shot convinced the project team of her ability to work outside the studio while retaining her singular vision.

The slow, calm process associated with von Zwehl's 10x8 plate camera and precise lighting brings a luminous quality to her sitters that is intensified by the reduction of detail in the background, often reminiscent of a painted nineteenth-century studio backdrop. Jessica Ennis stands proud and strong against a wall of grass at the Sheffield stadium where she started her career; Rebecca Adlington is pictured in front of the rich, muted tones of the rockery garden at Nottingham University, an area she dreaded tackling on her training runs in the university grounds; and Savannah Marshall is captured in a gridded corner of ExCel, where the women's boxing squad will compete in the Olympic Games.

'I felt the intensity of Bettina's work would give us what we were looking for,' explains Braybon. 'We wanted portraits that gave the viewer a sense of an encounter with the sitters, as if you were meeting the athletes and could ask who or what inspired them.'

With the completion of *Setting Out*, the project's first thirty portraits were unveiled at the Gallery in July 2010 to mark the two-year countdown to the Games, accompanied by an installation that underlined the theme of inspiration with a series of video interviews in which athletes recounted their various sources of motivation.

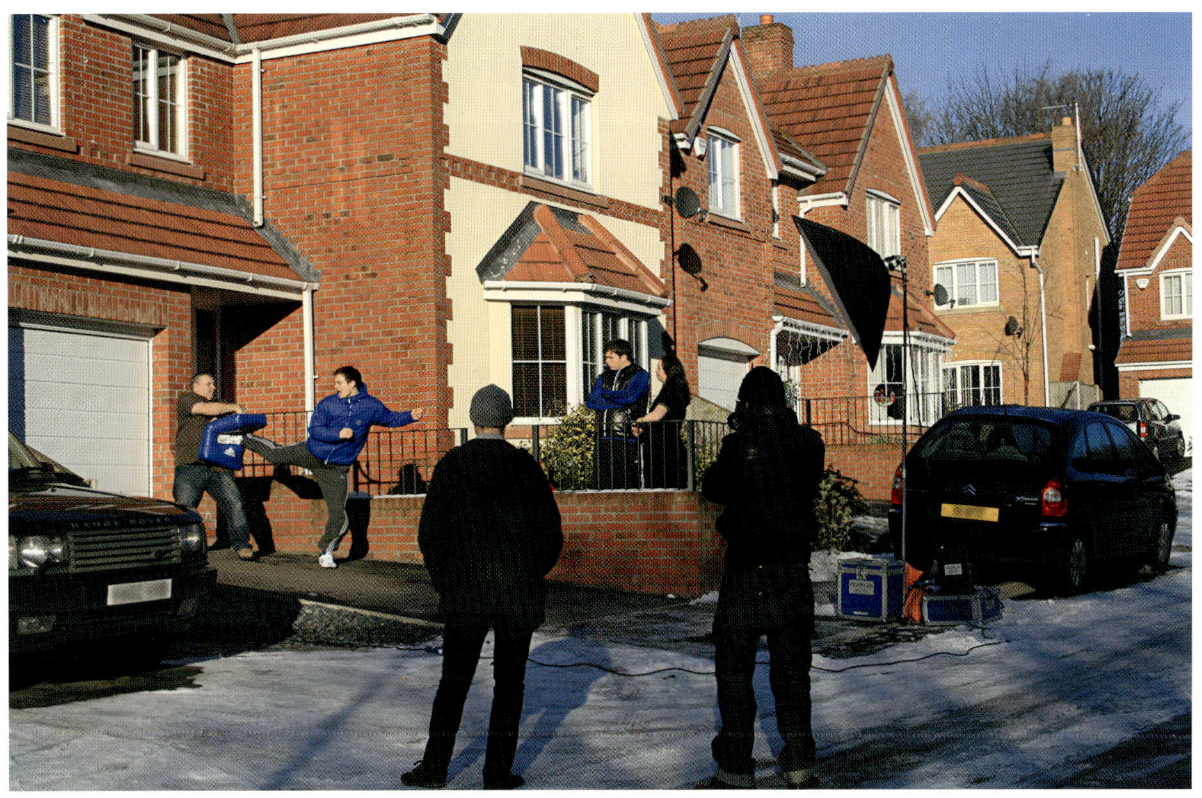

CHANGING PACE

Griffin and von Zwehl's studio-style portraits informed the choice of photographers for the next stage, *Changing Pace*, with a decision that the next phase of work should provide a contrasting experience for the audience. As Braybon puts it: 'We needed energy after the stillness; empathy after the formality.'

Finlay MacKay provided an abundance of that energy and vigour with his highly crafted scenarios that portray athletes in dramatic training moments or pictured alongside their coaches, depicting what Braybon calls 'the hard graft and crucial relationships behind competition'. For the project, MacKay moved away from the high-octane, tightly directed images of his advertising campaigns to produce both single shots and diptychs exploring his new interest in 'a figure in a landscape'.

Like his later images of gymnast Louis Smith and boxer Khalid Yafai, MacKay's portrait of young taekwondo star Aaron Cook and his family references the grass-roots stories behind the success of leading athletes. The photographer met the Cook family in Manchester where they had moved to support Aaron's Olympic ambitions. He began with a portrait of the martial artist training in the gym his father had built at the back of the house, but struck by the radiance of

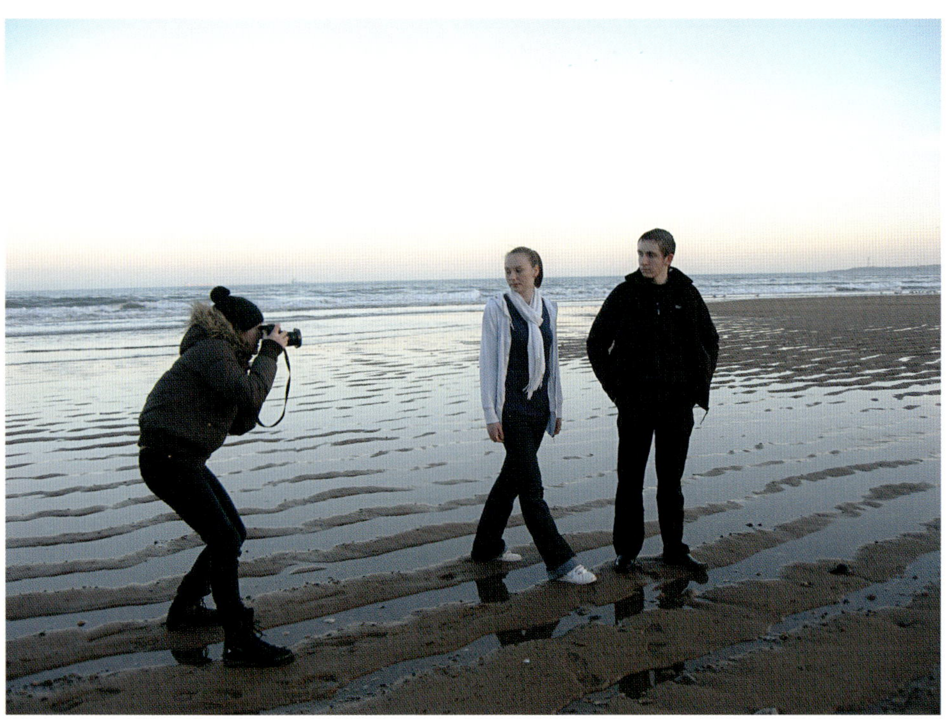

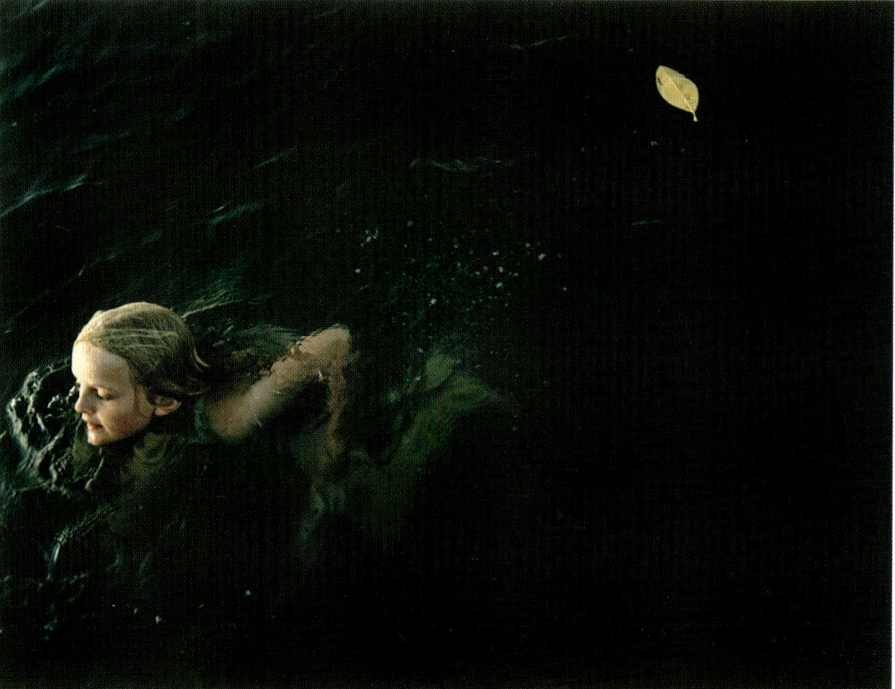

ABOVE, LEFT TO RIGHT
Emma Hardy on location with Lewis Bown and Stephanie Forbes
Little Leaf, by Emma Hardy
OPPOSITE, TOP TO BOTTOM
Anderson & Low on location
American Gothic, by Grant Wood

the blue skies, the snow and the new-build cul-de-sac, he recognised the potential for an extraordinary family portrait.

MacKay's large-scale scenarios were juxtaposed with Emma Hardy's quietly telling portraits of the directors, writers, designers and others involved in the staging of London 2012. 'Internationally renowned, Emma offered a very different mood to the work we had produced so far,' says Braybon. 'It is simpler and more empathetic. She strips back the process of portraiture to the essentials: film in her camera, natural light and her subject.'

This process depends on reciprocal trust and co-operation between Hardy and her sitter, which was important in convincing a hesitant Chris Holmes, Director of Paralympic Integration and a swimming gold medallist, to pose in a friend's pool. Hardy drew inspiration from her own portrait of her daughter, *Little Leaf*, for the setting. 'Emma wanted to allude to Chris's experience of the world as a blind person. She trusts her instinct, and that, together with her remarkable ability to create a safe and intimate atmosphere is critical to her work.' Hardy and Holmes worked together for nearly two hours to create the spare and powerful image. Holmes later recalled the 'flow of emotion and mood, and the connectivity that Emma created'.

During this commissioning period, producer and sound artist Martyn Ware collaborated with students at Goldsmiths, University of London, to explore the use of sound as an evocative medium in the creation of portraiture. 'The notion of examining and reinterpreting the inspirational stories and fascinating narratives of *Road to 2012* using sound as a tool was a genuine inspiration,' says Ware. The idea led Ware to suggest a competition for his students using digital media.

In July 2011, the *Changing Pace* exhibition opened at the Gallery. 'By this stage, we saw that we were creating a body of work that reflected a range of approaches,' says Braybon. 'It was exciting to recognise the depth this gave the commission and how it provoked reflections on contemporary photography.' A selection from the Goldsmiths students' work was shown at a themed *Late Shift* evening in August. Beyond the Gallery, Katherine Green's portraits of grass-roots sports enthusiasts were exhibited at the View Tube space overlooking the Olympic Park that summer, giving weight to the stories of those most affected by the Games. 'People felt a sense of disconnection from what was going on,' Green said. '*Road to 2012: A Local Story* has helped to change that.'

AIMING HIGH

As *Road to 2012* moved towards its conclusion with the final phase, *Aiming High*, photographic partners Anderson & Low were invited to contribute to this last strand by documenting athletes and their support staff. The duo's unique body of work draws upon their fascination with athletes' extraordinary physical and emotional qualities, and Braybon highlights their tableau of the women's hockey team as a sublime example of the formal style and naturalistic palette that they brought to the project.

Like Brian Griffin, Anderson & Low looked to fine art for inspiration. At the rowing headquarters in Hammersmith, their keen eye saw traces of Grant Wood's painting *American Gothic* in the demeanour of their sitters, the particular pitch of the roof an old boat tank and the shape of a shortened oar hanging inside the building. 'They brought all these elements together under some duress: the batteries for their lights froze in the snow, and the sitters, David Tanner and Maggie Netto, struggled with the cold,' recalls Braybon. 'But their fine double portrait expresses the quiet pride and resolve of the performance director and his assistant, who have overseen the ascendancy of British rowing.'

For *Aiming High*'s final, behind-the-scenes portraits, Jillian Edelstein was commissioned to photograph the Games' facilitators and those responsible for the ongoing regeneration plans for east London. As well as introducing a verve and freshness, Edelstein's versatility and ability to work quickly resulted in three evocative portraits of the ceremonies team taken one Sunday at Three Mills Studio as they prepared for a six-week period of casting for the Opening Ceremony.

In the prop studio, Edelstein was drawn to a rectangle of artificial turf and plastic

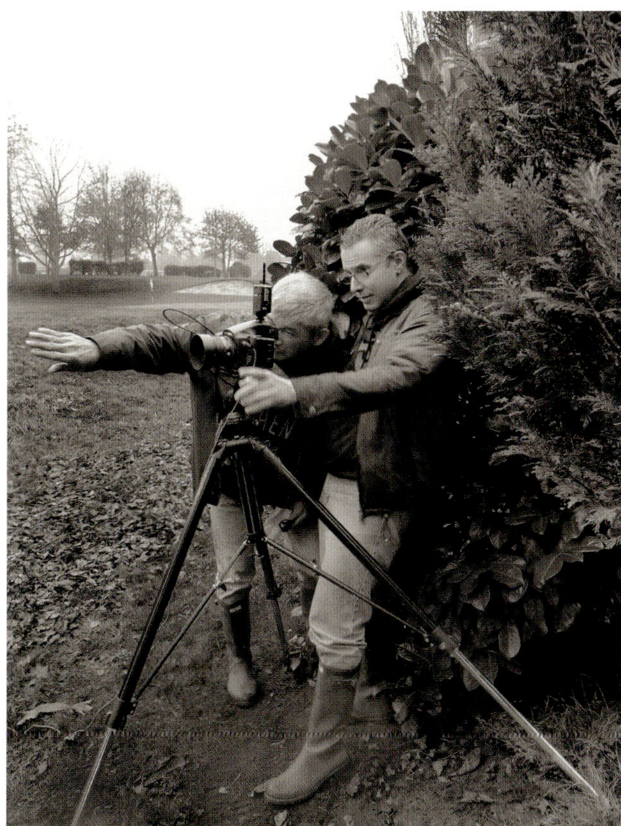

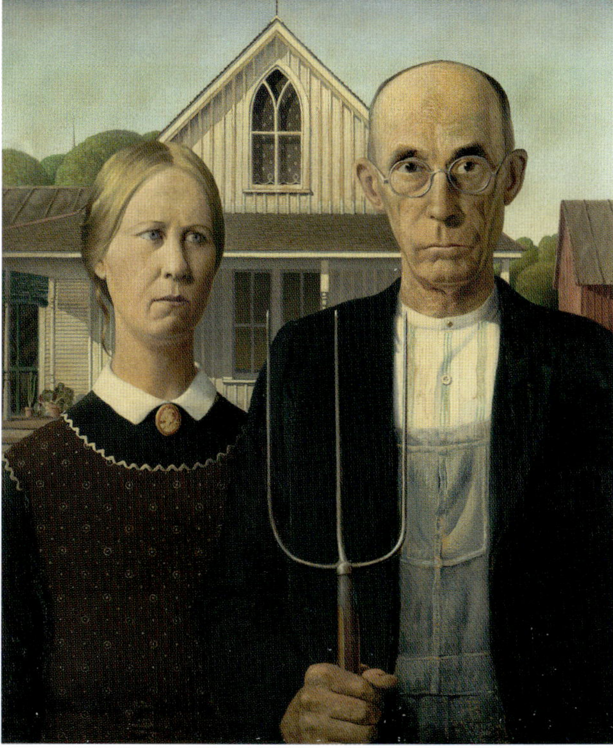

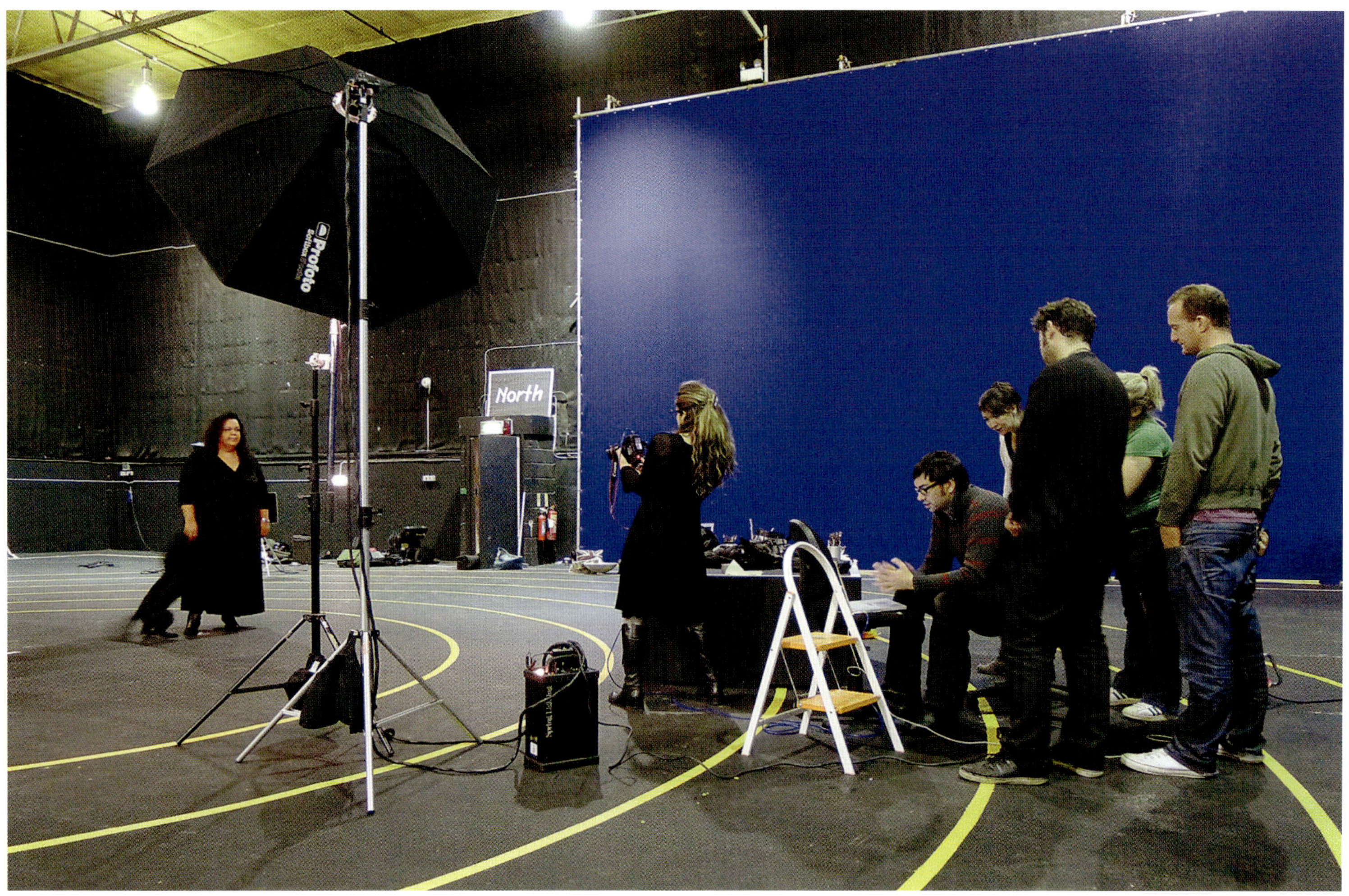

ABOVE
Jillian Edelstein on location with Catherine Ugwu

OPPOSITE
Nadav Kander in his studio with Jodie Williams

flowers. The ambiguous setting, Martin Green's relaxed pose and intense concentration combined to produce an enigmatic portrait of the head of ceremonies. 'Martin lay in the moment, as if he were in a real meadow,' says Edelstein. 'I was struck that someone with his massive responsibilities could be so giving and trusting.'

As a culminating commission for *Road to 2012*, Nadav Kander, a central figure in contemporary British photography, was asked to make two series of studio portraits. His four head-and-shoulder shots of prodigiously talented young athletes are accompanied by portraits of Torchbearers selected to carry the Olympic flame on the relay across the UK. Both series sum up the inspirational stories of determination, courage and aspiration that underpin the project, while the studio setting signalled another mood for the commission. 'The subjects look away from the camera, as if caught in reverie,' notes Braybon. 'Each portrait is produced with breathtaking attention to technical detail.'

Whereas Kander's images of the athletes explore the drama of heightened black-and-white tonal interplay, his deceptively simple approach to the Torchbearer portraits belies a carefully considered concept. 'He floats Rhyania Blackett-Codrington above the ground, isolated from the world that a location conveys. His portrait is honest to her, while conferring a particular status and respect. Seen together with the story behind her selection for the relay, it is profoundly moving.'

As the last portraits were completed, each photographer ran a series of masterclasses for students from the University of East London, who were creating their own documentary portraiture on themes of local inspiration and achievement. '*Road to 2012* has been a catalyst,' comments artist and UEL lecturer Faisal Abdu'Allah. 'It has brokered those private conversations, struggles and aspirations of the diverse collectives of East London.'

Taking the project to audiences outside London was always part of the Gallery's plan. In the spring of 2012, an outdoor touring exhibition showing thirty selected images on large printed panels opened in Cardiff, before moving to Edinburgh and Birmingham. It is the first National Portrait Gallery commission to be exhibited in an outdoor public space.

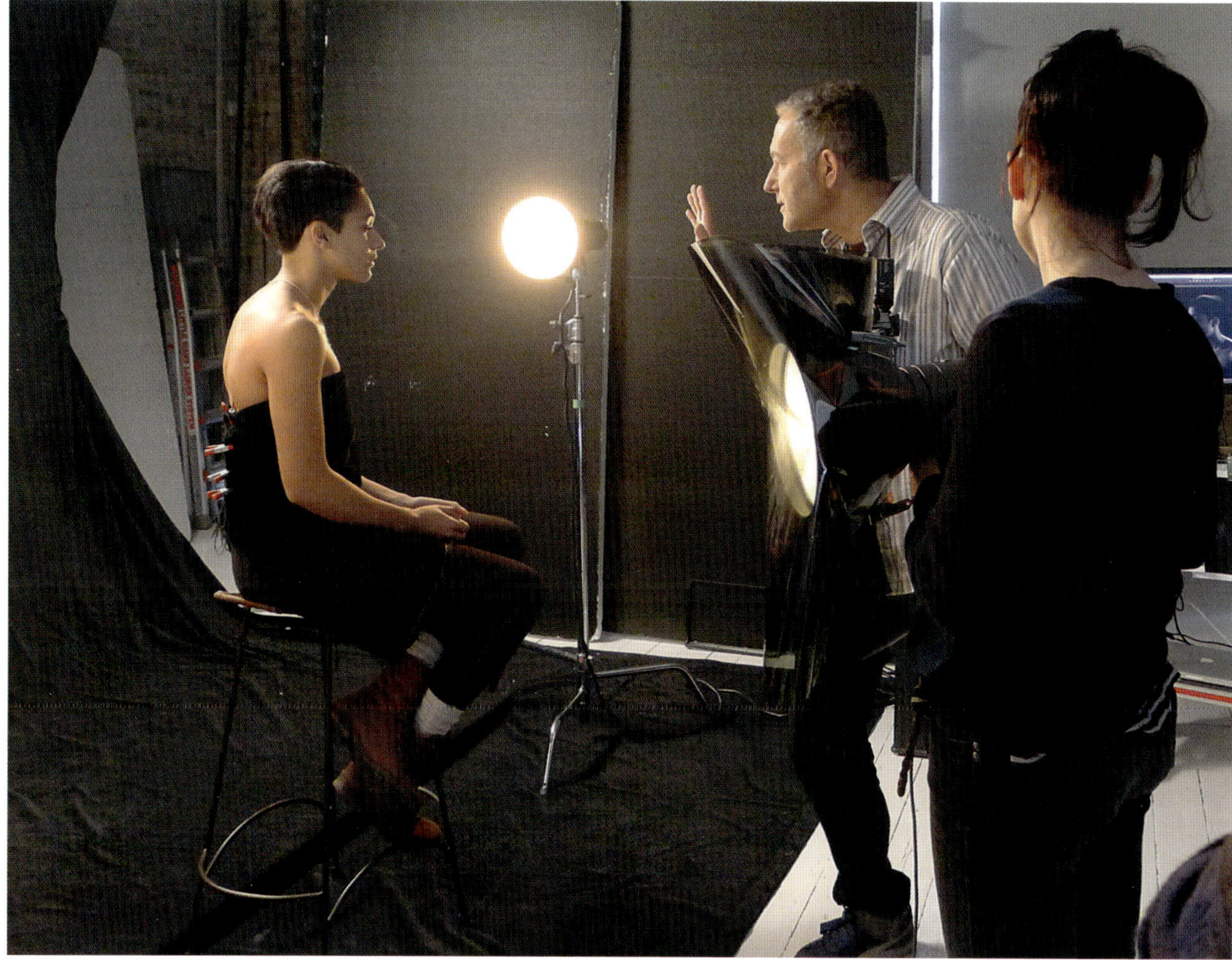

The final *Road to 2012* exhibition opened at the Gallery in the summer of 2012, comprising the new portraits, a selection of earlier work and Katherine Green's local stories. '*Road to 2012* celebrates the sitters, those individuals, both high-profile and less well-known, from multiple disciplines and backgrounds, who came together for a limited time collectively to make 2012 happen,' concludes Braybon. 'It also celebrates the creative vision of the photographers who shaped the project and brought it to life.' The portraits now form part of the National Portrait Gallery's permanent collection in perpetuity. Digitally archived for online accessibility, they will create a lasting record of a very special period in the history of the capital and of the nation.

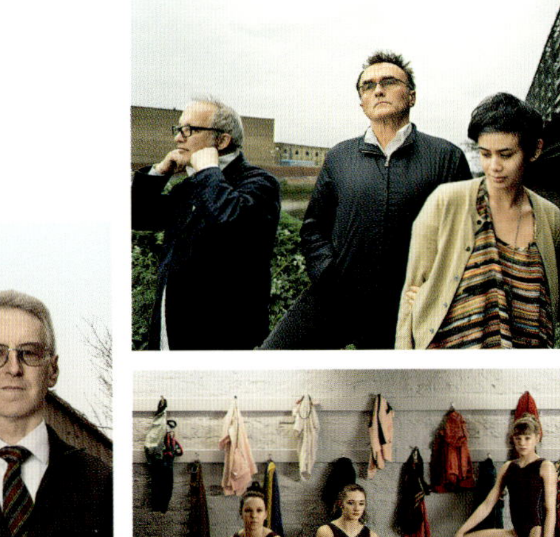
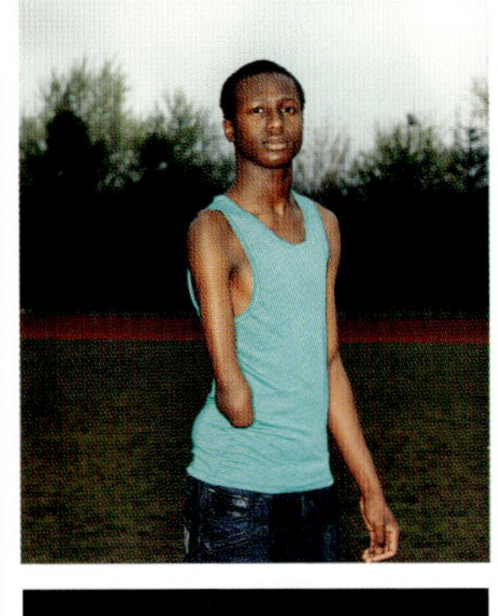
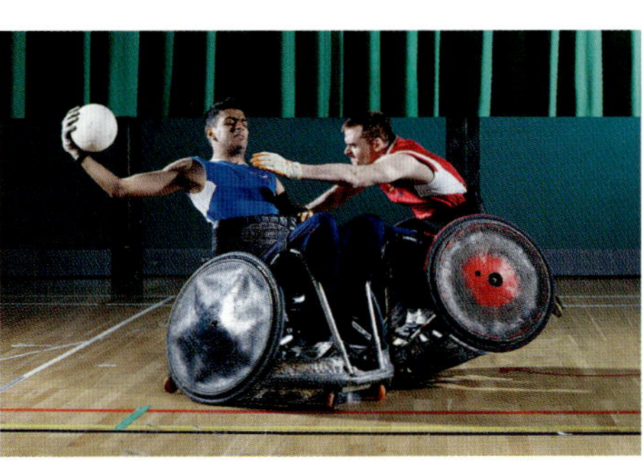
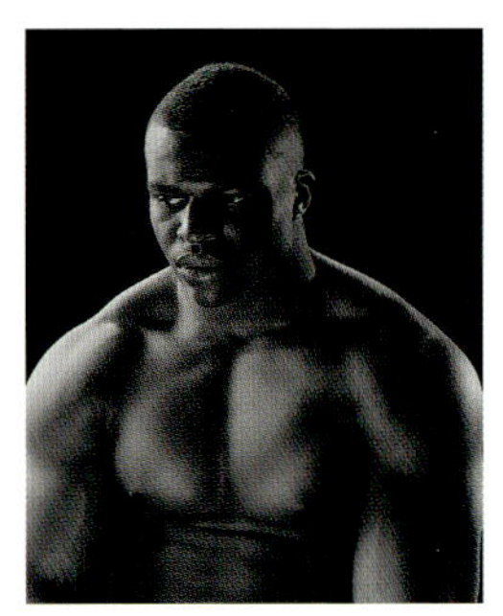
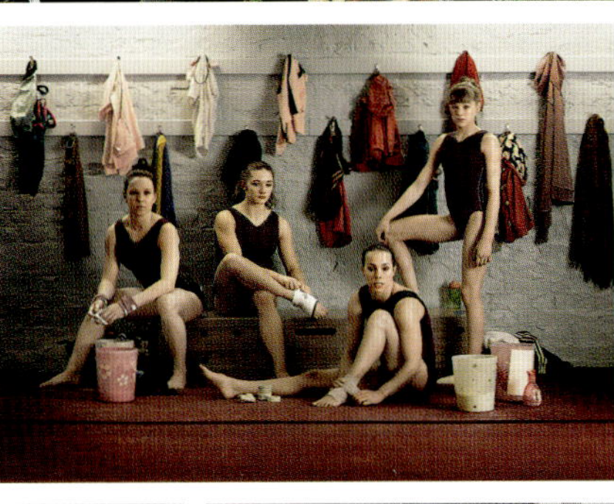
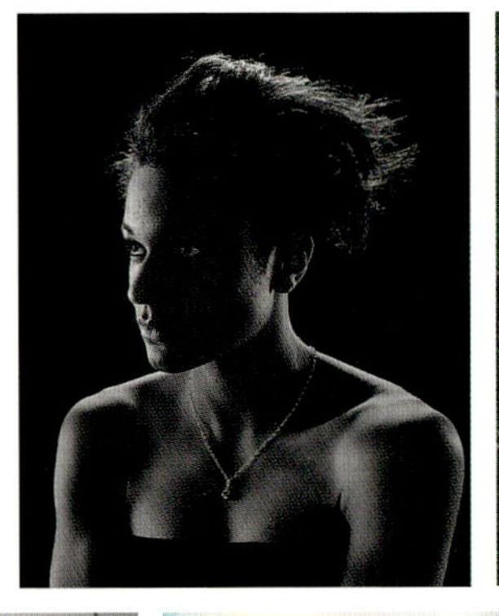
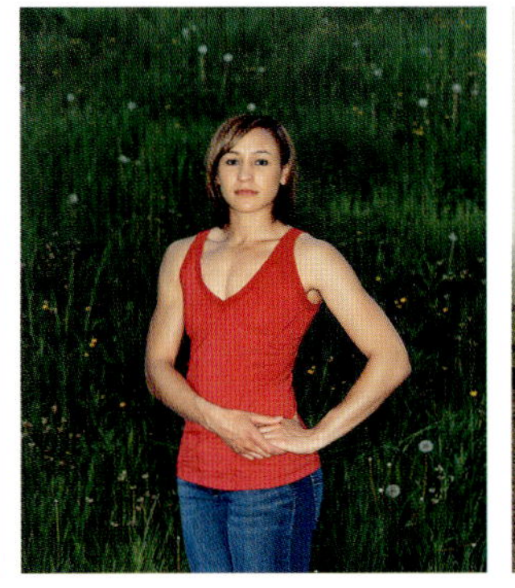
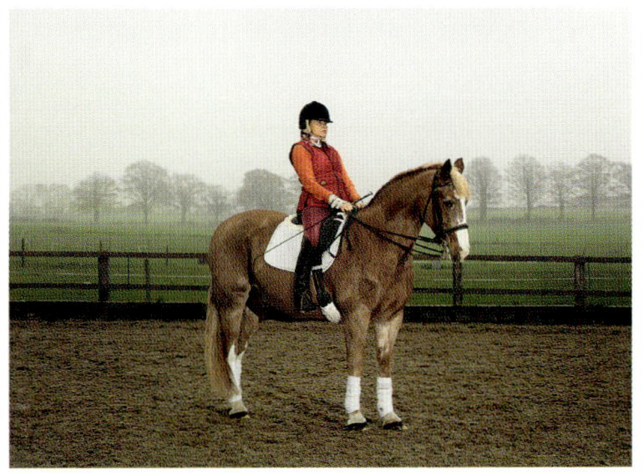
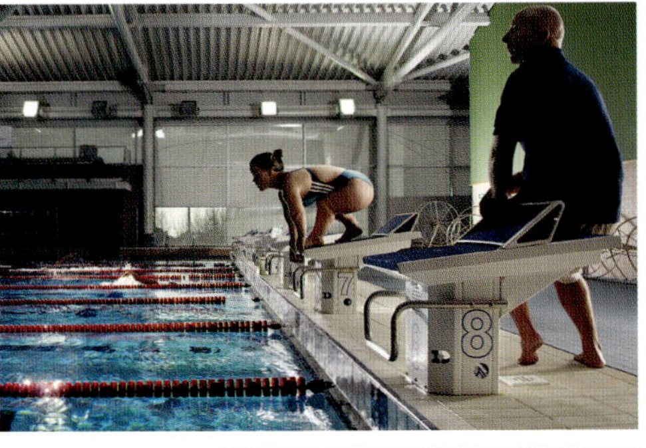
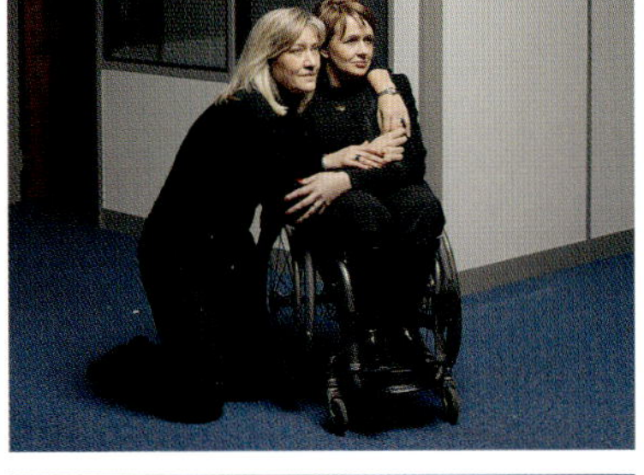
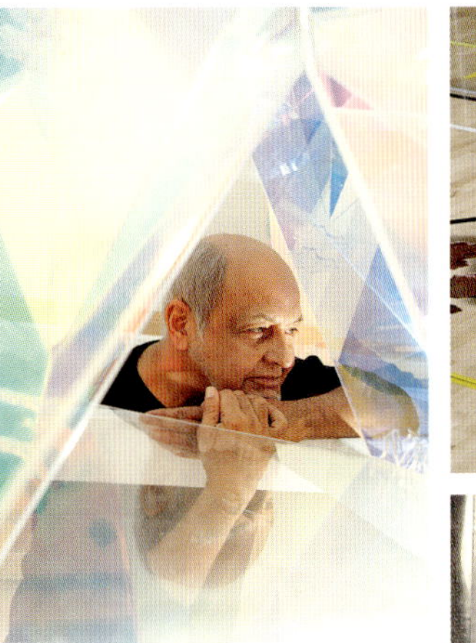
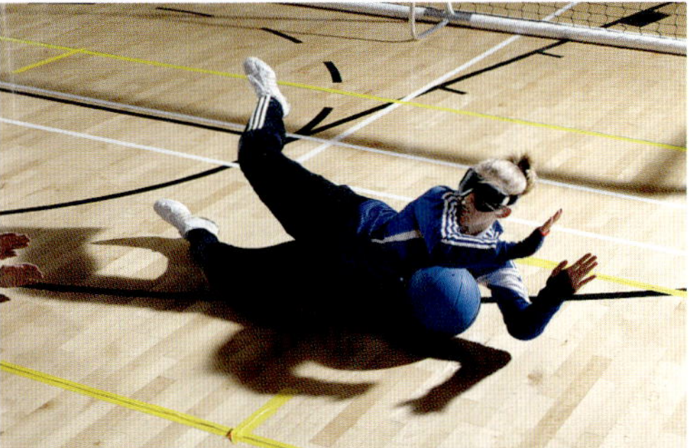
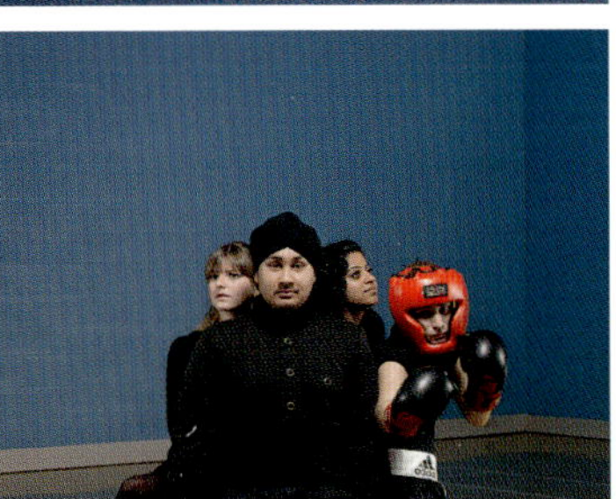
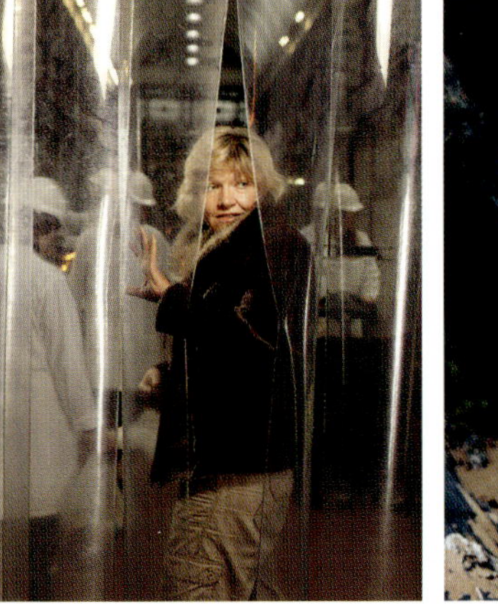
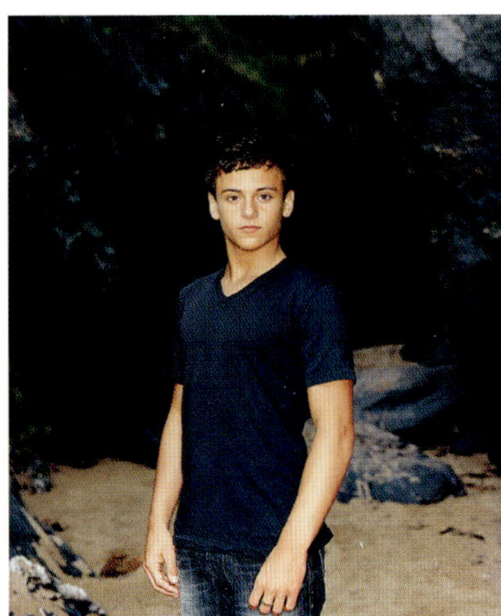
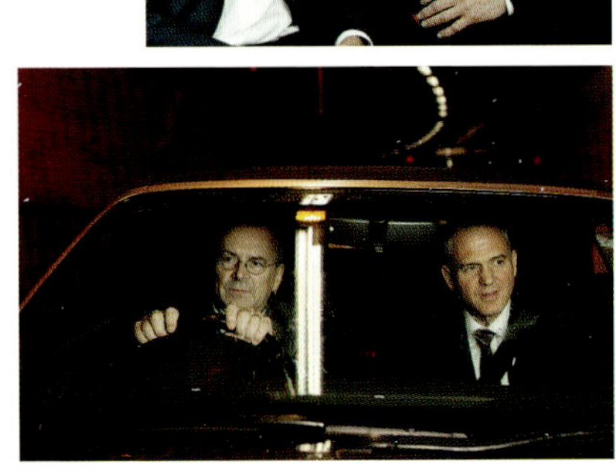
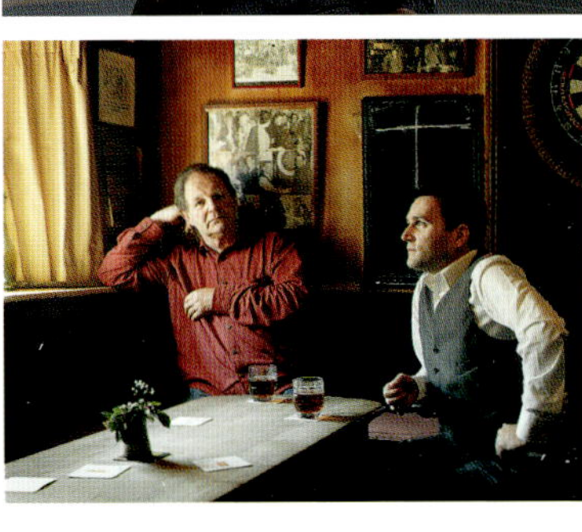
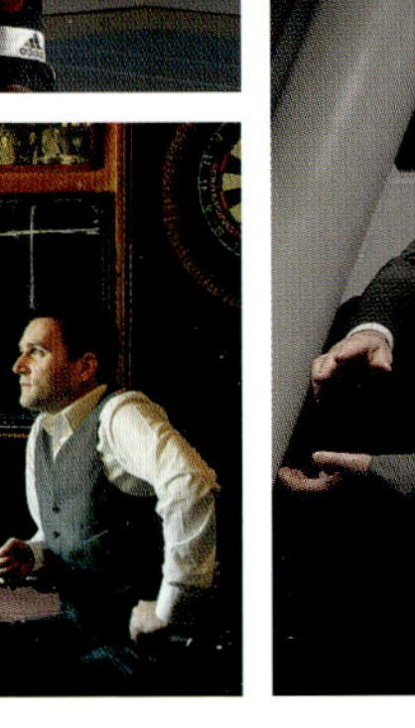
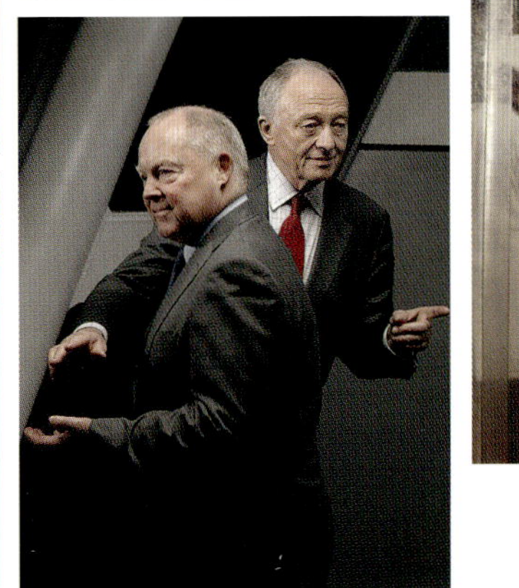

THE PORTRAITS

ICONS

Broadcasters, designers and gold-medal hopefuls are among the many iconic individuals who have played a major part in contributing to the success of the London 2012 Olympic and Paralympic Games. These exceptional people have inspired others to make the Games a fantastic and memorable occasion for London and the world.

SEBASTIAN COE KBE
Photographed by Emma Hardy
21 March 2011, Greenwich Park, London

Sebastian Coe chairs the London Organising Committee of the Olympic and Paralympic Games (LOCOG), the company responsible for preparing and staging the London 2012 Olympic and Paralympic Games. The middle-distance runner and double Olympic gold medallist (1980 and 1984) was appointed Chair of the London 2012 bid team in 2004. From the outset, Coe's vision for London 2012 was to inspire the youth of the world through sport. Retiring from athletics in 1990, the twelve-time world record holder became an MP (1992–7). He was made a life peer in 2002, becoming Lord Coe of Ranmore, and was knighted in 2006.

'I am a runner. It's what I do.'
SEBASTIAN COE

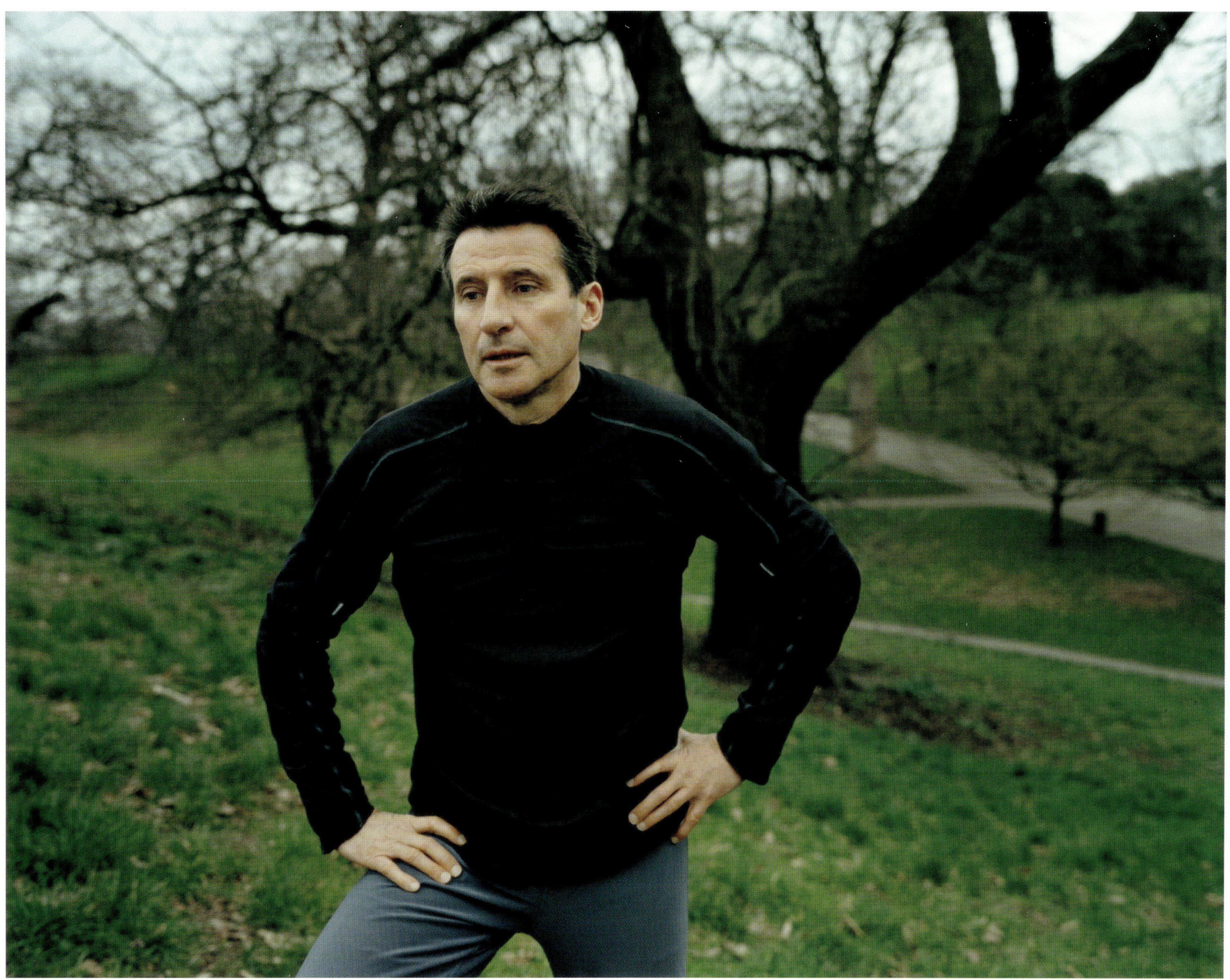

ELEANOR SIMMONDS WITH BILLY PYE

Photographed by Finlay MacKay
1 December 2010,
Wales National Pool, Swansea

Eleanor Simmonds is the youngest-ever individual Paralympic or Olympic gold medallist. At the age of thirteen, she won the 100m and 400m freestyle swimming events in Beijing 2008. Simmonds, who was born with achondroplasia (dwarfism), began swimming at the age of five. She currently competes in multiple events, and is World Champion and world-record holder in four. Simmonds moved to Swansea in 2007 to train with Billy Pye. The former miner and award-winning coach for British Disability Swimming was part of ParalympicsGB, who enjoyed one of their most successful performances at a Paralympic Games at Beijing 2008.

'She might have qualified, she might have gone, but she wouldn't have achieved what she achieved in Beijing without Billy.'

VAL SIMMONDS, ELEANOR'S MOTHER

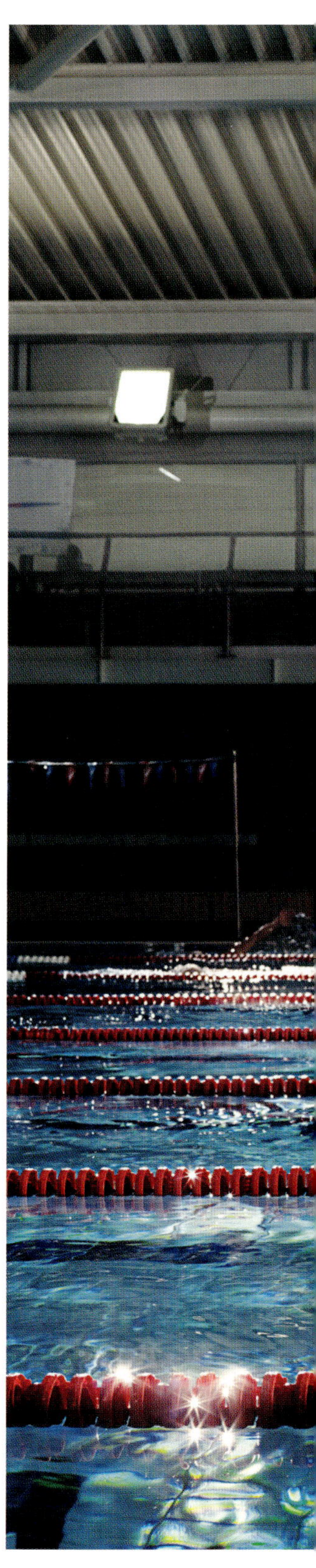

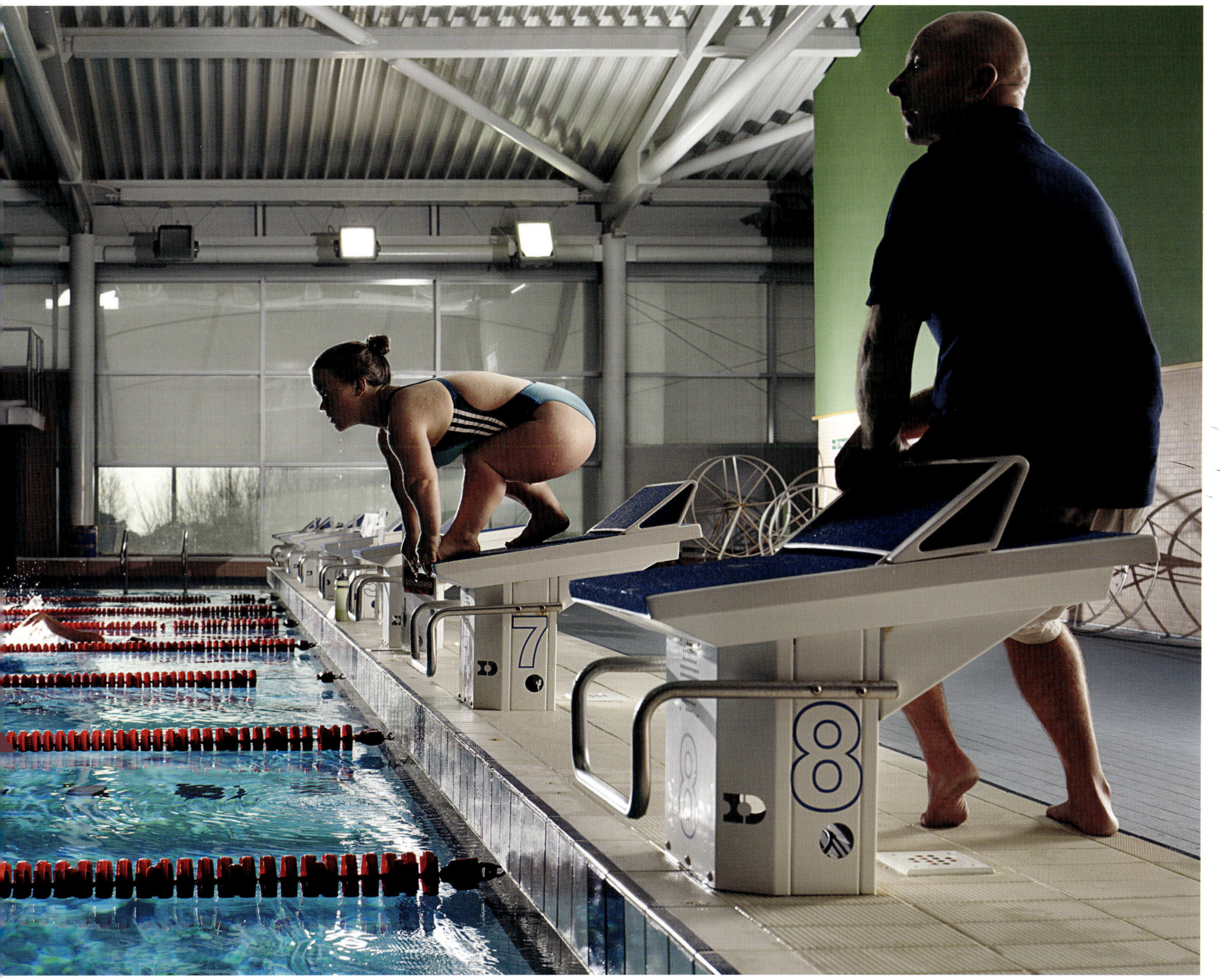
7
8

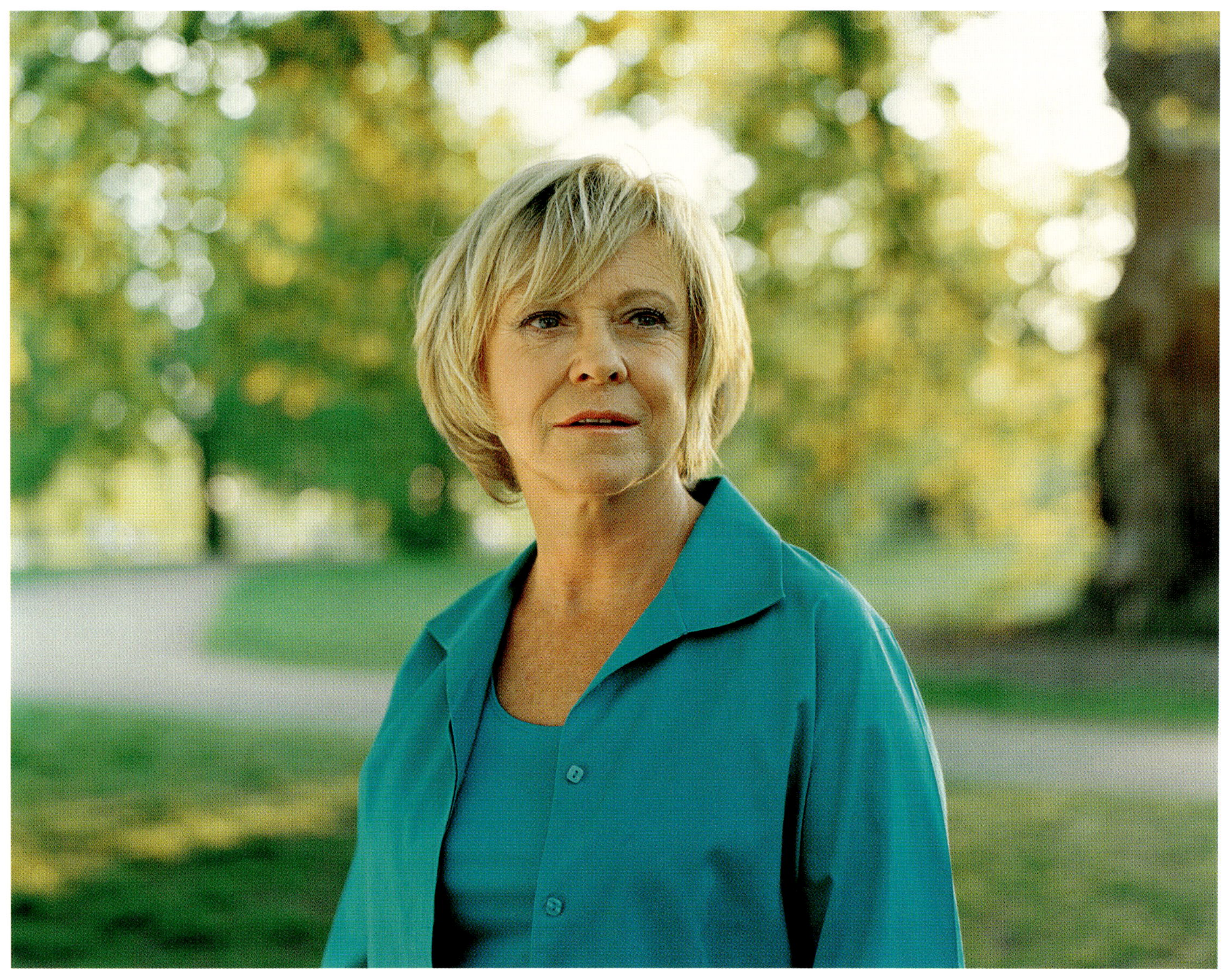

SUE BARKER
Photographed by Emma Hardy
19 April 2011, Serpentine, London

Former world number three tennis player and presenter Sue Barker will anchor the London 2012 Olympic Games for the BBC. Barker began sports broadcasting in 1985 and has presented the summer and winter Olympic Games, Commonwealth Games, the Wimbledon Championships and other world-class competitions. Barker's involvement with London 2012 began in 2004 when she presented the promotional film for the official announcement of London's bid to host the 2012 Olympic and Paralympic Games.

RHYANIA BLACKETT-CODRINGTON

Photographed by Nadav Kander
8 February 2012, London

'My daughter Rhyania has completely turned her life around from her teenage years, and in doing so has done everything that she can to help the young people in her community. She has gone from being involved in the wrong crowd at fourteen to first helping disadvantaged youths at mentoring schemes such as Dalston Youth Project and Mentoring Plus, then teaching in male prisons, completing two degrees (whilst being a single mother) and becoming a secondary school teacher trying to help the lives of inner-city young people. She is truly inspirational.'

Quoted from Olympic Torchbearer nomination by Daphne Blackett, Rhyania's mother.

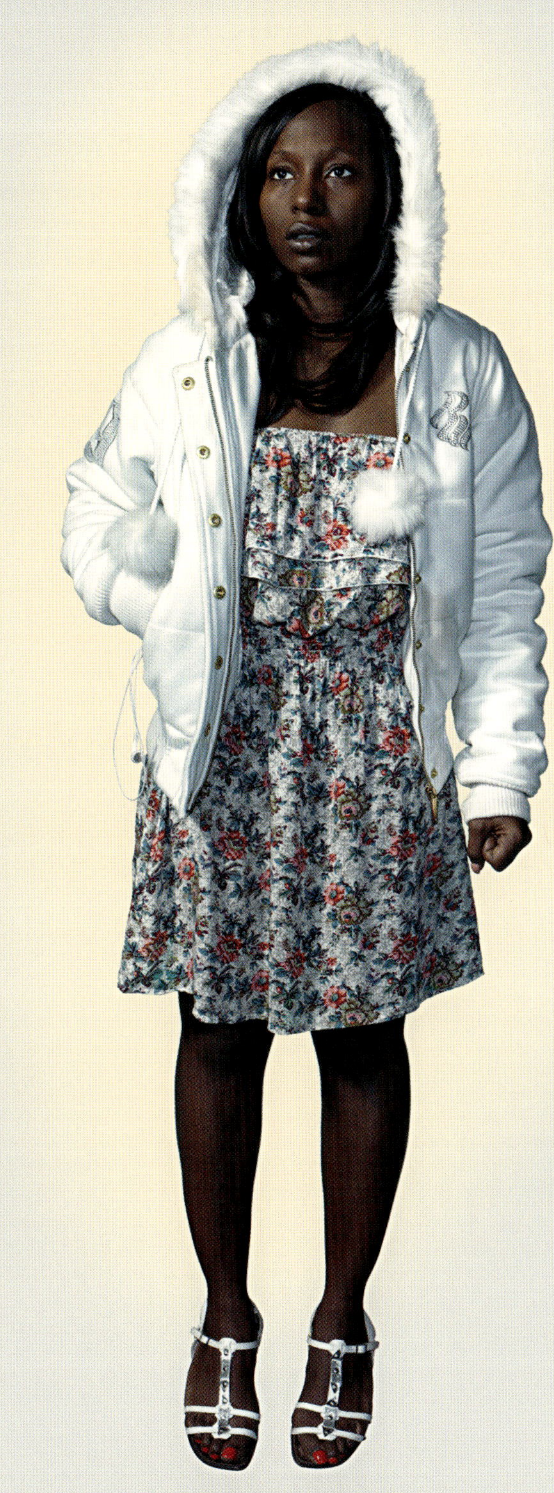

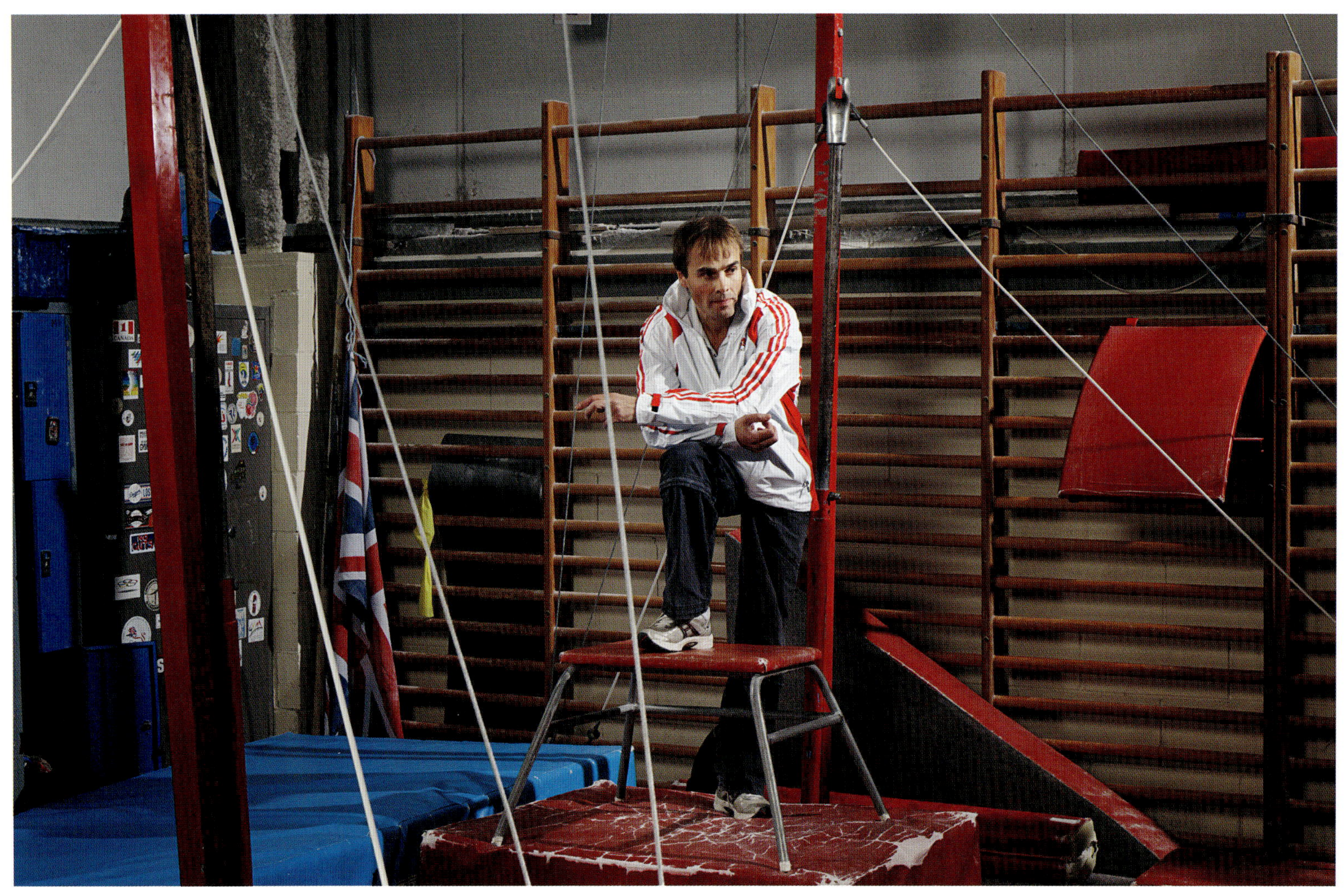

'Louis has been coming here since he was six. He didn't really stand out until he was thirteen. It's his mental attitude, not just talent and hard work.'
PAUL HALL, HEAD COACH, HUNTINGDON GYM

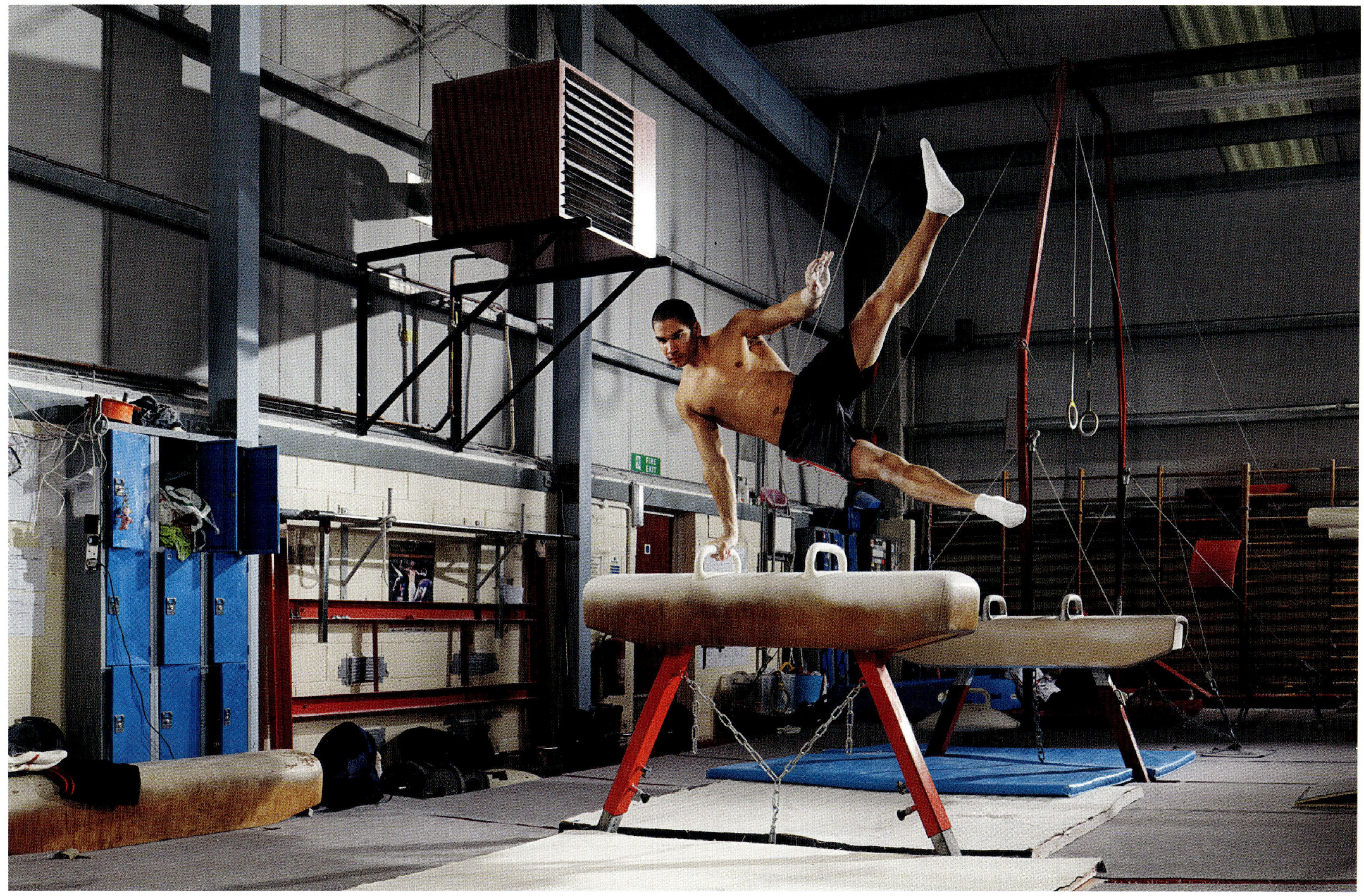

LOUIS SMITH WITH PAUL HALL

Photographed by Finlay MacKay
10 March 2011, Huntingdon Gymnastics Club, Huntingdon

Louis Smith (above) began gymnastics at the age of four, and is the first British gymnast to win an individual Olympic medal for one hundred years. Specialising in the pommel horse, he has since won medals at the World Championships (2010) and in the World Cup Series (2010 and 2011). Paul Hall (opposite) has coached the national team for over ten years and the Olympic squad for the last four years, nurturing some of the most successful gymnasts in British history, including Daniel Keatings and Luke Folwell.

JUDE KELLY AND SIR STEVE REDGRAVE

Photographed by Brian Griffin
4 February 2010,
South Bank, London

As Chair of Culture, Ceremonies and Education (2003–6), Jude Kelly (left) developed the cultural chapter of the London 2012 bid proposal. Currently Artistic Director of the Southbank Centre, London, she also sits on the Cultural Olympiad Board. Oarsman Steve Redgrave (right) is the UK's greatest Olympian and one of only five people to have won gold medals in five consecutive Olympic Games. He was the first athlete to join the London 2012 bid team, and is currently advising government as a 2012 Sports Legacy Champion.

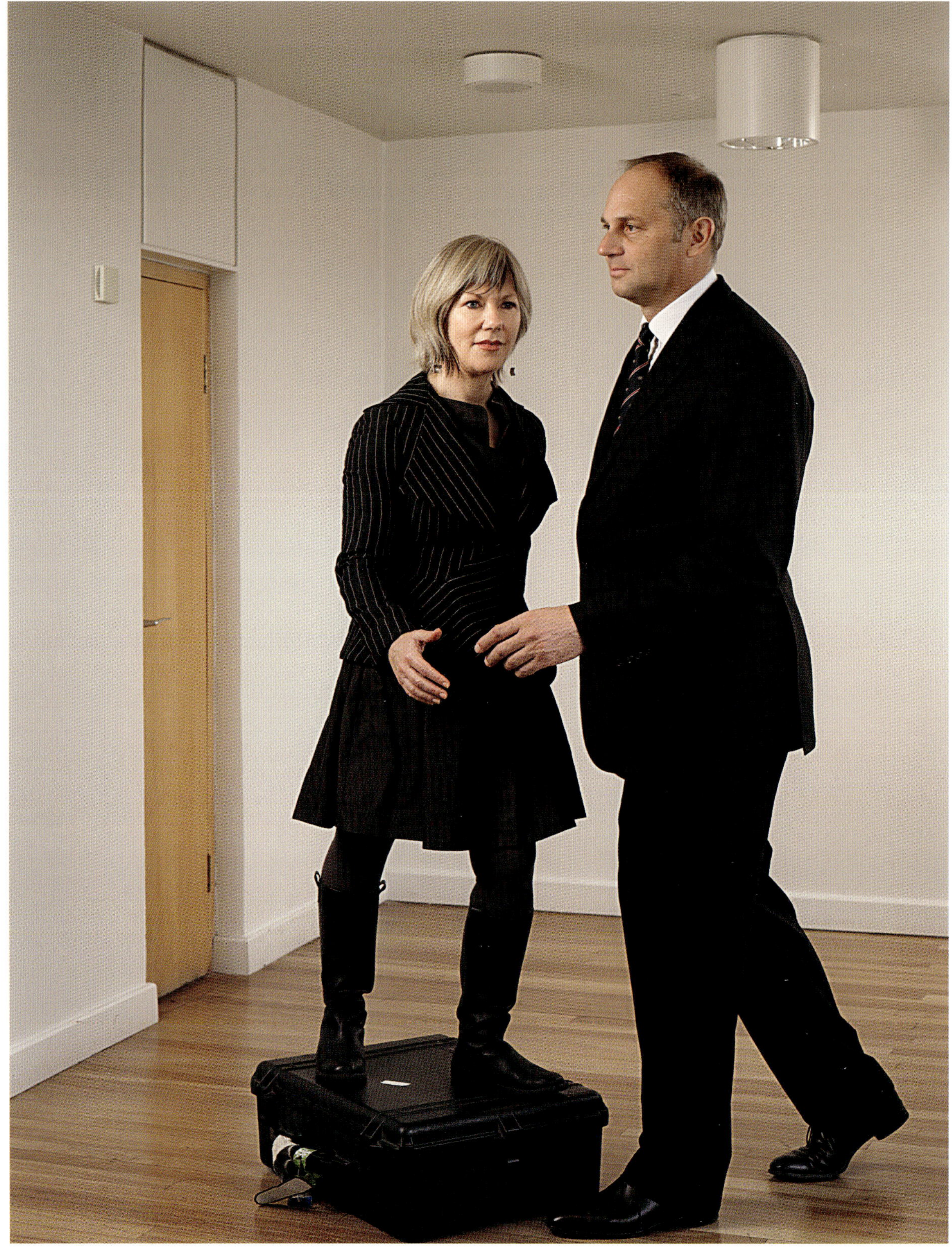

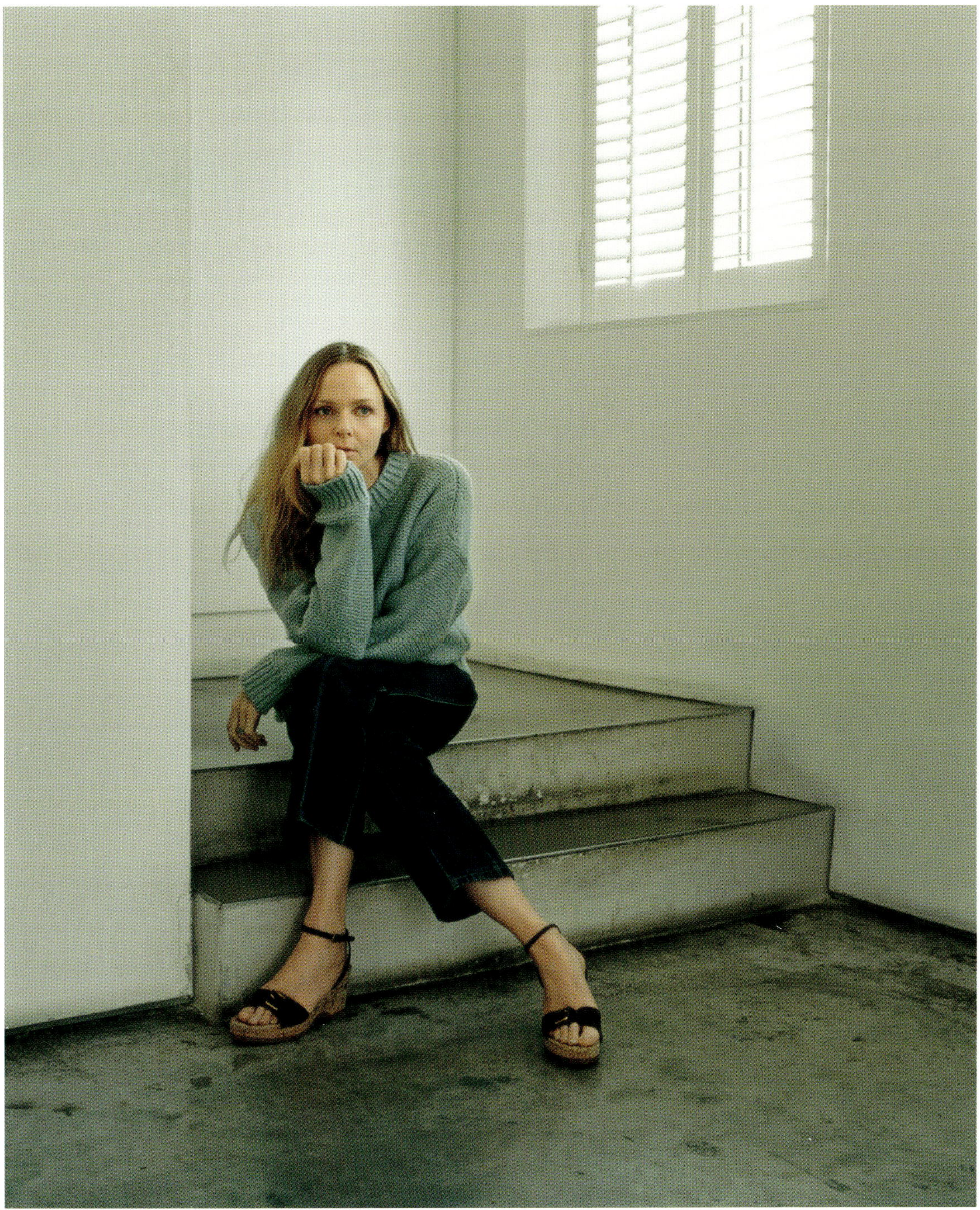

STELLA McCARTNEY

Photographed by Emma Hardy
24 May 2011, London

Stella McCartney is adidas's Creative Director for Team GB and ParalympicsGB, overseeing the design of both athlete kit and fan wear. She is the first internationally renowned designer to work with a sports brand on competition wear at a summer Olympic Games. She set up her own label, Stella McCartney, in 2001, and it is currently distributed in over fifty countries. McCartney has collaborated with adidas since 2004, designing critically acclaimed sports collections.

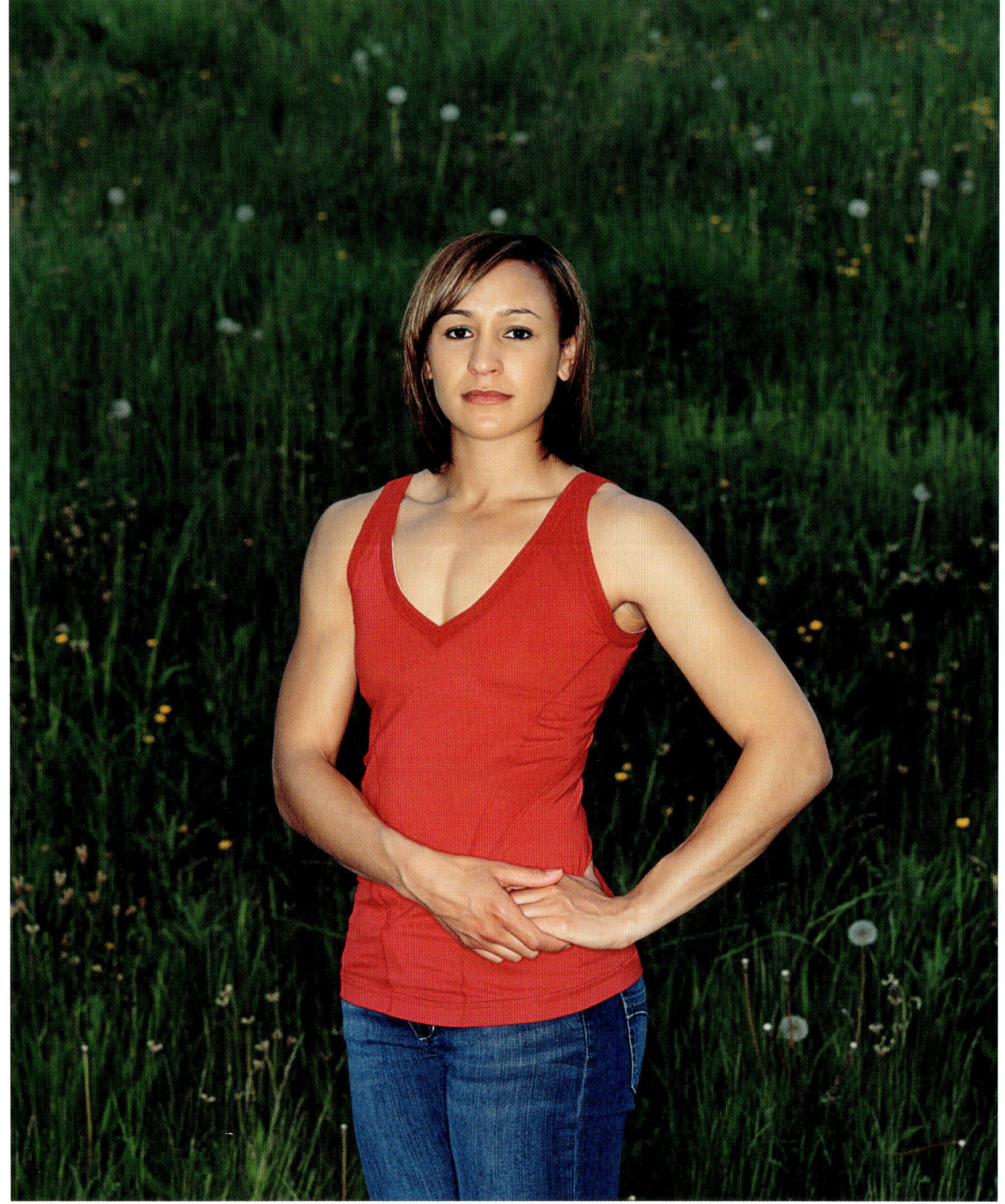

JESSICA ENNIS

Photographed by Bettina von Zwehl
20 May 2010, Don Valley Stadium, Sheffield

Jessica Ennis is a double World Champion in the heptathlon (2009) and the indoor pentathlon (2010). In her first senior championship at the 2006 Commonwealth Games she won a bronze medal. Five weeks before the Beijing 2008 Olympic and Paralympic Games, Ennis fractured her ankle. With the help of her coach, Toni Minichiello, she re-trained to compete using her other foot. Sheffield-born Ennis is training at the Don Valley Stadium in preparation for London 2012.

'I personally draw inspiration from my injury ... When I think about those days, it makes me feel really thankful for what I've got.' **JESSICA ENNIS**

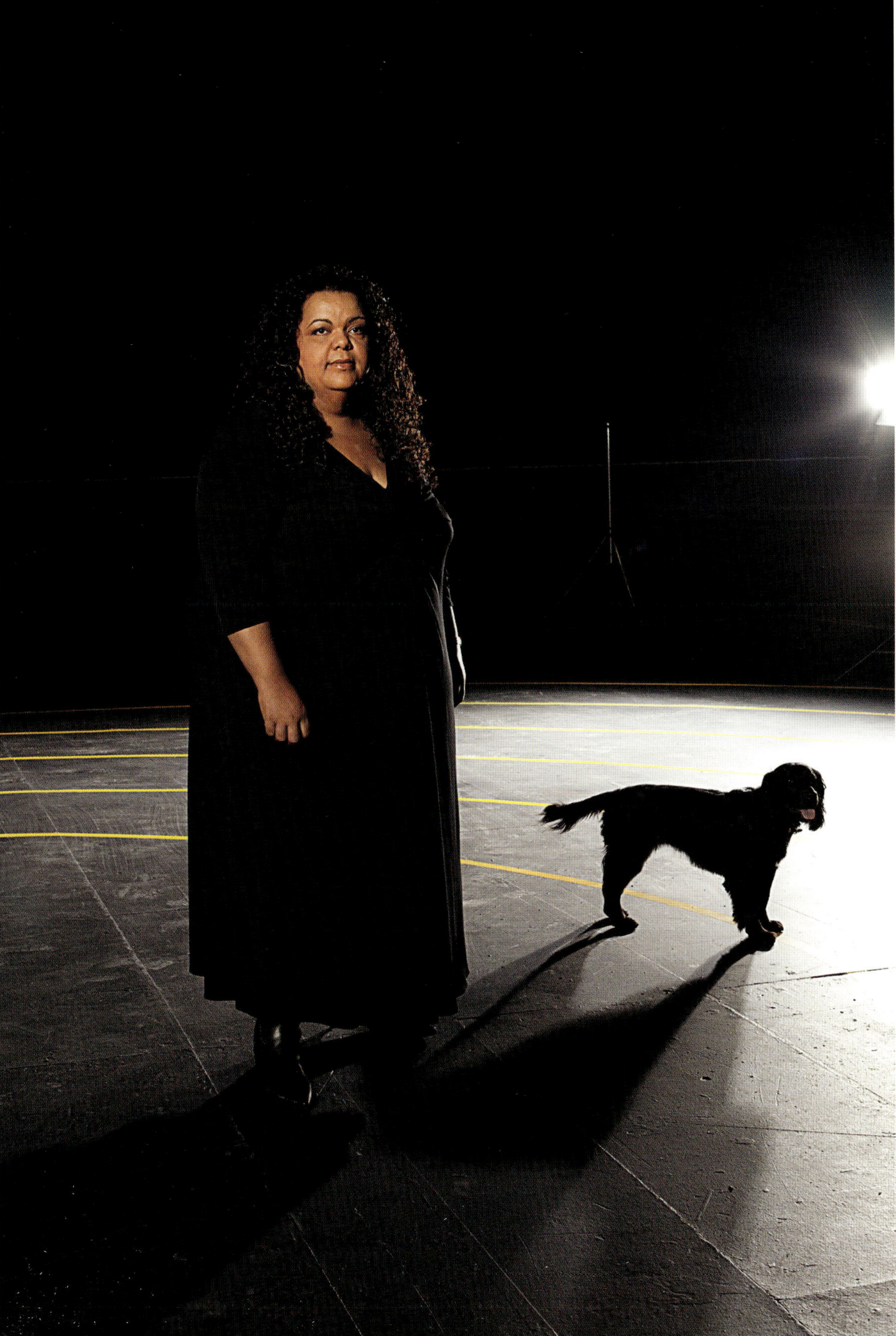

CATHERINE UGWU

Photographed by Jillian Edelstein
30 October 2011, Three Mills Studio, London

Catherine Ugwu is one of four executive producers for the London Organising Committee of the Olympic and Paralympic Games (LOCOG). She worked on the opening, closing and victory ceremonies of the Vancouver Winter Olympics in 2010, produced the opening ceremony for the 2006 Asian Games in Doha, the closing ceremony for the 2002 Commonwealth Games in Manchester and a large-scale performance spectacle to mark the opening of the Millennium Dome. In 1997 she co-founded the Live Art Development Agency in London.

'This experience can be compared to no other.'
CATHERINE UGWU

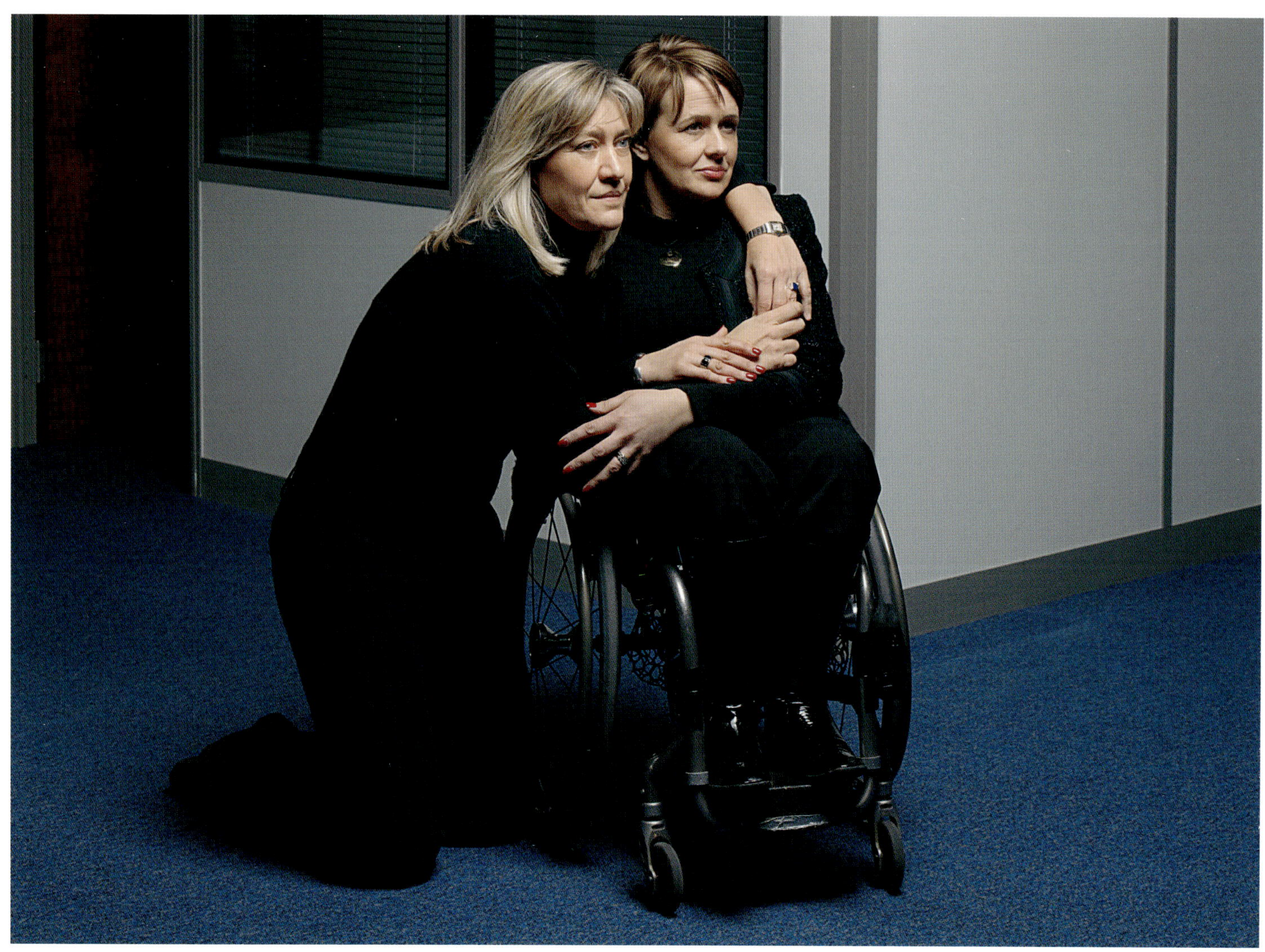

DEBBIE JEVANS AND DAME TANNI GREY-THOMPSON
Photographed by Brian Griffin
27 February 2010,
Canary Wharf, London

Former GB tennis player Debbie Jevans (left) is the first woman to reach the top in UK sports administration. Drawing on her experience at the International Tennis Federation, she worked with the London 2012 bid team before becoming Director of Sport for the London Organising Committee of the Olympic and Paralympic Games (LOCOG). With fifteen Paralympic medals, including eleven golds, Tanni Grey-Thompson (right) is the UK's most successful Paralympian. She was an Ambassador for the London 2012 bid team, and is a crossbench peer in the House of Lords.

'It's giving back – to your city, to your country.' DEBBIE JEVANS

BORIS JOHNSON

Photographed by Jillian Edelstein
13 January 2012, City Hall, London

As Mayor of London, Boris Johnson received the Olympic flag on behalf of the city at the closing ceremony of the Beijing Olympic Games in 2008. He has served as co-chair of the Olympic Board, with a key role in ensuring that a sustainable legacy of new jobs, homes, communities and infrastructure improvements is created from the 2012 Games. As the executive of the Greater London Authority, Johnson's role directs economic development, transport and oversees policing for the capital. Formally a journalist and editor of the *Spectator*, he served as a Conservative MP from 2001–7.

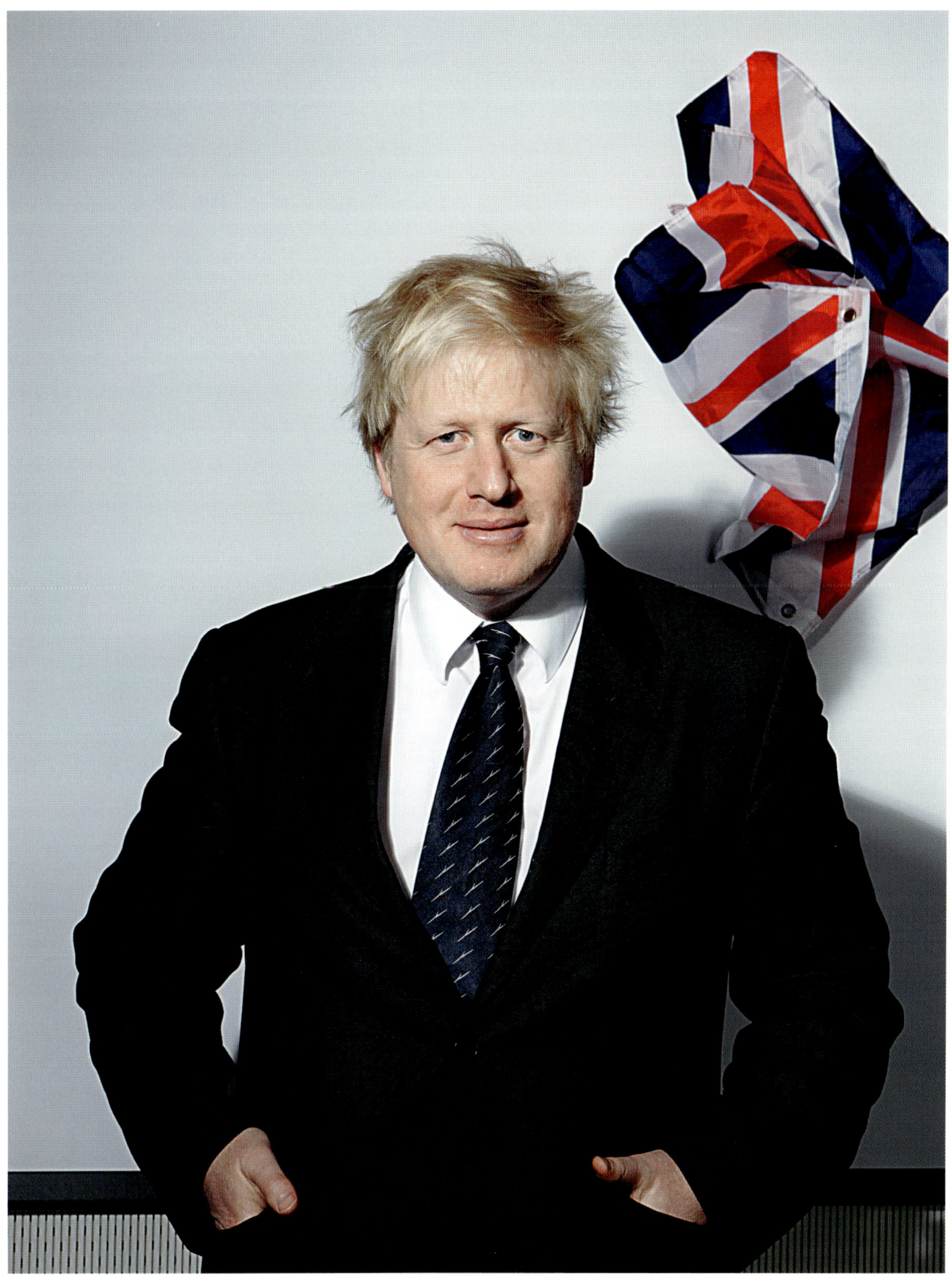

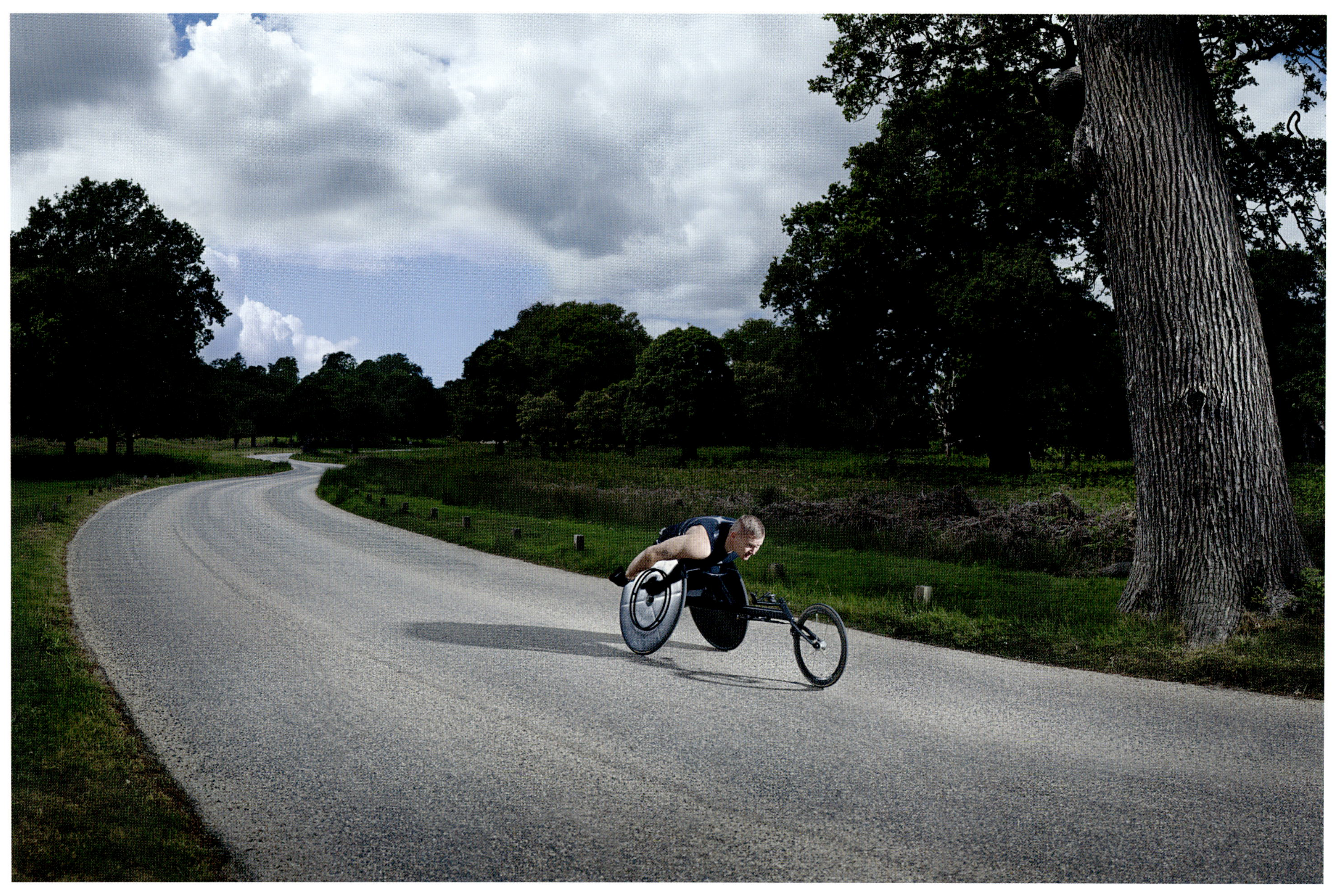

‘When David came to me and said he wanted to win gold at the Paralympic Games and become World Champion, I said, “I’ll take you on. I’ll make you laugh and I’ll make you cry.”’

JENNY ARCHER, PERSONAL COACH TO DAVID WEIR

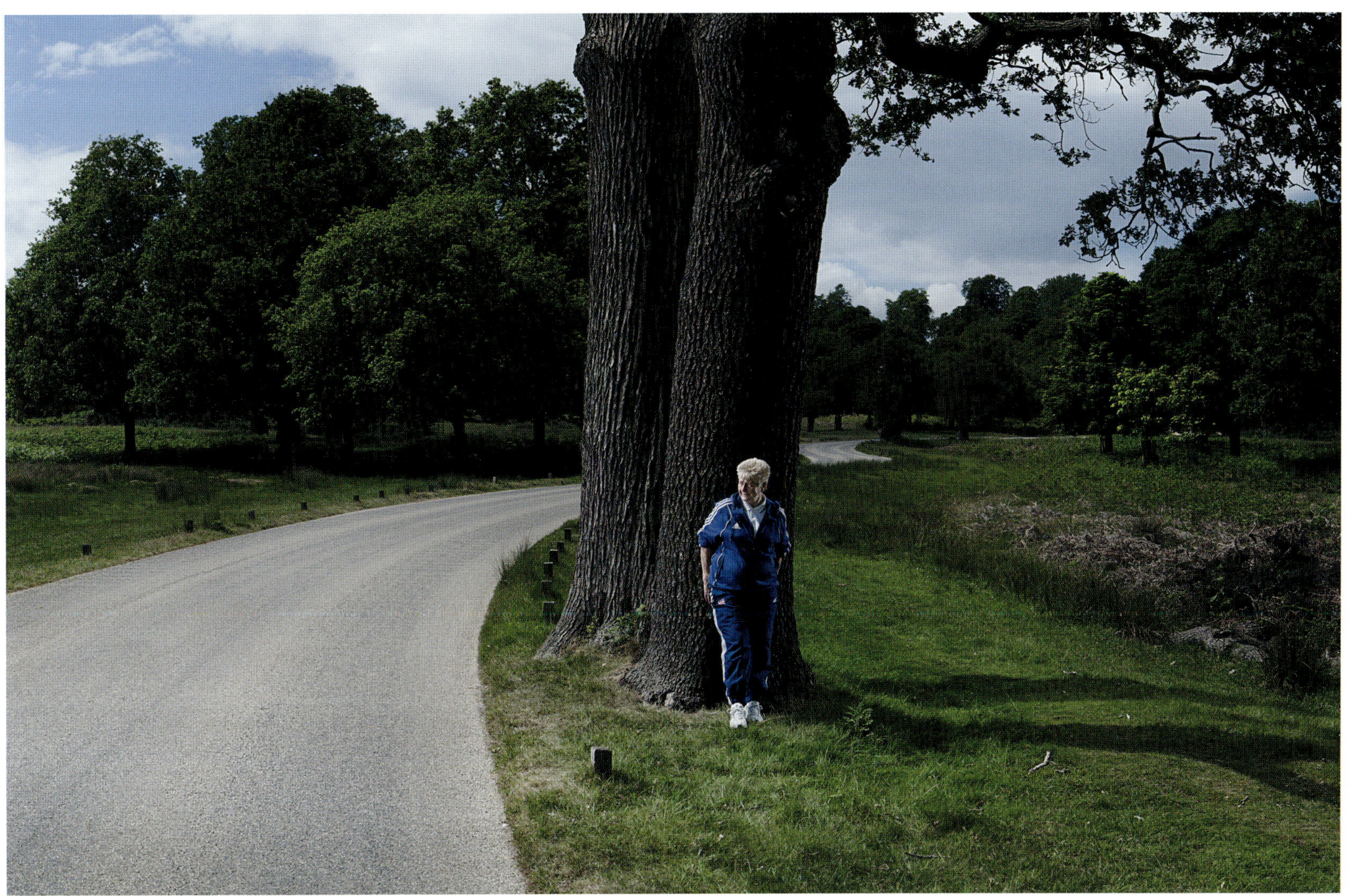

DAVID WEIR WITH JENNY ARCHER

Photographed by Finlay MacKay
12 May 2011, Richmond Park, London

David Weir was introduced to wheelchair racing at primary school and first competed in the London Mini Marathon at the age of eight. He met Jenny Archer at the London Youth Games and she became his coach in 2002. Archer guided him to double gold in Beijing 2008, triple gold at the 2011 World Championships and a record fifth title at the 2011 London Marathon. Formerly a teacher, Archer was a fitness coach with Wimbledon Football Club for eleven years before working with Weir to achieve his Paralympic ambitions.

LEADERS

Whether by spearheading the bid for the London 2012 Olympic and Paralympic Games, creating the masterplan for the Olympic site or co-ordinating the largest peacetime catering operation in the world, these inspirational individuals have organised and motivated their teams to ensure the success of every aspect of the Games.

PETER HENDY AND GRAHAM JONES
Photographed by Jillian Edelstein
14 October 2011, Blackwall Tunnel, London

Transport for London's (TfL) Commissioner, Peter Hendy (left), is responsible for all transport in the capital apart from local roads, airports and the national railway network. He has overseen £15.9 billion of capital investment in London's transport system, including major improvements to boost capacity before the London 2012 Olympic and Paralympic Games. Civil engineer Graham Jones (right) is TfL's Games Programme Director for Surface Transport, leading the preparation, design and delivery of road and traffic operations within London.

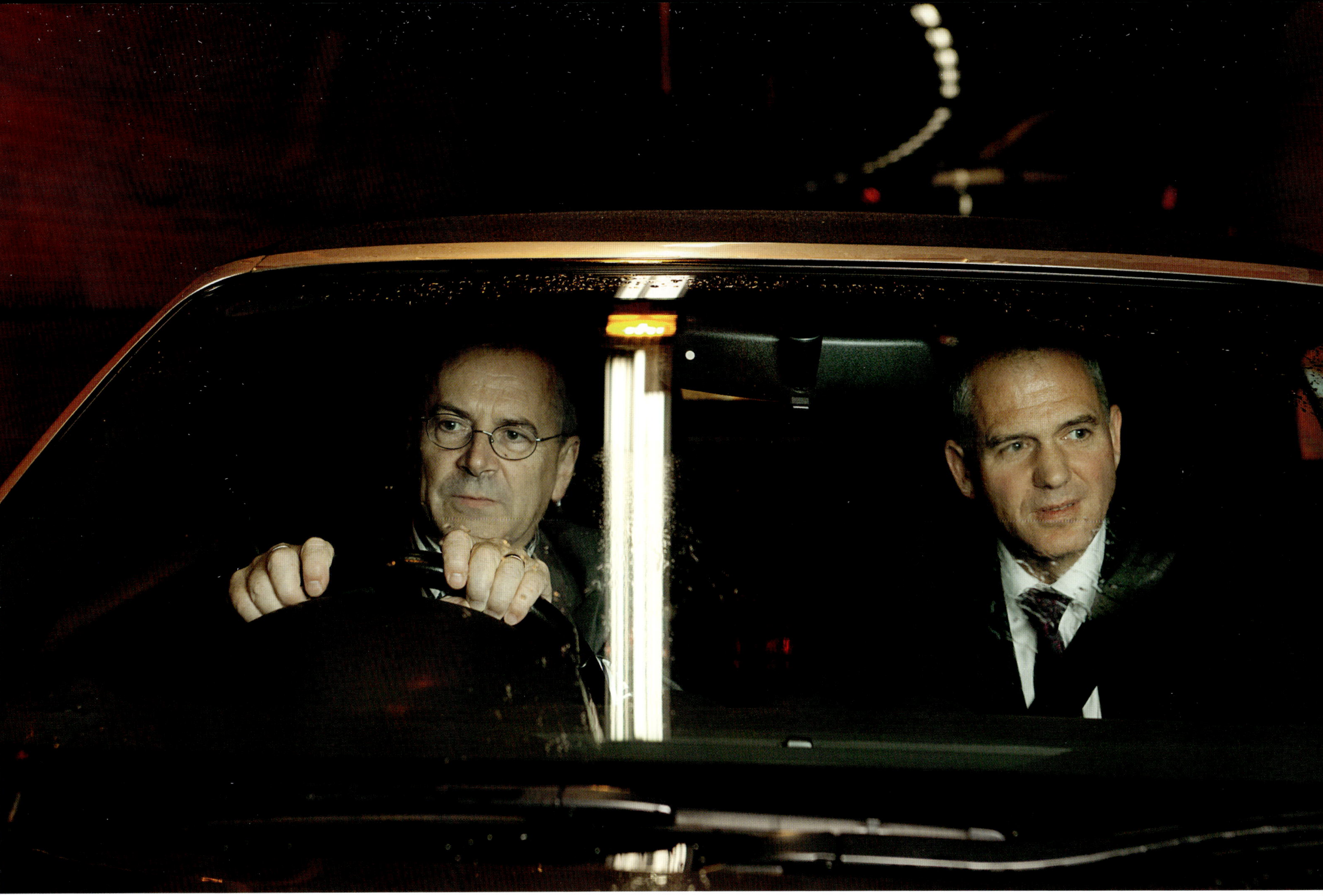

'We have two objectives: to make sure that London 2012 transport is successful and to ensure that the city continues to function.' **PETER HENDY**

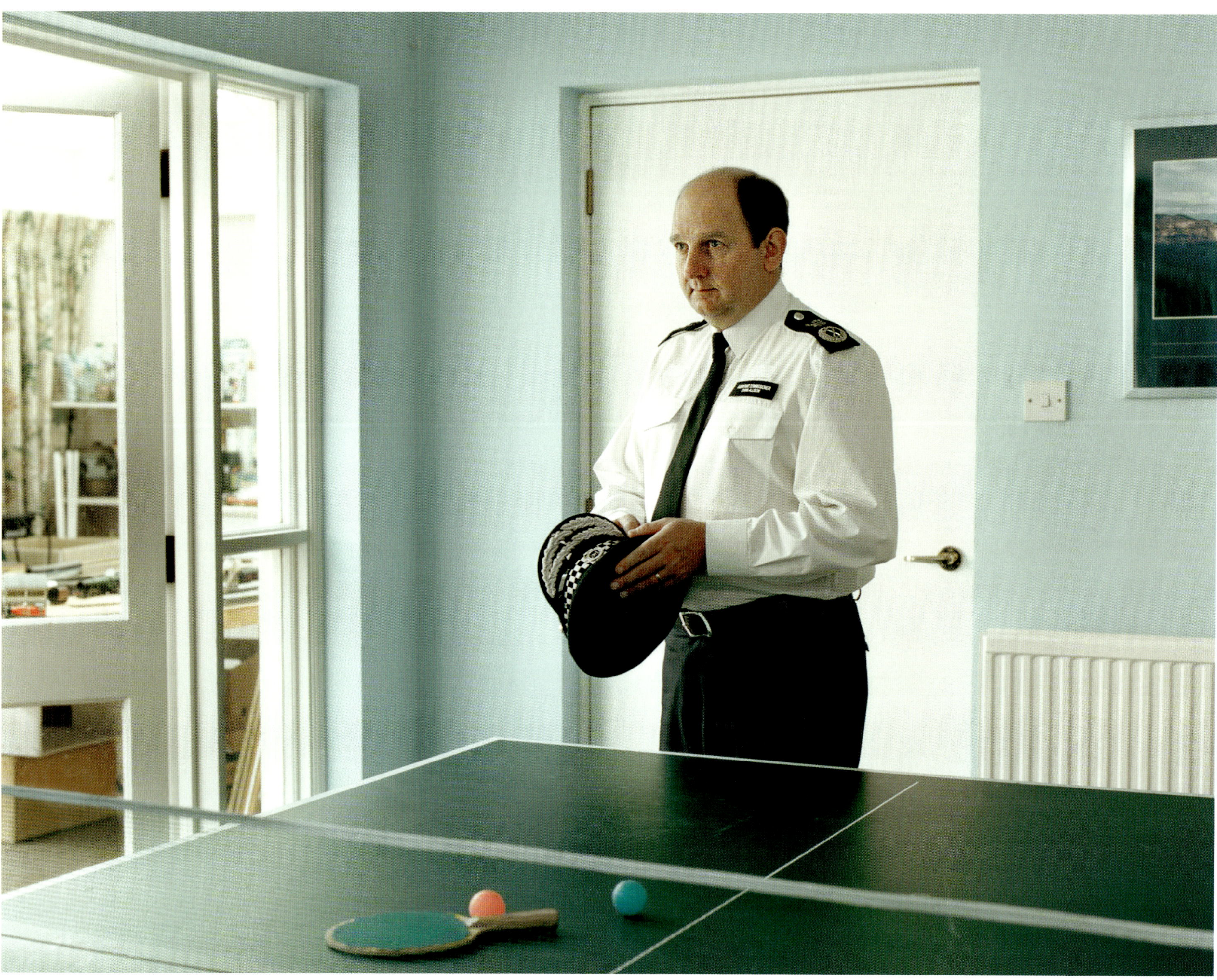

CHRIS ALLISON

Photographed by Emma Hardy
15 April 2011, London

Assistant Commissioner Chris Allison has been a uniformed officer with the Metropolitan Police for most of his twenty-seven-year career. He was appointed National Olympic Security Coordinator in 2009 and is responsible for delivering the national safety and security plan. Allison will lead the UK's largest-ever peacetime policing operation, which will have an impact on every police force in the country.

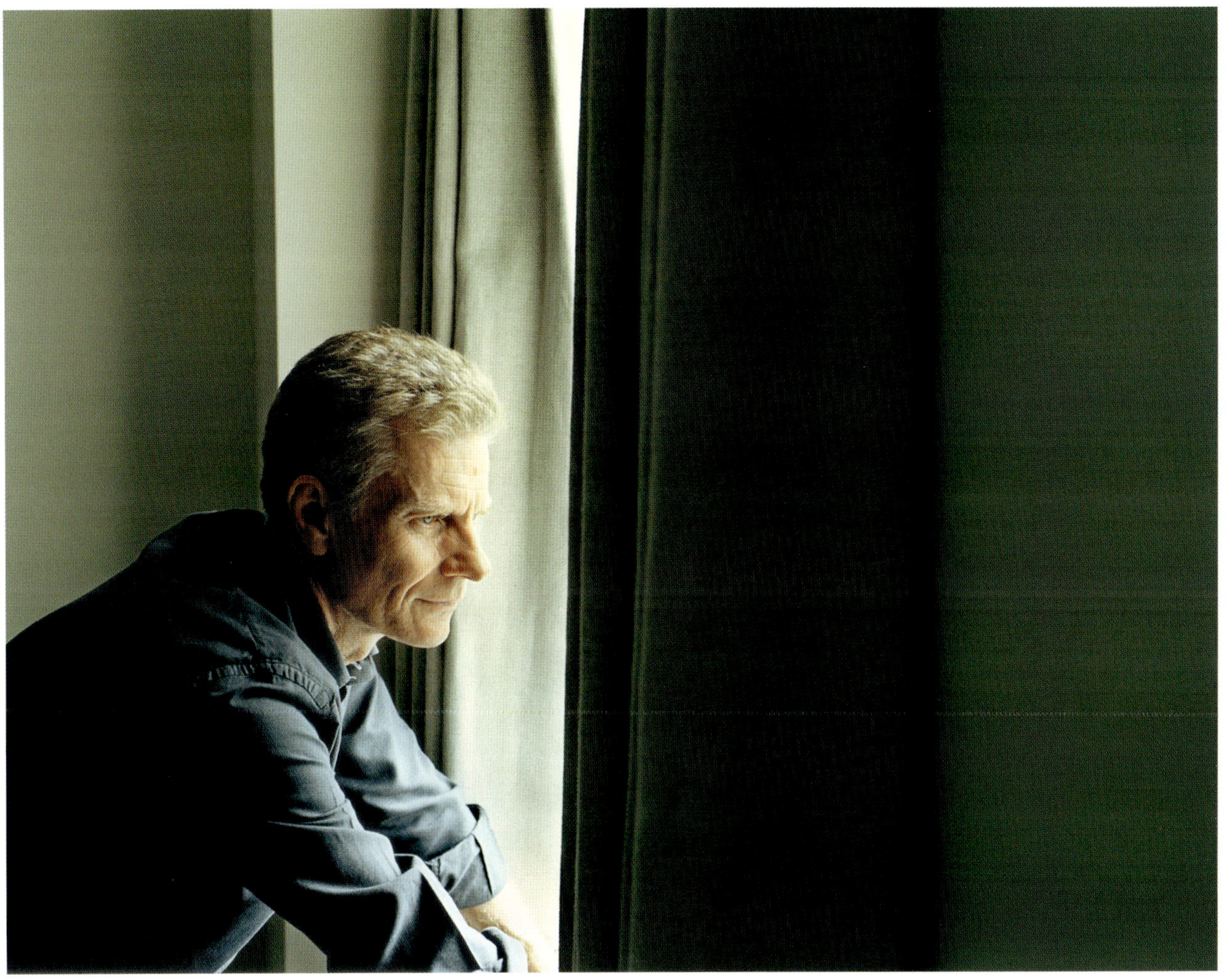

PAUL DEIGHTON

Photographed by Emma Hardy
16 April 2011, London

Paul Deighton was appointed CEO of the London Organising Committee of the Olympic and Paralympic Games (LOCOG) in 2006. He is in charge of day-to-day operations, from raising the £2 billion budget from the private sector to working closely with the Olympic Delivery Authority and meeting all the requirements for a successful Olympic and Paralympic Games in 2012. Deighton also leads LOCOG's relationships with key stakeholders including the Government, the Mayor of London, the British Olympic Association and the British Paralympic Association.

MARTIN GREEN

Photographed by Jillian Edelstein
30 October 2011,
Three Mills Studio, London

Martin Green is Head of Ceremonies for the London Organising Committee of the Olympic and Paralympic Games (LOCOG). He joined LOCOG in 2007 to produce the handover ceremony in Beijing in 2008, and now leads the teams responsible for the opening and closing ceremonies of the London 2012 Olympic and Paralympic Games, as well as the torch relays, victory ceremonies and medal ceremonies.

'This portrait captures the essence of the job. It is at once magical and terrifying.'
MARTIN GREEN

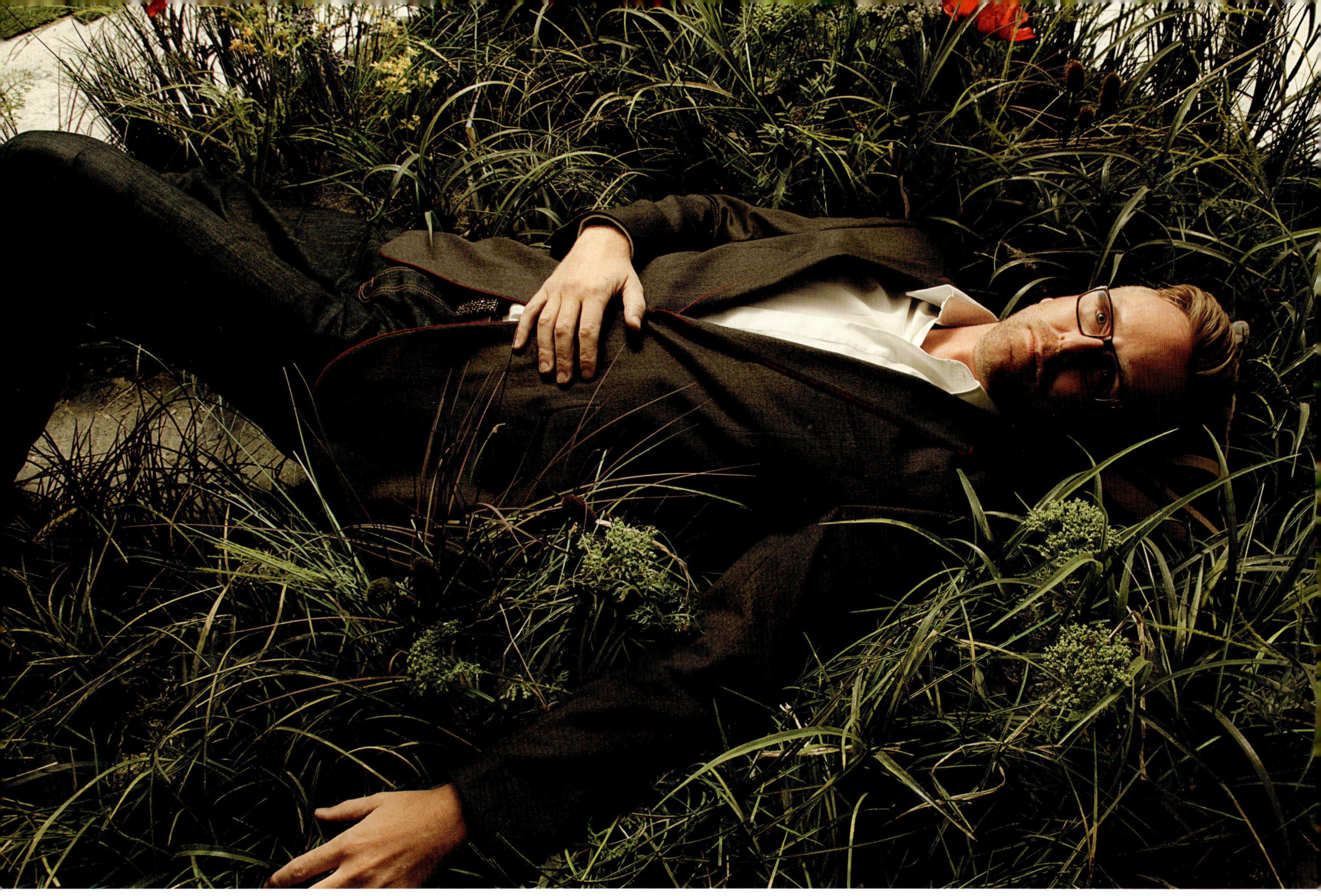

DAVID TANNER WITH MAGGIE NETTO

Photographed by Anderson & Low
31 January 2012, The Old Rowing Tank,
GB Rowing Headquarters, London

David Tanner has been British rowing's Performance Director since 1996, making him the most experienced leader of Britain's Olympic and Paralympic programmes. He was a medal coach at the 1980 Moscow Olympic Games, and more recently head teacher of a London comprehensive school. He has overseen British rowing's increasing success on the water, culminating in Great Britain heading the rowing medal tables in both the Olympic and Paralympic Games in Beijing 2008. Maggie Netto has been Tanner's assistant throughout, and together they form a formidable and successful partnership.

'It's a privilege working with elite athletes. They're unique. It's about the end prize, gold standard. As a support team we are the same. You couldn't operate in any other way.'
MAGGIE NETTO

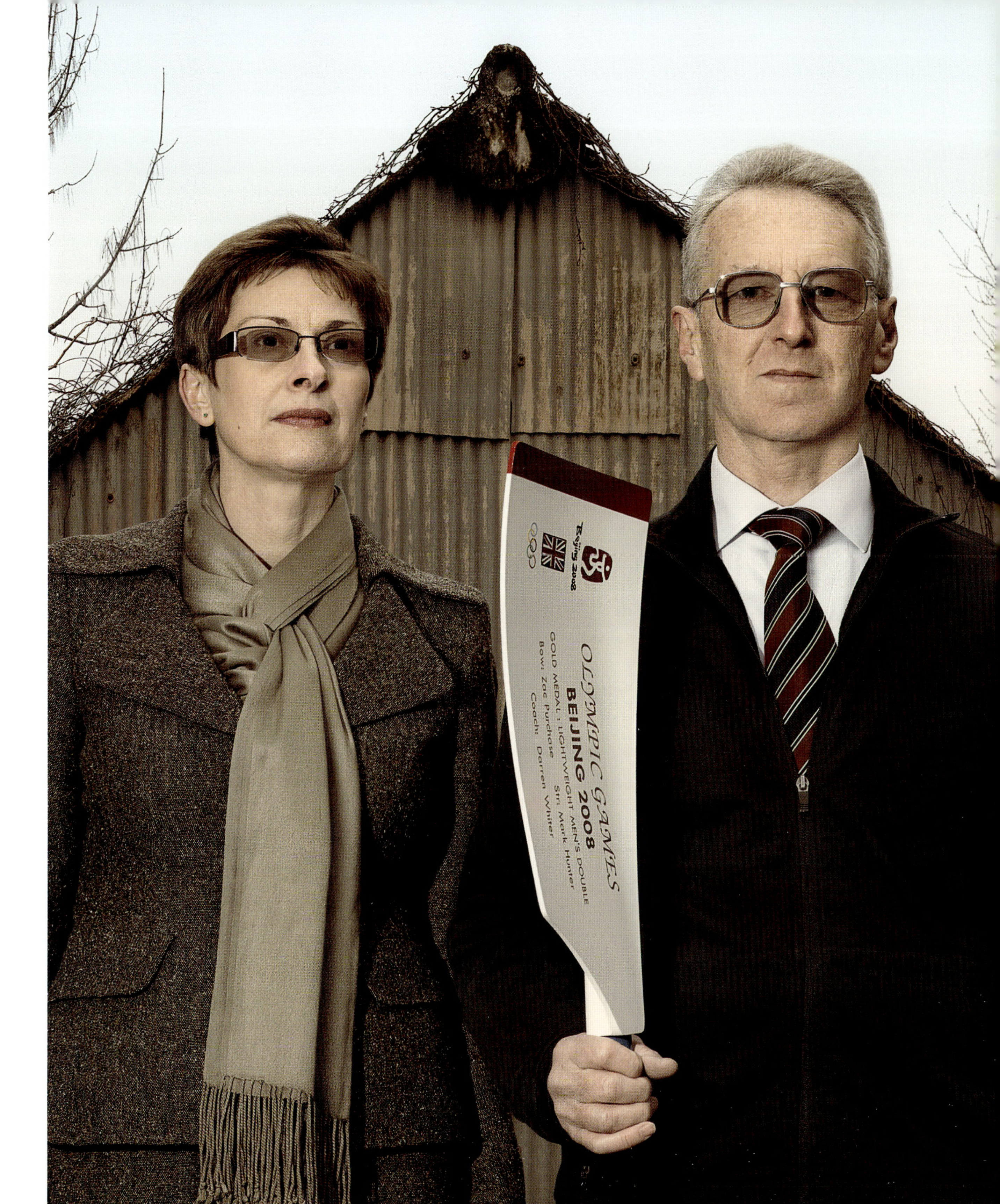
Beijing 2008
OLYMPIC GAMES
BEIJING 2008
GOLD MEDAL : LIGHTWEIGHT MEN'S DOUBLE
Bow: Zac Purchase
Str: Mark Hunter
Coach: Darren Whiter

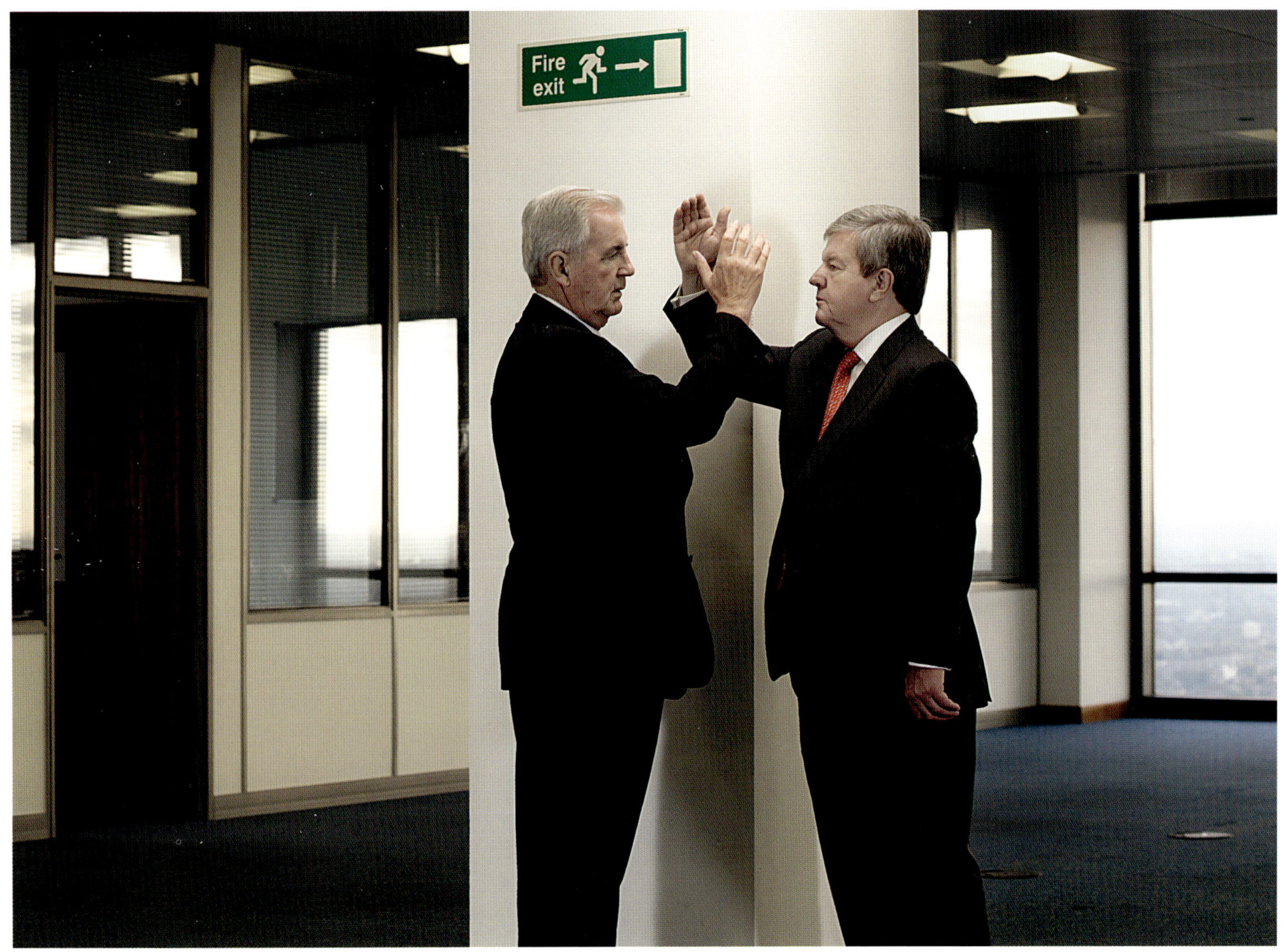

**SIR CRAIG REEDIE
AND SIR KEITH MILLS**

Photographed by Brian Griffin
19 October 2009,
Canary Wharf, London

'Keith Mills is my mentor.'
SEBASTIAN COE

Craig Reedie (left) is a British representative on the International Olympic Committee and an executive board member since 2009. As Chair of the British Olympic Association (1992–2005), Reedie was a driving force behind the bid to host the 2012 Olympic and Paralympic Games. While working in marketing, Keith Mills (right) devised the Air Miles and Nectar incentive schemes, positioning him at the forefront of British business. In 2003 he was appointed Chief Executive of London 2012 to lead the bid team. He later became deputy chair of the London Organising Committee of the Olympic and Paralympic Games (LOCOG).

TONY WINTERBOTTOM AND KEN LIVINGSTONE

Photographed by Brian Griffin
25 January 2010, City Hall, London

During his seven years as Executive Director, Major Projects at the London Delivery Agency (LDA), Tony Winterbottom (left) was at the centre of significant London developments, including Wembley Stadium. He played a key role in the delivery of London's bid to host the 2012 Olympic and Paralympic Games. In 2001, Ken Livingstone (right), then Mayor of London, saw the project's potential for the regeneration of east London and offered the British Olympic Association essential and unequivocal support in their bid campaign. Subsequently, Livingstone's financial agreement with Tessa Jowell, then Minister for Culture, Media and Sport, enabled her to gain full Cabinet endorsement in 2003.

'The Olympic bidding process was a real team effort, but Ken was the driver.' TONY WINTERBOTTOM

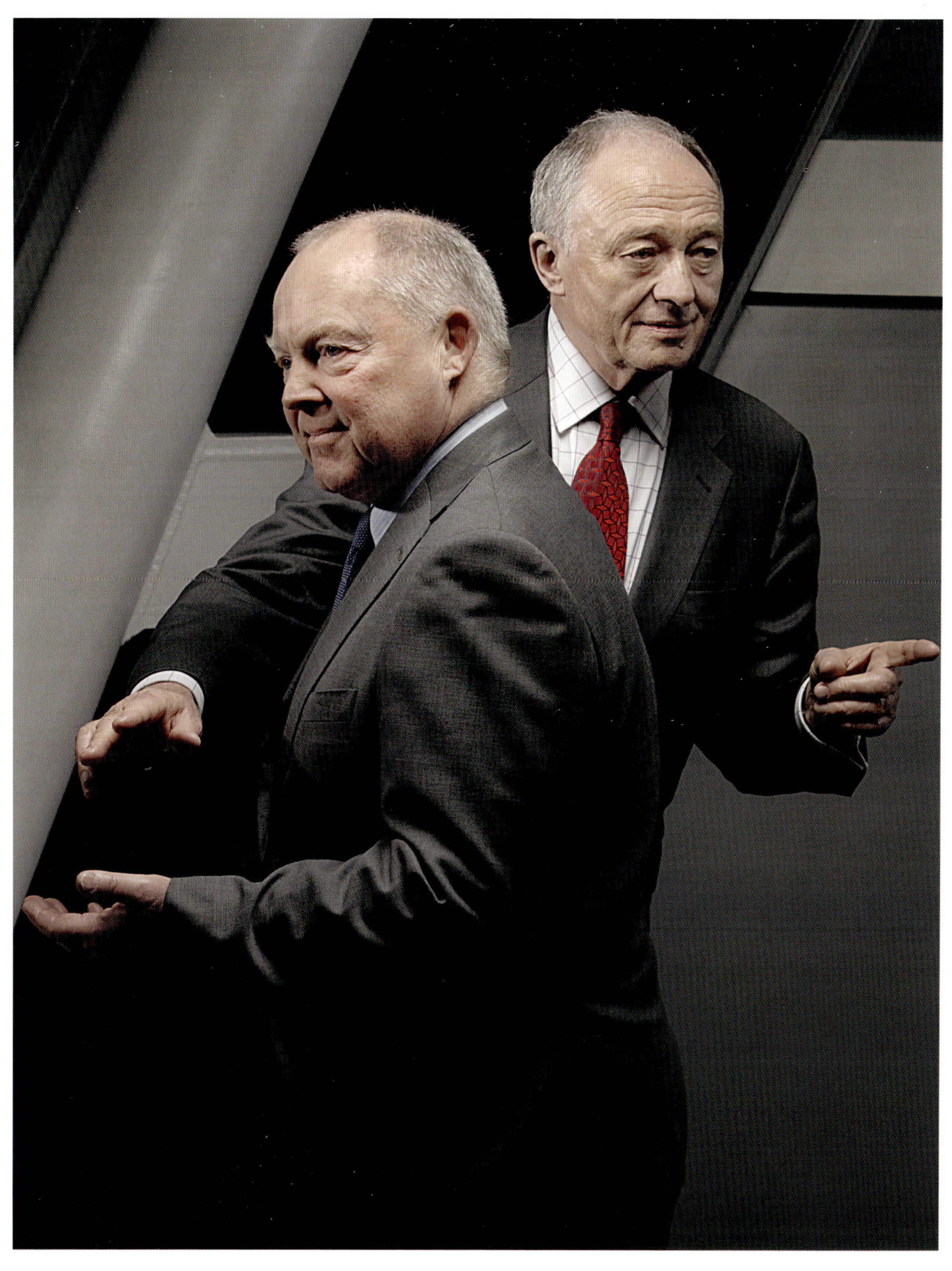

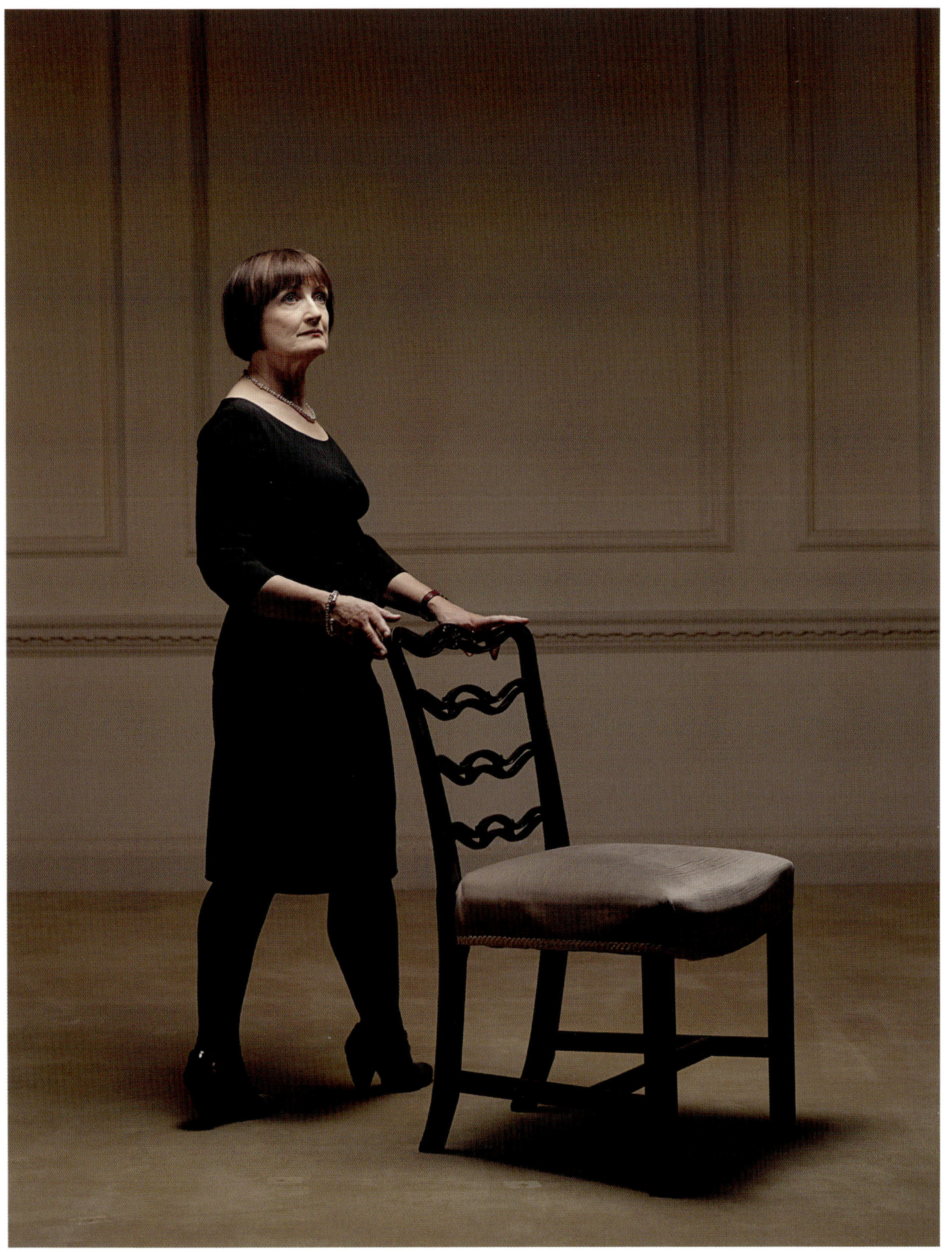

TESSA JOWELL

Photographed by Brian Griffin
2 February 2010, Cabinet Office, London

Tessa Jowell played a critical part in London's bid to host the 2012 Olympic and Paralympic Games. In 2003, after a two-year campaign, she gained the required endorsement of the entire Cabinet to support the proposal. Jowell entered Parliament as a Labour MP in 1992 and was a member of both the Blair and Brown Cabinets, with roles including Secretary of State for Culture, Media and Sport (2001–7) and Minister for London (2009–10). The role of Minister for the Olympics was added to her portfolio in July 2005, which she has shadowed in opposition since 2010.

'We are all so proud to be part of this. It's a passion.'
TESSA JOWELL

JAN MATTHEWS

Photographed by Jillian Edelstein
8 November 2011, Smithfield Market, London

As Head of Catering, Cleaning and Waste for the London Organising Committee of the Olympic and Paralympic Games (LOCOG), Jan Matthews is responsible for the world's largest peacetime catering operation, serving 14 million meals over seventy-seven days. LOCOG's Food Vision Plan focuses on sustainability and local procurement, and has set new industry standards that will leave a lasting legacy. Matthews is working with third-party partners to deliver the London 2012 zero-waste-direct-to-landfill pledge, and was previously responsible for supplying catering, retail and leisure facilities to the British armed forces.

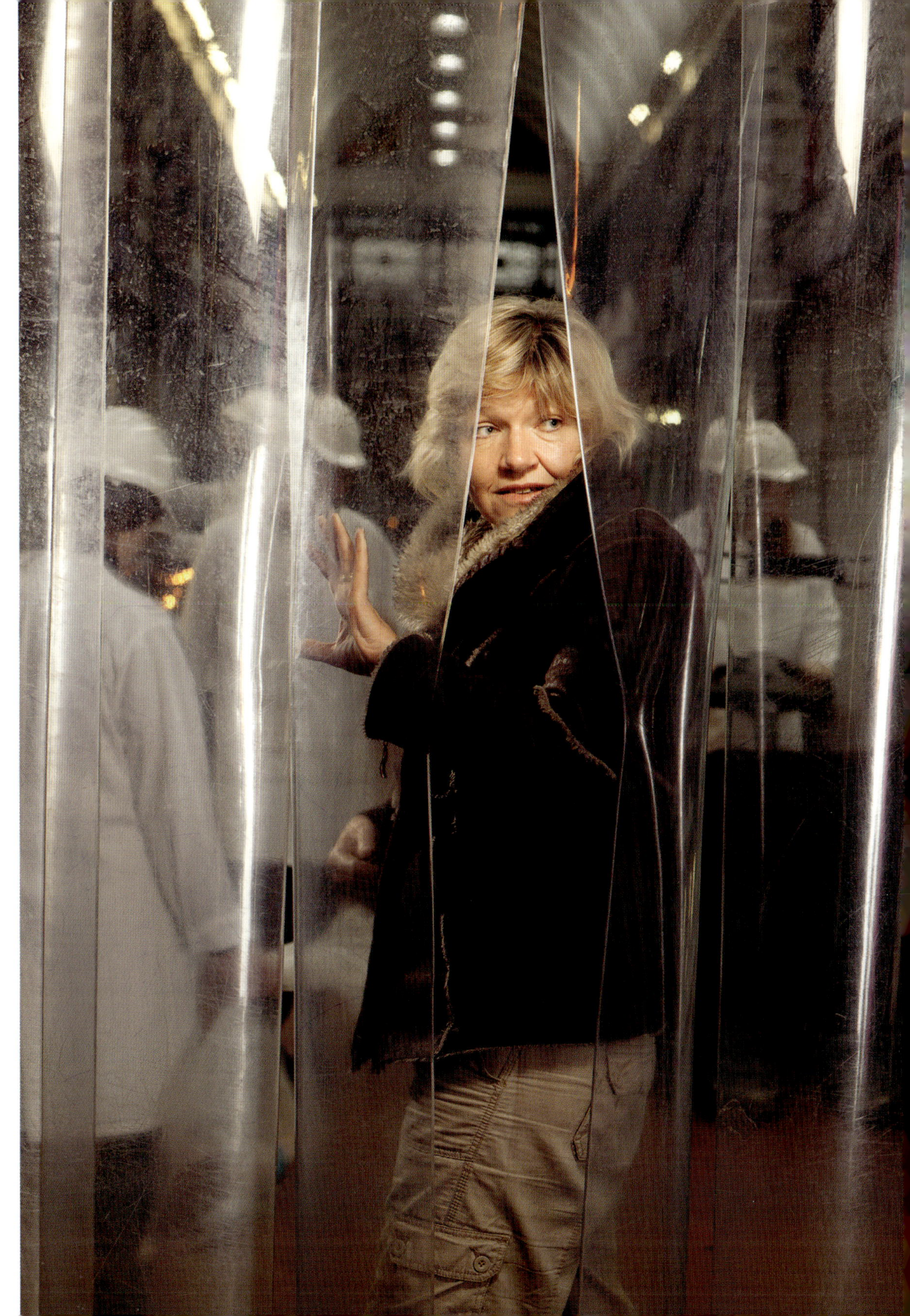

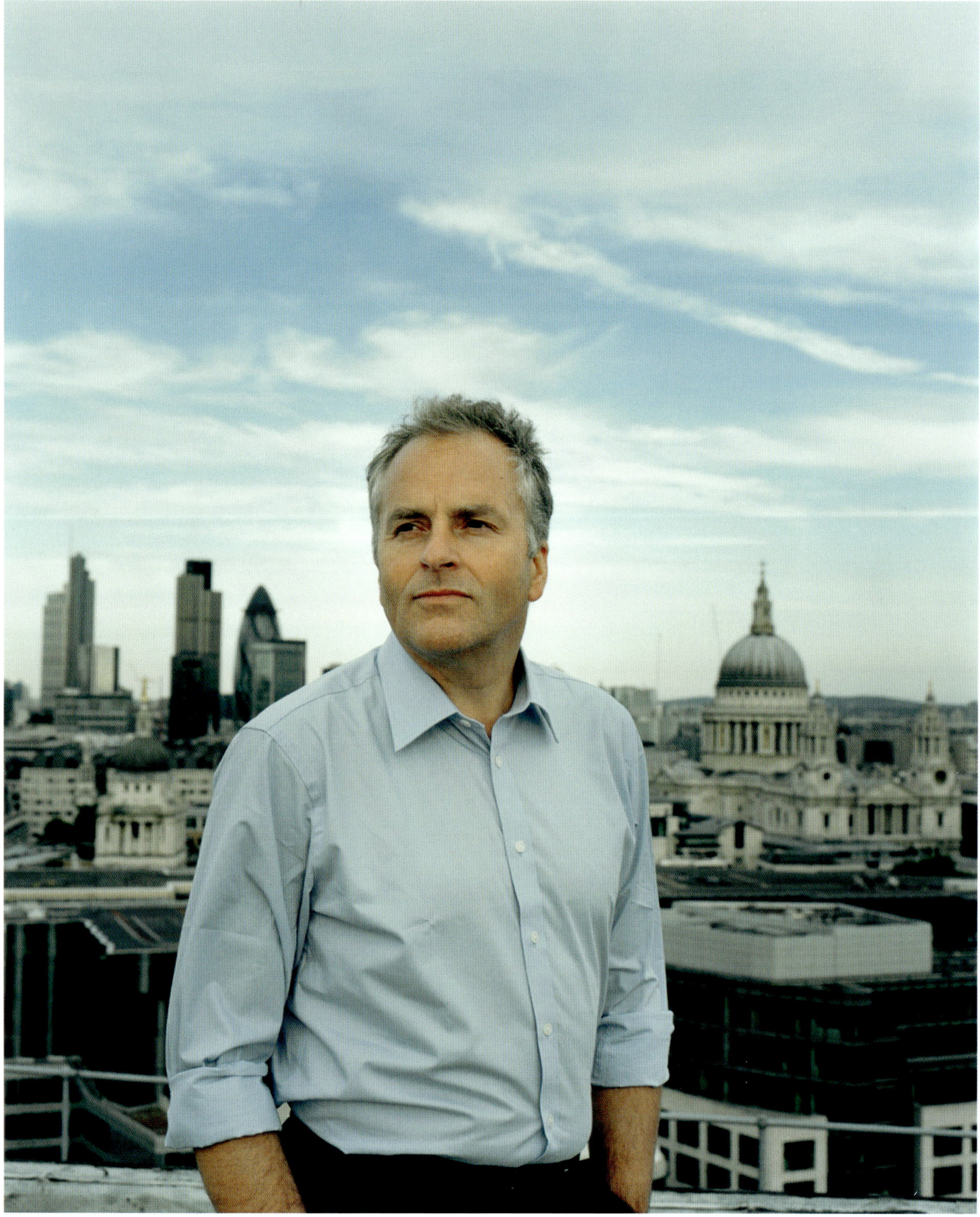

GERRY PENNELL

Photographed by Emma Hardy
25 May 2011, London

Chief Information Officer Gerry Pennell leads the London Organising Committee of the Olympic and Paralympic Games (LOCOG) and their partners in delivering IT, telecommunications and audio-visual, results, timing and scoring technologies, all vital to the staging of London 2012. His role encompasses everything from the infrastructure network and provision of hardware to the distribution of results. Pennell was Director of Technology for the 2002 Commonwealth Games, and previously led large-scale projects at the Co-operative Group and PricewaterhouseCoopers.

'It is big and it is complex and it has to work right first time – that's a challenge worth getting out of bed for!'
GERRY PENNELL

DAVID HIGGINS,
IAN GALLOWAY
AND SIR JOHN ARMITT

Photographed by Brian Griffin
3 March 2010,
Bow Yard East, London

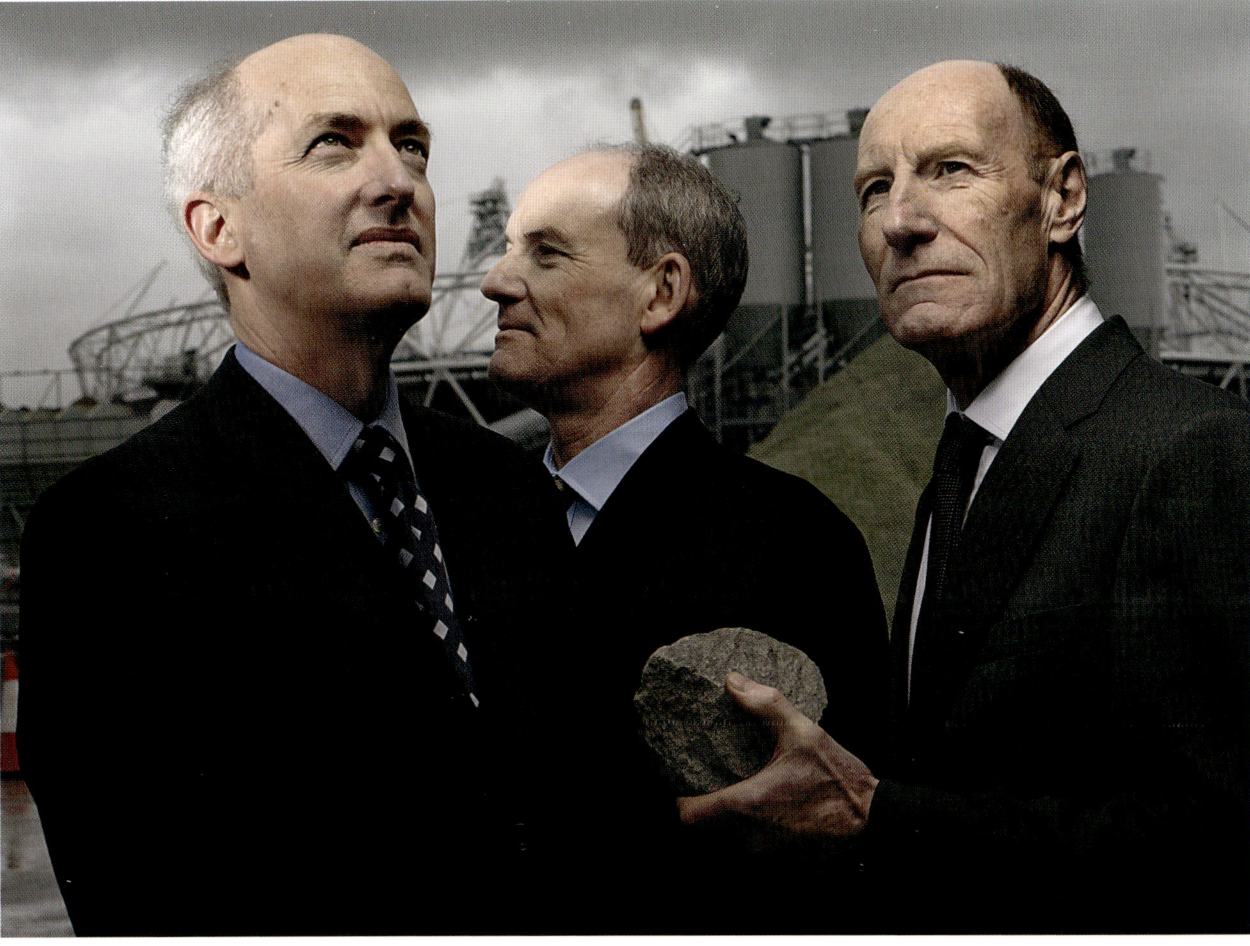

'The genius of the London 2012 Olympic and Paralympic Games is David Higgins. He is building the Olympic Park on budget and on time.'

TESSA JOWELL

Australian-born David Higgins (left) was chief executive of the Olympic Delivery Authority (ODA) from 2006 to 2011, with responsibility for the design and construction of London 2012 venues and infrastructure. He joined Network Rail as chief executive in February 2011. Ian Galloway (centre) brought his experience of large-scale infrastructure projects, including the Channel Tunnel Rail Link, to his position as head of the construction consortium, CLM. Created to work on the 2012 bid, CLM was later appointed by the ODA as their delivery partner. ODA Chair Sir John Armitt (right), a former civil engineer, joined the organisation following his retirement as chief executive of Network Rail in 2007, and worked closely with Higgins on ODA strategy.

SIMON WRIGHT, MARGARET HICKISH, MORAG STUART, HUGH SUMNER AND HOWARD SHIPLEE

Photographed by Brian Griffin
5 March 2010,
Stratford International, London

Simon Wright (far left), the Olympic Delivery Authority (ODA) Director of Infrastructure and Utilities, headed up the environmental, geotechnical and civil engineering programme across the 2012 Olympic Park. Margaret Hickish (second from left), a civil engineer and wheelchair user since 1997, was the ODA Principal Access Officer, responsible for making London 2012 the most accessible Olympic and Paralympic Games ever. Morag Stuart (centre) was ODA Head of Procurement (2006–9). Hugh Sumner's (second from right) transport planning played a critical part in London's successful bid. He went on to deliver this as ODA Director of Transport. Howard Shiplee (far right), as ODA Director of Construction, led the construction contracts, budgets and schedules.

'Looking at the picture now tells me that Brian Griffin is a very good judge of personality, as he depicts us in ways that reflect our behaviours.' **HOWARD SHIPLEE**

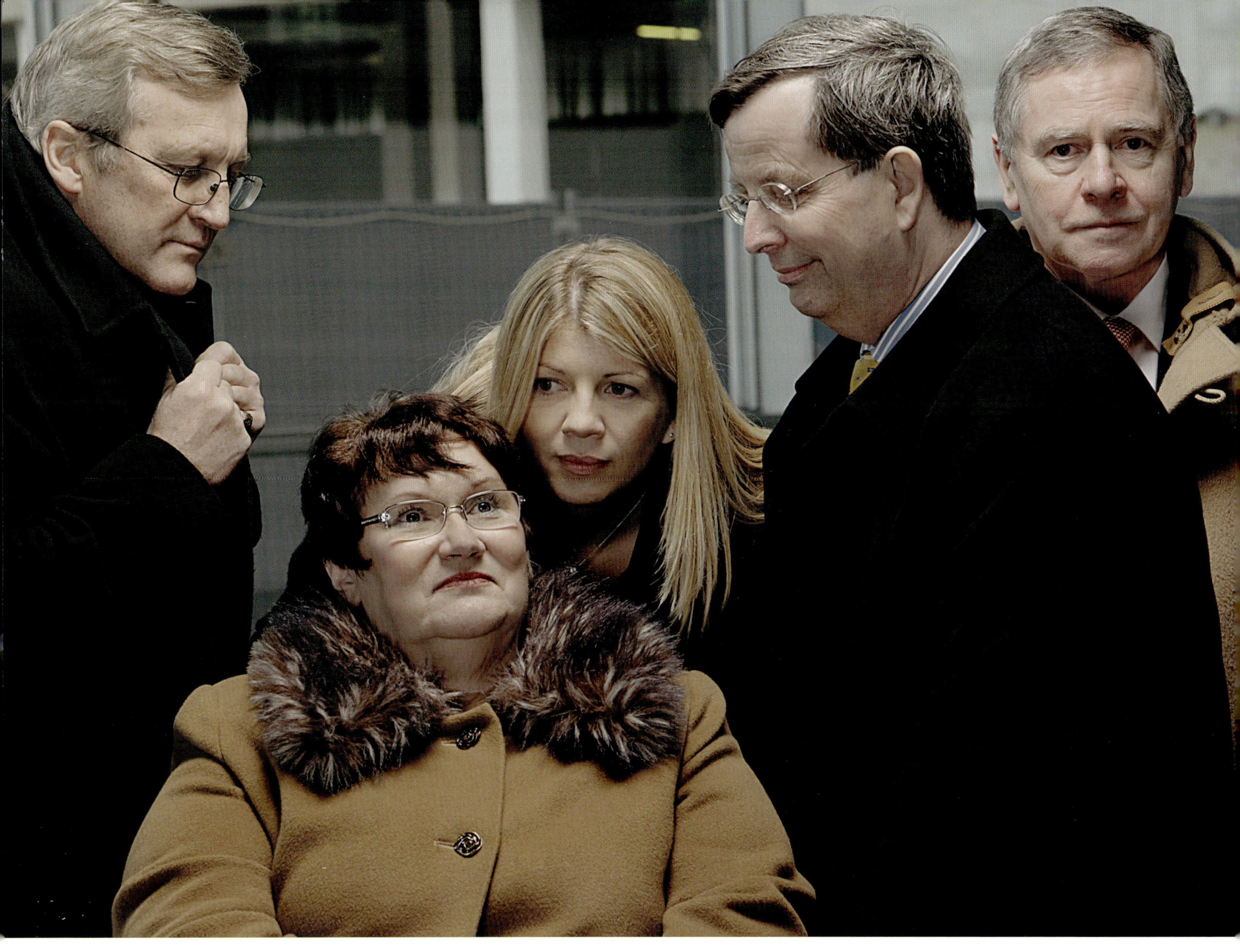

ALISON NIMMO AND JASON PRIOR

Photographed by Brian Griffin
30 September 2009,
AECOM/EDAW offices, London

Alison Nimmo, a chartered surveyor and town planner, joined the bid team in 2003 and was later appointed Director of Design and Regeneration for the Olympic Delivery Authority (ODA). Jason Prior is a landscape architect, urban designer and environmental planner. As European President of international planning, design and environmental firm EDAW he led a consortium to produce the bid masterplan for the Olympic Park. In 2006 the ODA appointed Prior and the EDAW consortium as delivery partners for the development and implementation of the plan.

'He has the vision. I make it happen.' **ALISON NIMMO**

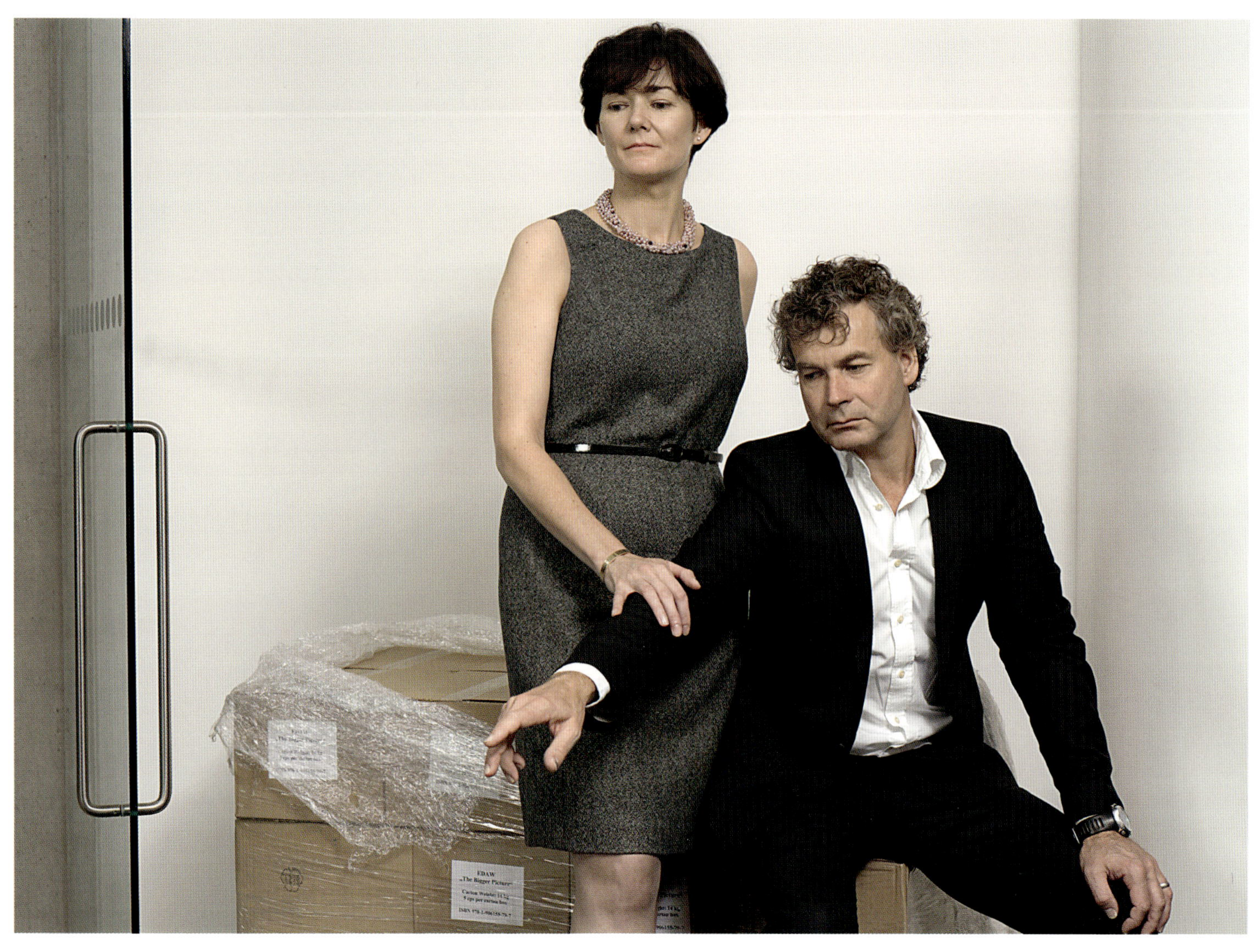

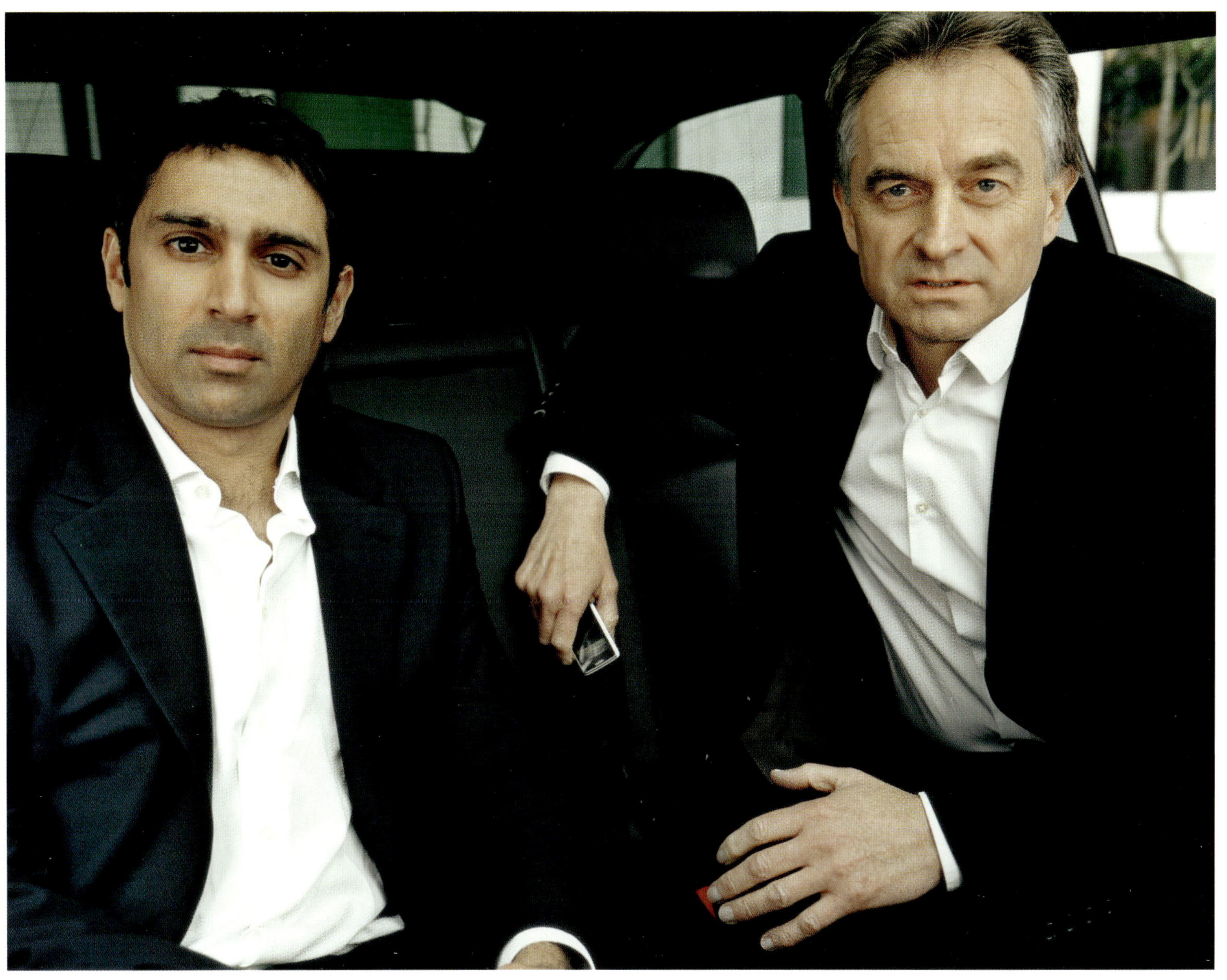

CHARLIE WIJERATNA AND CHRIS TOWNSEND
Photographed by Emma Hardy
15 April 2011, London

Charlie Wijeratna (left) was a key member of the London 2012 executive team from 2003 to 2010, working first on the corporate structures of the bid and the London Organising Committee of the Olympic and Paralympic Games (LOCOG), and then with the commercial team. Chris Townsend (right) is Commercial Director of LOCOG. He leads the commercial team responsible for generating the £2 billion revenue and procurement necessary to stage the London 2012 Games.

TEAM PLAYERS

All Olympic and Paralympic athletes, whether competing as a team or individually, benefit from the essential support of coaches and administrative staff as well as their fellow Team GB and ParalympicsGB athletes. Similarly, teams of dedicated experts come together to design and build stadiums, improve transport and turn around the fortunes of individual sports, all the time encouraging each other to greater Olympic success.

GB WOMEN'S HOCKEY TEAM
Photographed by Anderson & Low
22 November 2011, Bisham Abbey, National Sports Centre, Marlow

Back row (left to right): Rebecca Herbert, Sally Walton, Nicola White, Emily Maguire, Laura Unsworth. Front row (left to right): Helen Richardson, Laura Bartlett, Maddie Hinch, Kate Walsh (captain), Alex Danson, Sarah Thomas.

Coming together solely to compete at the Olympic Games, London 2012's Great Britain women's hockey squad brings together twenty-nine players from England, Scotland and Wales, all of whom compete under their own flags in the intervening three years. The GB women's hockey team is currently ranked fourth in the world.

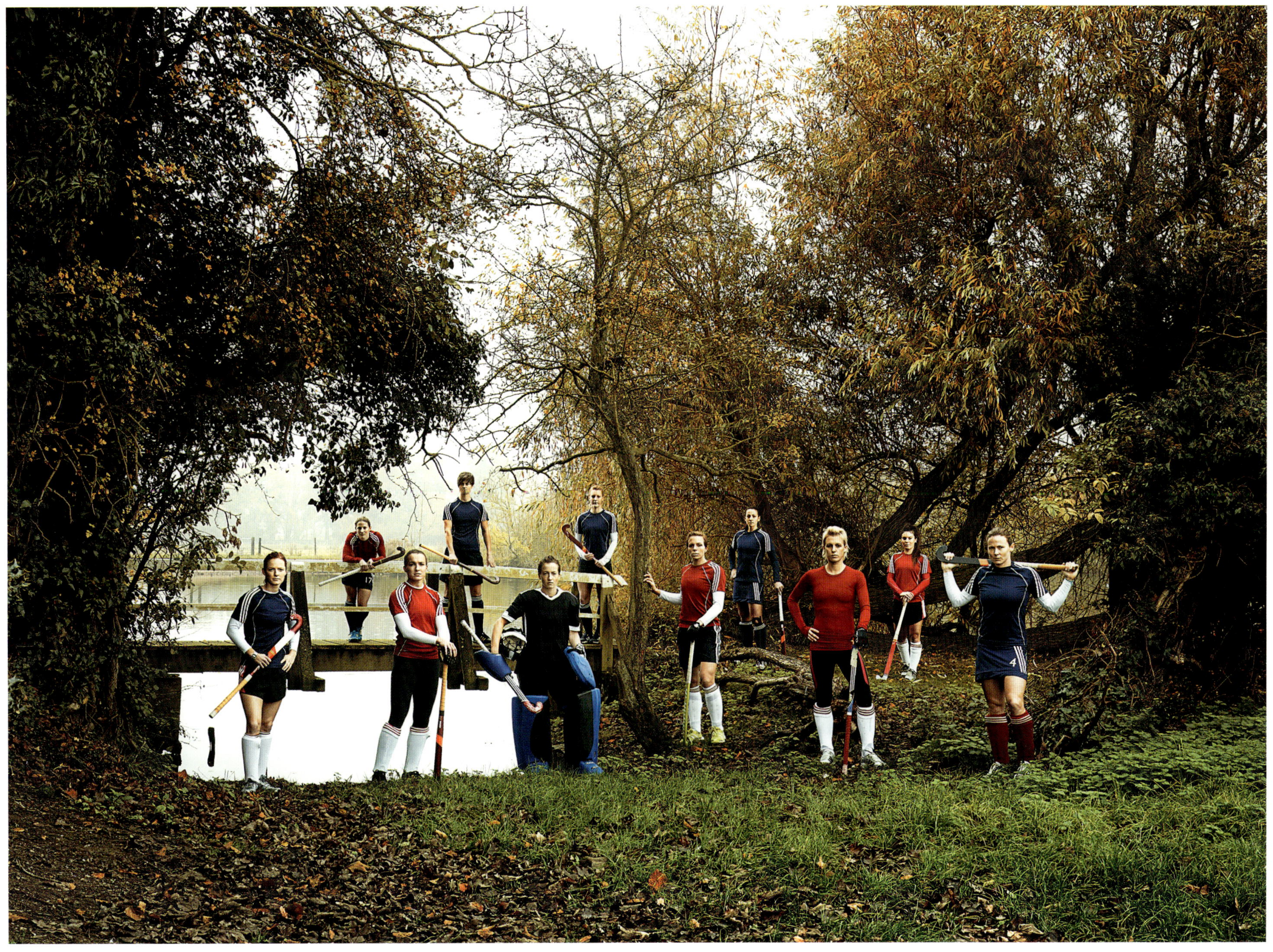

JIM HEVERIN, ZAHA HADID, STUART FRASER AND MIKE KING

Photographed by Brian Griffin
21 May 2010,
Olympic Park, London

The Aquatics Team – Jim Heverin, Zaha Hadid, Stuart Fraser and Mike King (left to right) – has worked to deliver the spectacular venue designed by internationally acclaimed architectural practice Zaha Hadid Architects. Heverin has worked with Zaha Hadid Architects for thirteen years, and has led the design on the London Aquatic Centre since 2005. Baghdad-born Hadid, recognised for her innovative designs and pioneering research, trained in London and founded her practice in 1980. Fraser, the Balfour Beatty project director, draws on forty-five years of experience in the construction industry, including the completion of London Heathrow's Terminal 5. Arup project director King is a structural engineer. His professional focus on long-span structures began with the Olympic Aquatic Centre in his native Sydney.

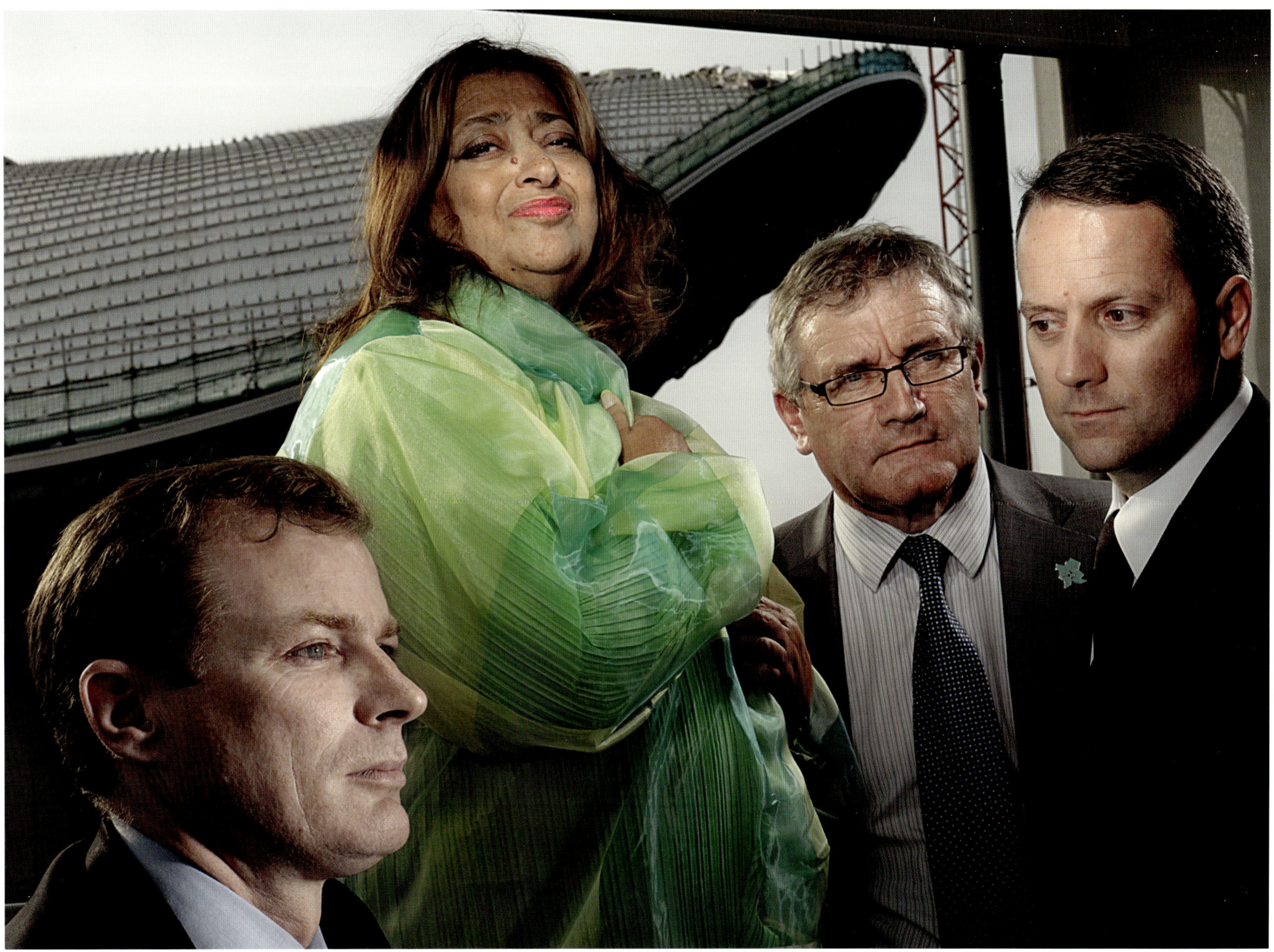

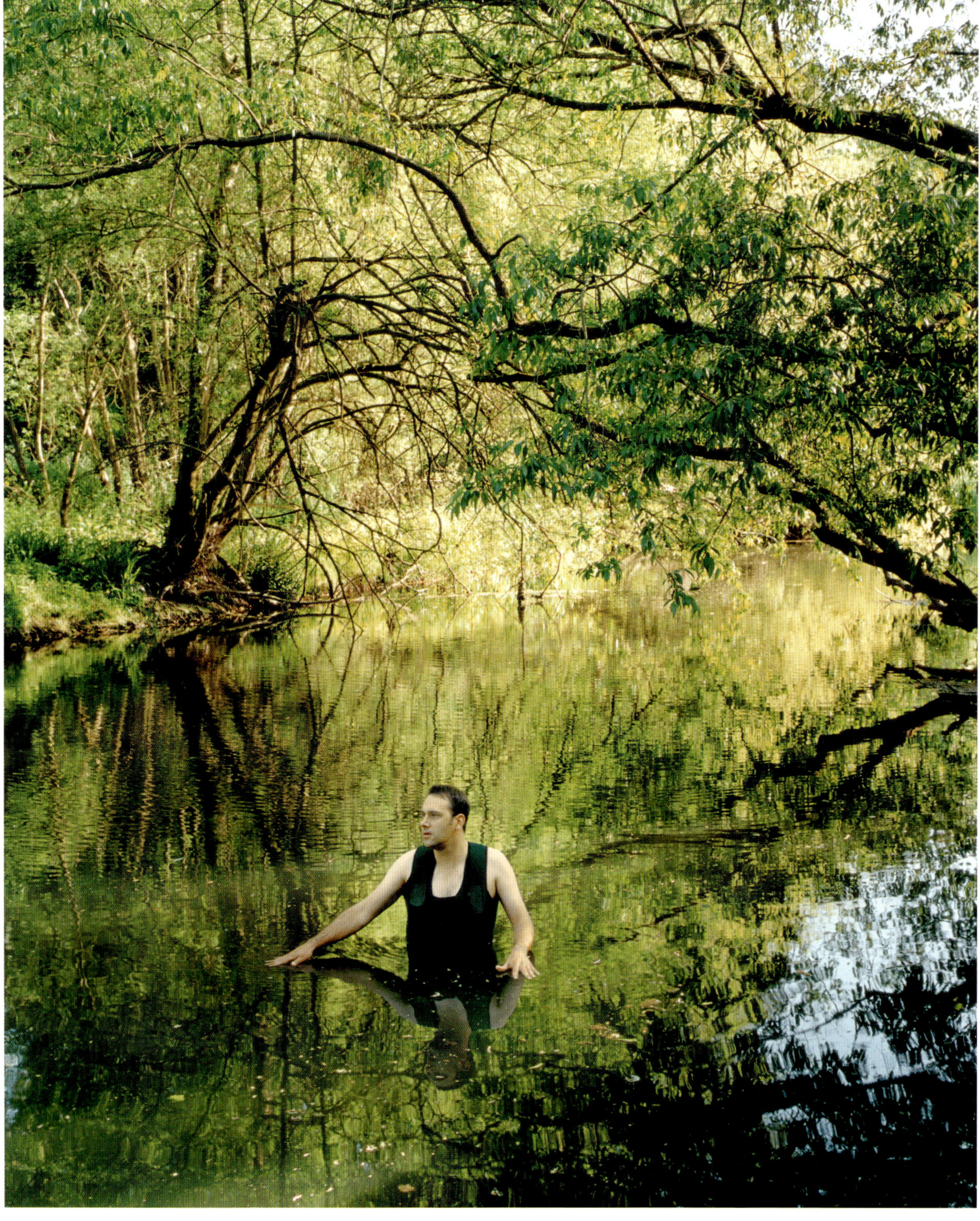

IAN MORRISSEY
Photographed by Emma Hardy
April 2011, Dorking, Surrey

Ian Morrissey was the 2011 winner of BT's Everyday People on the Road to 2012 competition, which encouraged members of the public to nominate someone who was contributing behind the scenes, without public recognition, to the London 2012 Olympic and Paralympic Games. Morrissey is an environmental scientist and key member of Atkins' River Edge Engineering Team. He trialled and designed the species planting for the newly created wetland habitats in the Olympic Park, which contributes to the site's status as a place of particular environmental importance.

'Ian's spirit has helped us all through some hard deadlines and difficult decisions.'
MIKE VAUGHAN, PRINCIPAL ENGINEER AT ATKINS

RAY HAGGAN

Photographed by Bettina von Zwehl
4 June 2010, Barbican, London

Seventy-year-old Ray Haggan has worked with the Anaconda Swimming Club for twenty-five years, and was the 2010 winner of BT's Everyday People on the Road to 2012 competition. As the voluntary Competition Secretary his role involves choosing the teams and driving them to competitions. His work has contributed to the growth and success of the club, saving it from near closure to a membership of over 600, including thirty swimmers competing in Nationals as well as two former members who are tipped for Olympic success.

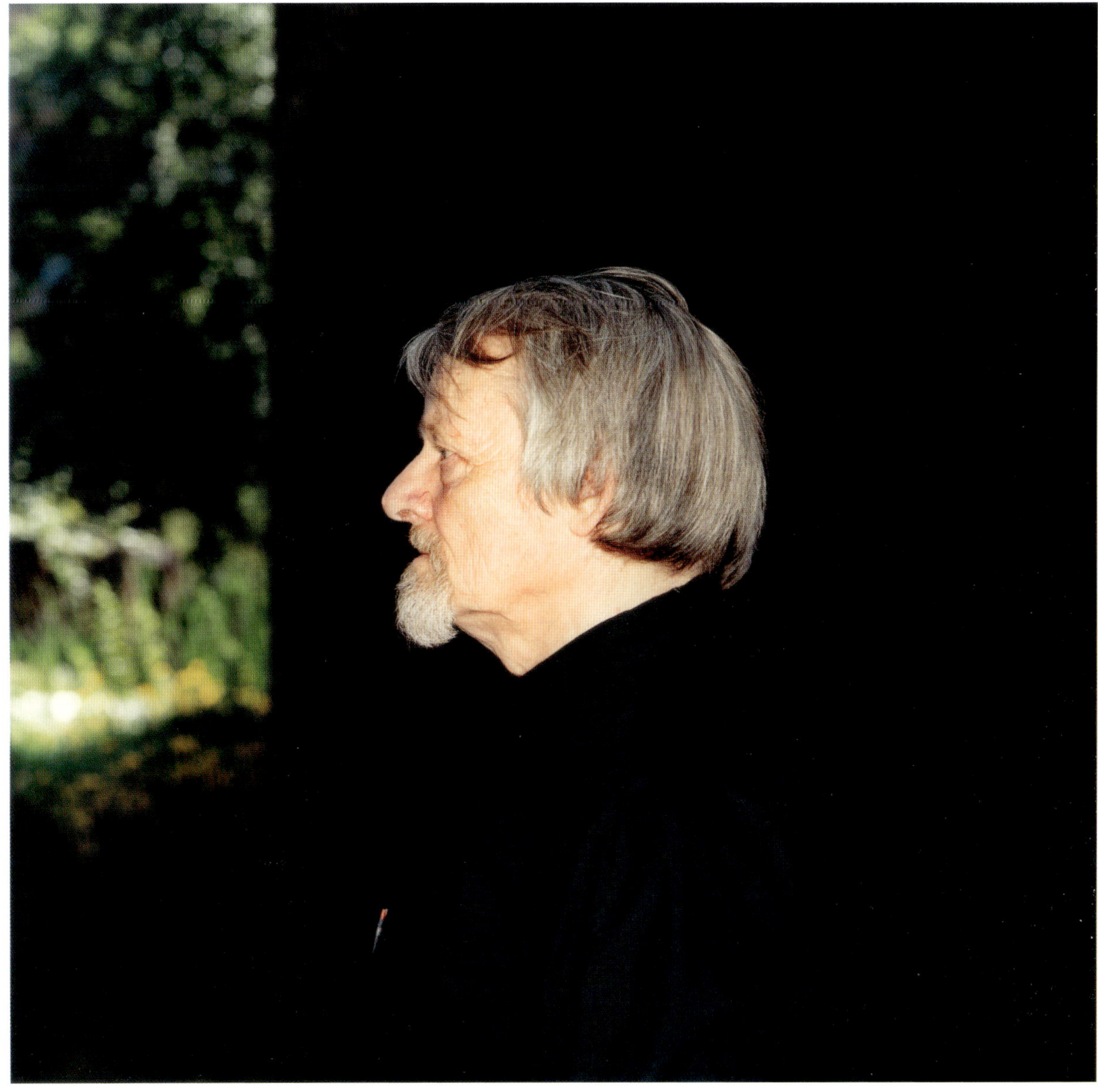

MARK BENSTED AND BILLY SMITH

Photographed by Jillian Edelstein
12 October 2011,
Olympic Park, London

Mark Bensted (left), former London Director of British Waterways, led the regeneration of east London's waterways, which included designing and constructing the new Three Mills Lock to enable freight and leisure boats to access the Olympic Park. Billy Smith (right) is British Waterways' Dockmaster and local tides supervisor. With fifty years' experience on the Thames, his skills and knowledge have been fundamental in the planning and transformation of the waterways network.

'The Lee was an absolute sewer when we started. It's a beautiful river now.' BILLY SMITH

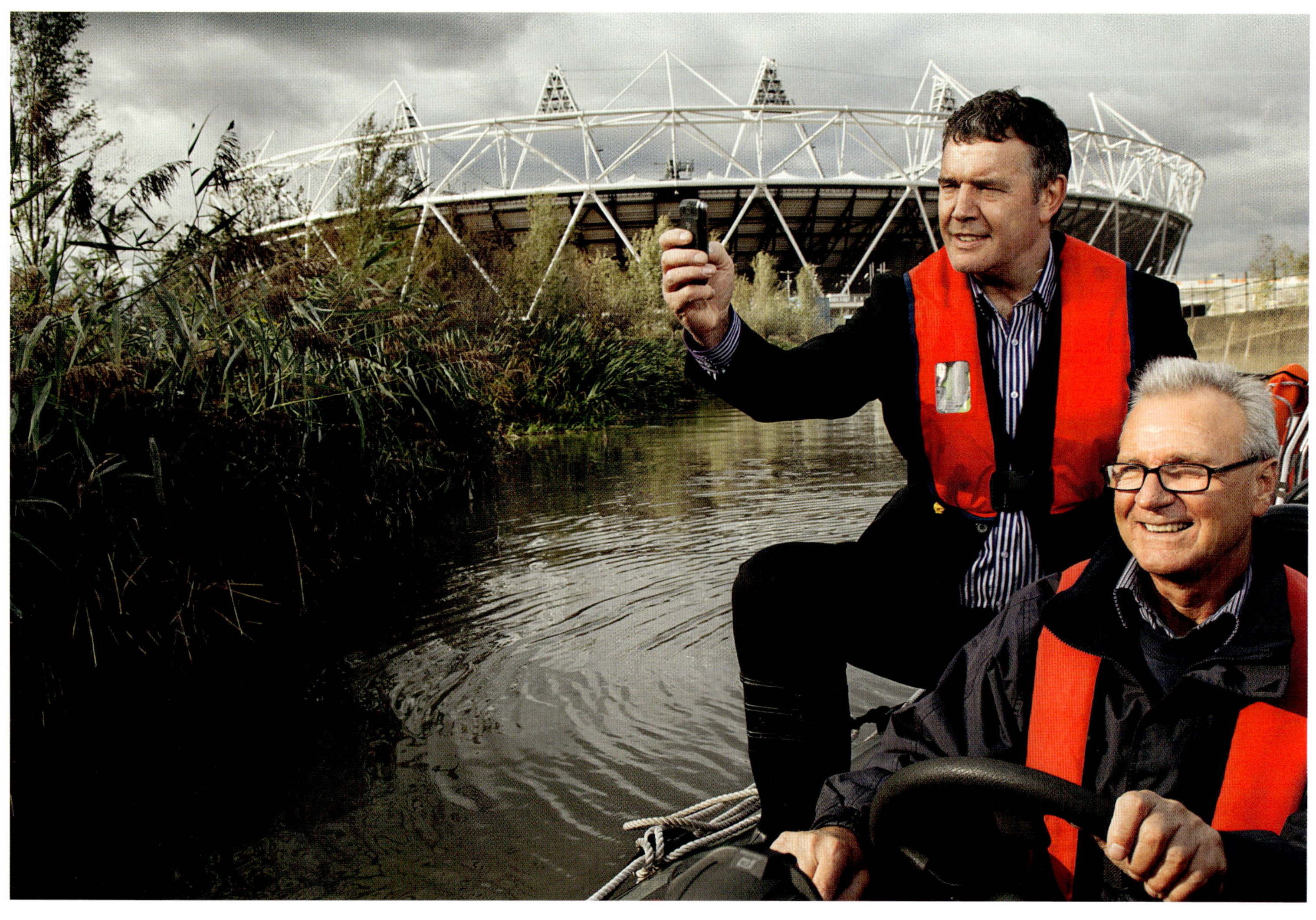

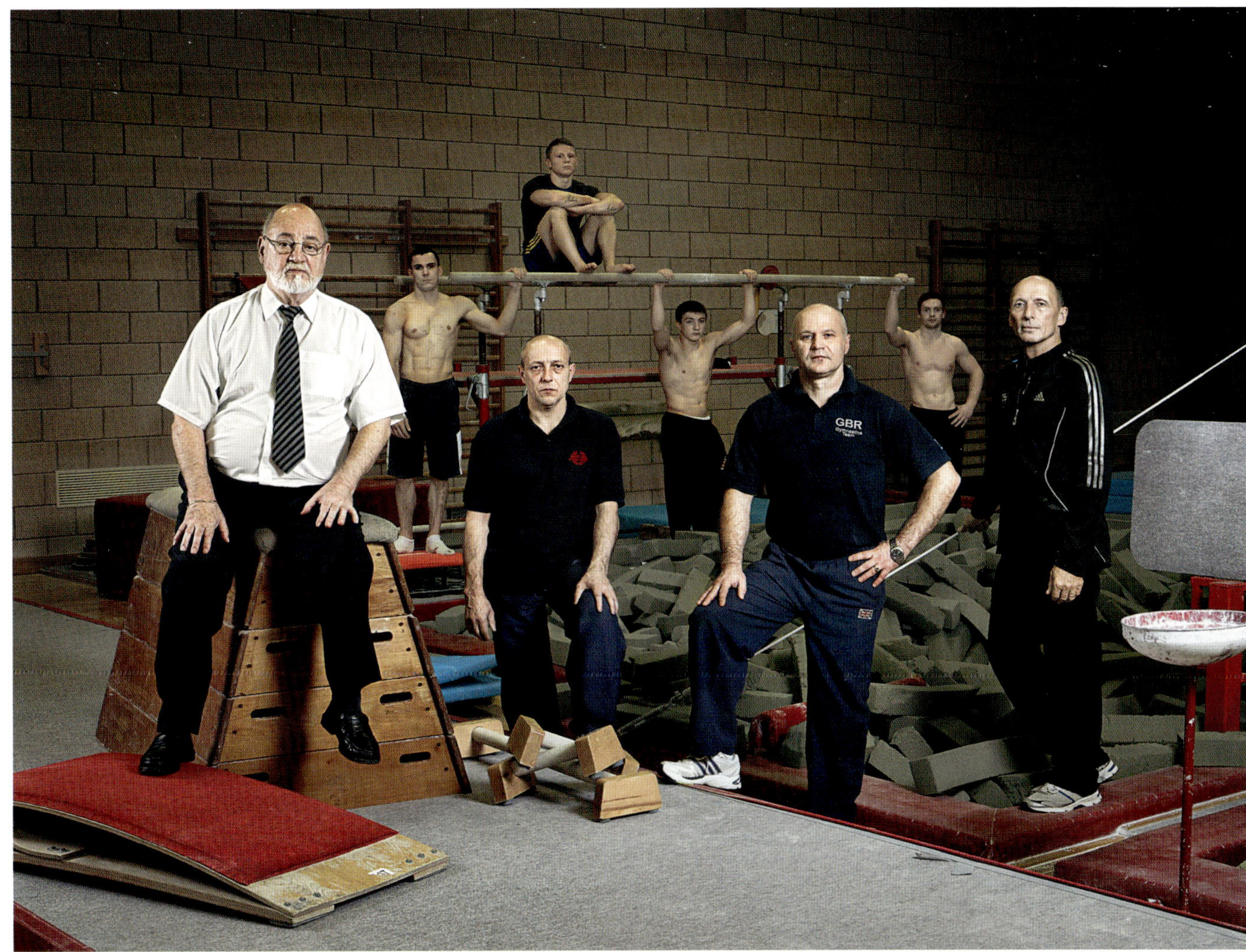

'John had the vision; he made the sacrifices, fought the establishment and broke through the glass ceiling.'

JANE ALLEN, CEO BRITISH GYMNASTICS

JOHN ATKINSON WITH SERGEI SIZHANOV, ANDREI POPOV, EDDIE VAN HOOF, SAM HUNTER, THEO SEAGER, SAM OLDHAM AND DANIEL PURVIS

Photographed by Anderson & Low
17 November 2011,
National Gymnastics Centre,
Lilleshall Hall, Newport

John Atkinson (far left) is seen here with British gymnastics men's coaches Sergei Sizhanov (left) and Andrei Popov (right), and technical director Eddie van Hoof (far right). Behind them (from left to right) are members of the men's elite squad, Sam Hunter, Theo Seager, Sam Oldham and Daniel Purvis. In the late 1960s, inspired by the professionalism he observed in Russia, Atkinson established a national development plan, assembled a team of top coaches and sports science support, and led the drive for the first dedicated facility for gymnastics, at Lilleshall Hall. He retired as performance director of British gymnastics in 2003.

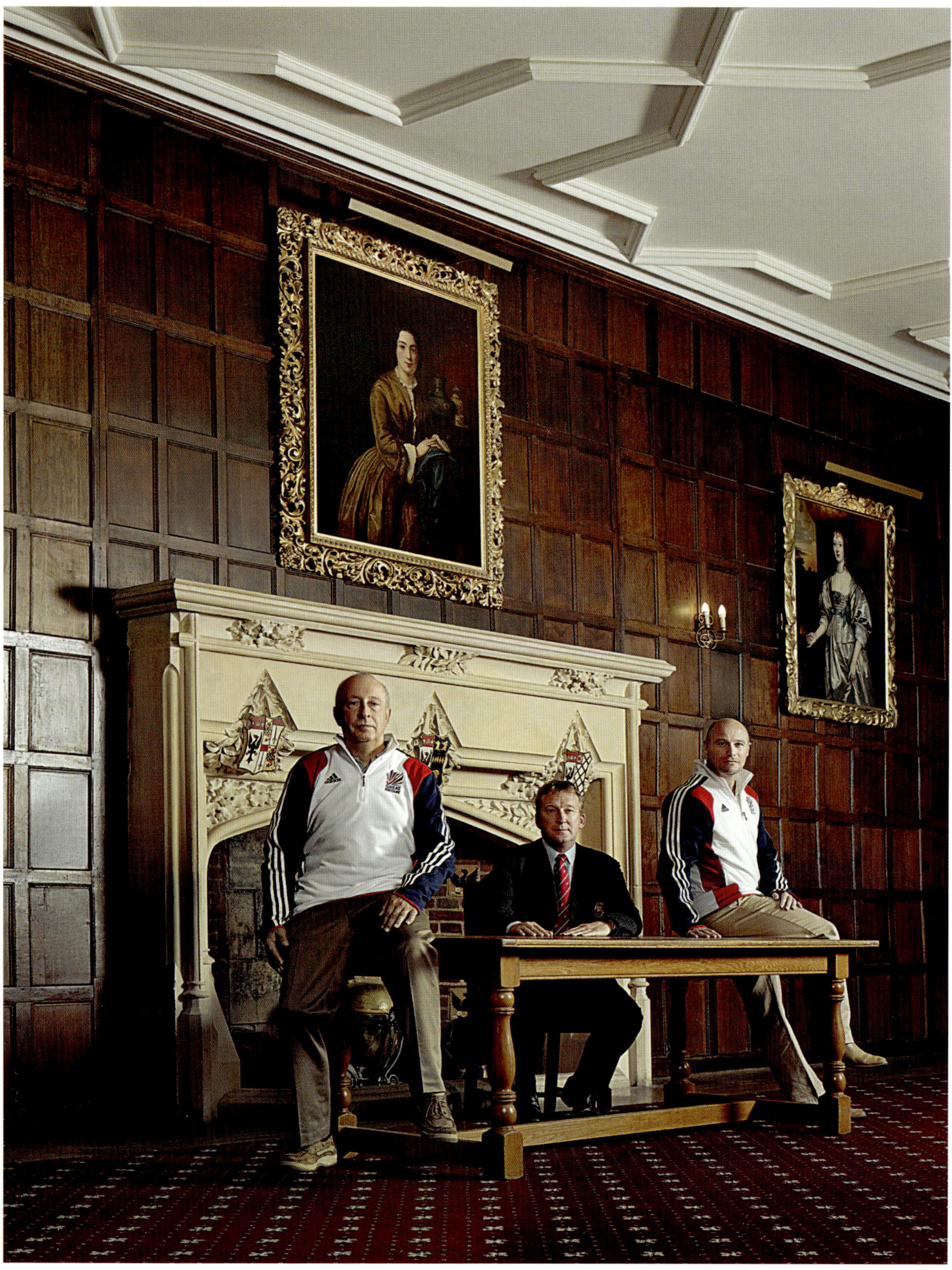

DAVID FAULKNER, DANNY KERRY AND JOHN HURST

Photographed by Anderson & Low
17 November 2011,
National Gymnastics Centre,
Lilleshall Hall, Newport

David Faulkner (left), former Olympic hockey gold medallist, joined England Hockey as Performance Director in 2005 and is responsible for the planning, strategy and logistics for the Great Britain hockey teams. Danny Kerry (centre) started coaching while studying at Loughborough University. He was appointed Head Coach of the England Women's senior team in 2004, and has led them to their highest world rankings since 1992. John Hurst (right) has been working with England and GB Hockey since 1989. He is a former England and Great Britain goalkeeper, winning over 100 caps between 1977 and 1988.

'The governing body of hockey was not performing and went bankrupt in 2003. Reborn the following year, England Hockey saw new structures and staff in place that have built success and won increased funding.'

DANNY KERRY, WOMEN'S COACH, GB HOCKEY

PAUL WESTBURY, TONY AIKENHEAD AND ROD SHEARD
Photographed by Brian Griffin
18 January 2010,
Olympic Stadium, London

Paul Westbury, Tony Aikenhead and Rod Sheard (left to right) led Team Stadium, the consortium responsible for the design and construction of the London 2012 Olympic Stadium. Structural engineer Westbury is an award-winning director of Buro Happold; his stadium projects include the Emirates Stadium for Arsenal FC. Aikenhead joined Sir Robert McAlpine in 2007 as construction Project Director for Team Stadium. Sheard is the Senior Principal at Populous. He is recognised internationally for his large venue designs, including the Sydney 2000 Olympic Stadium in his native Australia.

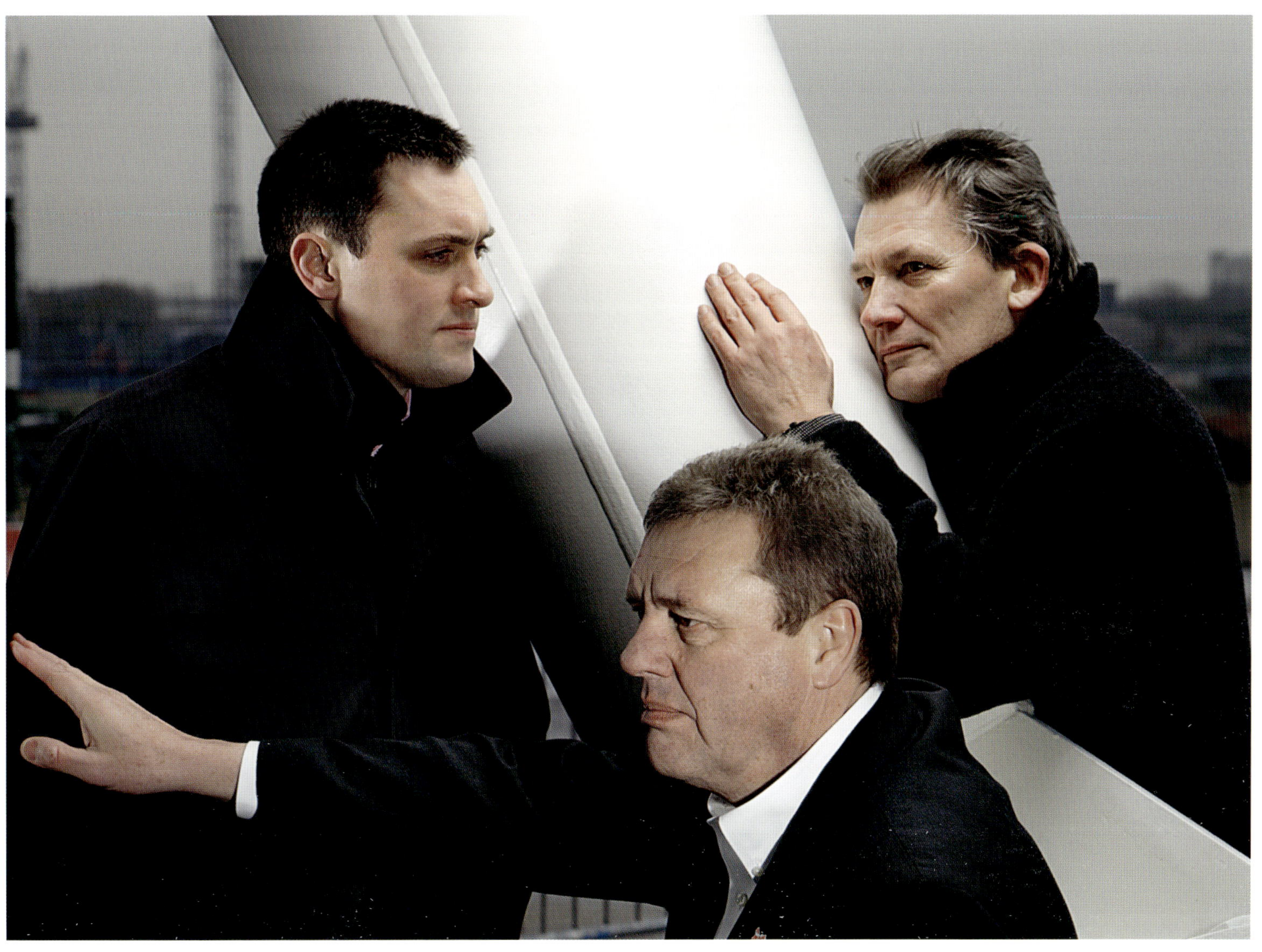

MEN'S ROWING EIGHT

Photographed by Anderson & Low
14 October 2011, Seville

Back row (left to right): Cameron Nichol, Greg Searle, Phelan Hill (cox), James Foad, Mo Sbihi. Front row (left to right): Ric Egington, Tom Ransley, Alex Partridge, Noddy Reilly-O'Donnell. The men's eight is the fastest rowing boat at the Olympic Games. The eight rowers and one cox race opposing crews over a 2,000-metre course, covering the distance in approximately five-and-a-half minutes.

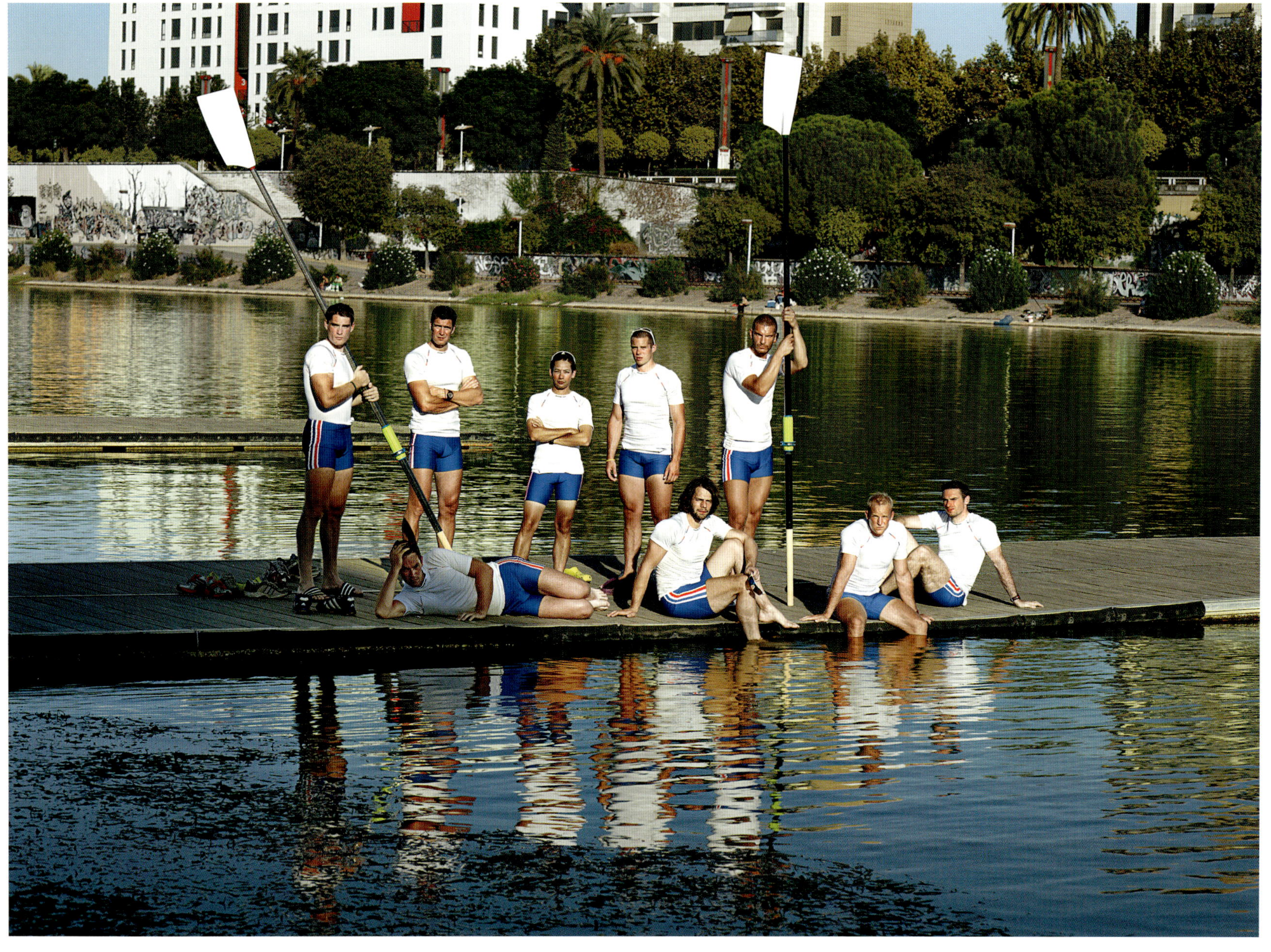

'Beth is a role model for pretty well all gymnasts in Britain. She is so strong mentally and she knows how to compete. She is clearly more experienced than any of us. She has done it all.'
HANNAH WHELAN

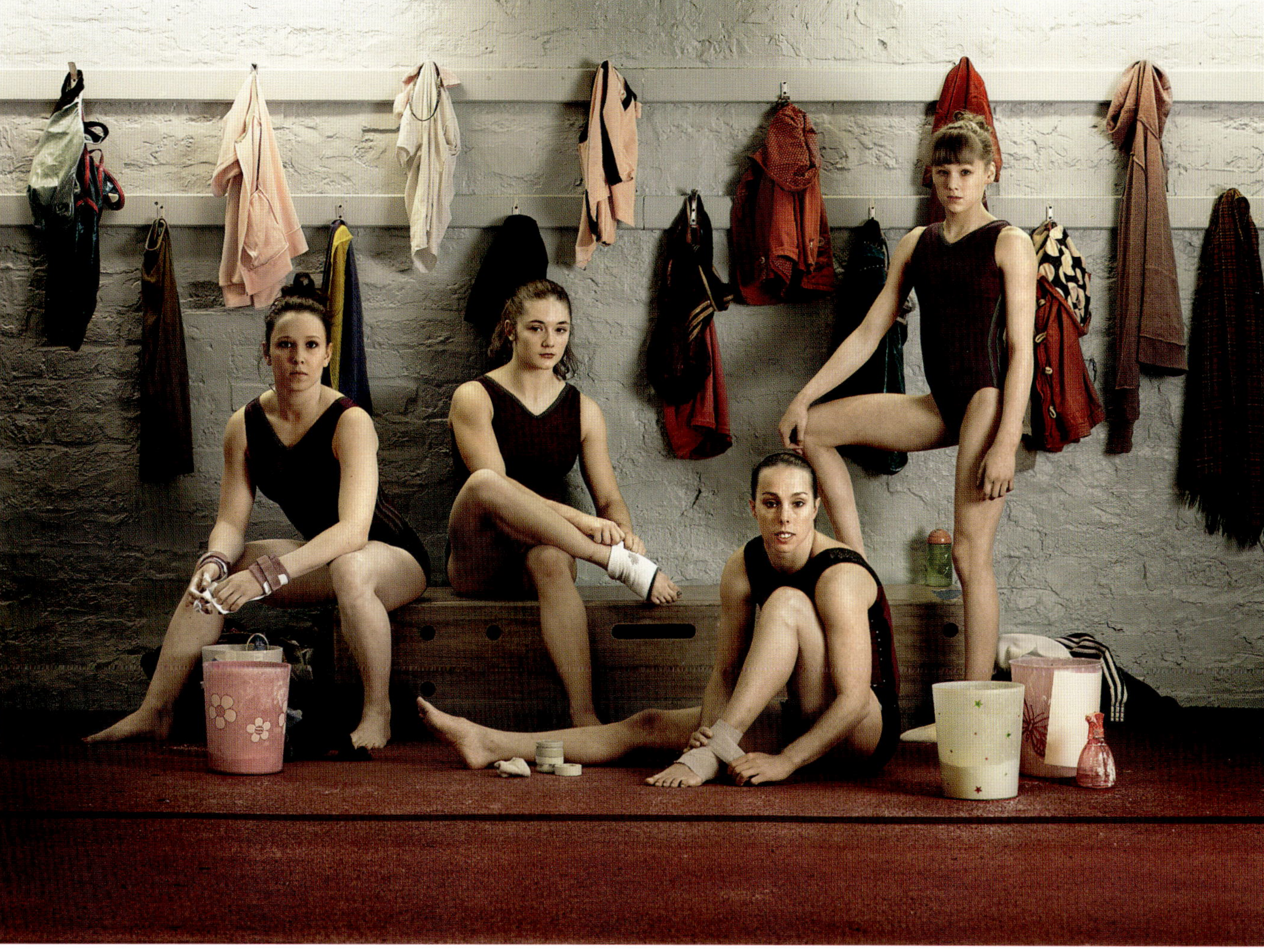

BETH TWEDDLE WITH HANNAH WHELAN, JENNI PINCHES AND REBECCA TUNNEY

Photographed by Anderson & Low
17 November 2011, Liverpool

Beth Tweddle (second from right) is seen here together with Hannah Whelan, Jenni Pinches and Rebecca Tunney (left to right). Tweddle became Britain's first ever World Champion in women's gymnastics in 2006. She began competing at the age of seven, and moved to Liverpool in 1997 to train with coach Amanda Reddin. Since 2002, Tweddle has won multiple medals at international level. She has competed at two Olympic Games and is now a three-time World Champion. Tweddle, current British Champion Whelan and Pinches are all members of the women's team who qualified for London 2012 at the World Championships in 2011. Rebecca Tunney is British Junior Champion 2011.

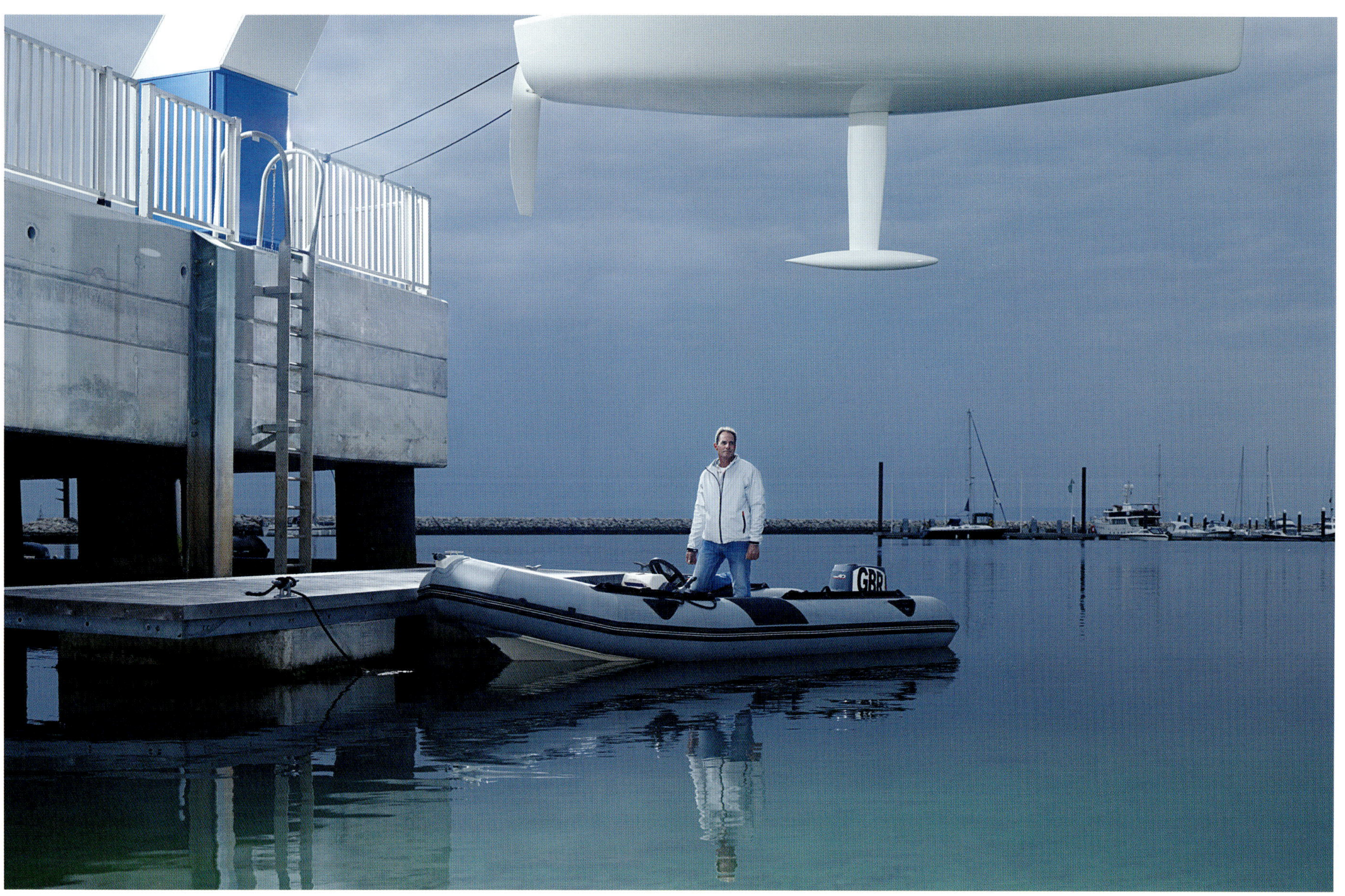

KATE MACGREGOR, ANNIE LUSH AND LUCY MACGREGOR, WITH MAURICE PAARDENKOOPER

Photographed by Finlay MacKay
16 April 2011, Weymouth and Portland National Sailing Academy, Weymouth

Kate Macgregor, Annie Lush and Macgregor's sister Lucy (opposite, left to right) are strong contenders for an Olympic medal in women's match racing. They all learnt to sail as children in Poole Harbour, and started sailing as a team in 2010. They have since won National, European and World Championship titles. Dutch coach and professional sailor Maurice Paardenkooper has coached Olympic sailing teams for fifteen years. He joined Lucy and her team in January 2011.

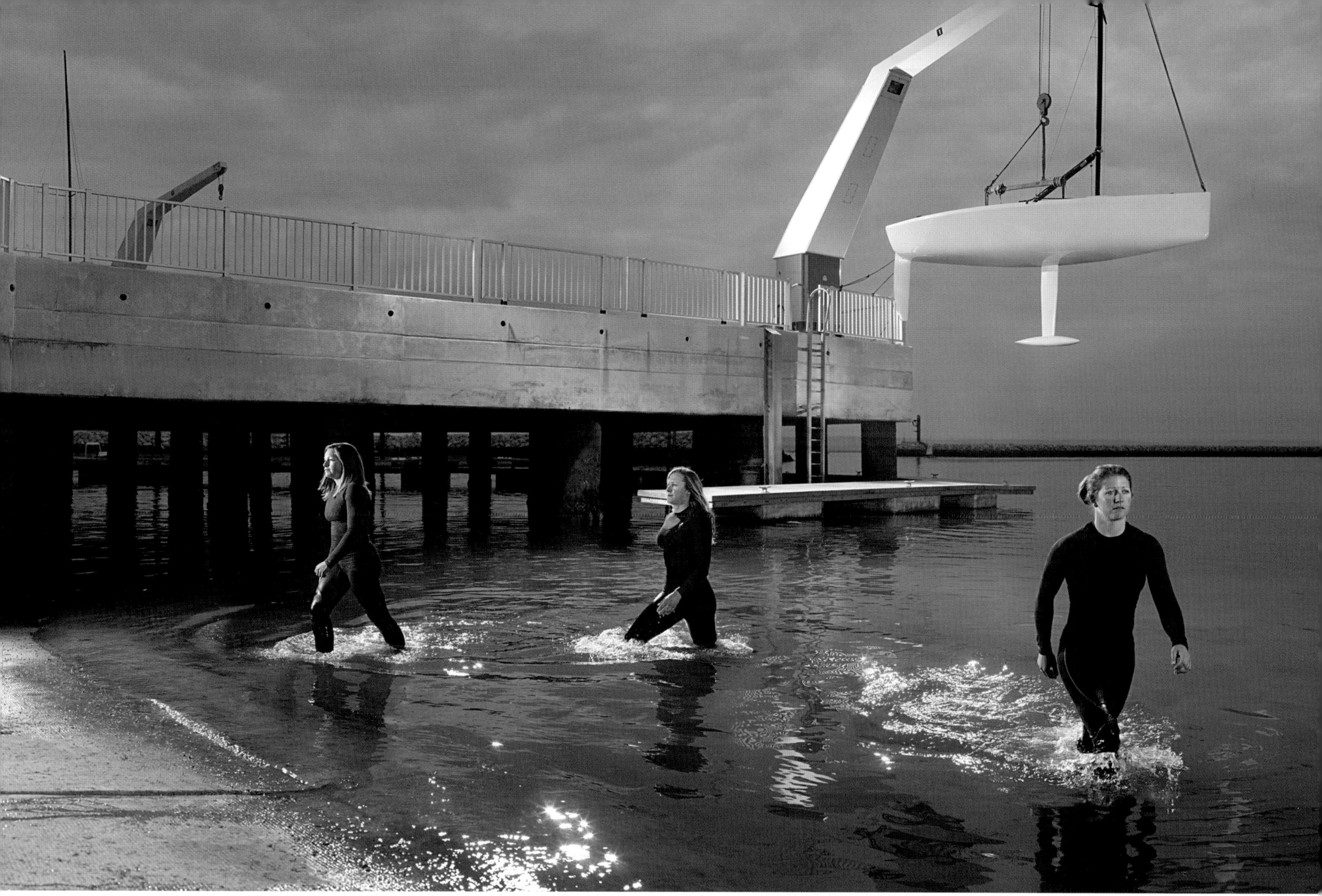

'The Olympics is a circus. What we do is out on the water.'
MAURICE PAARDENKOOPER

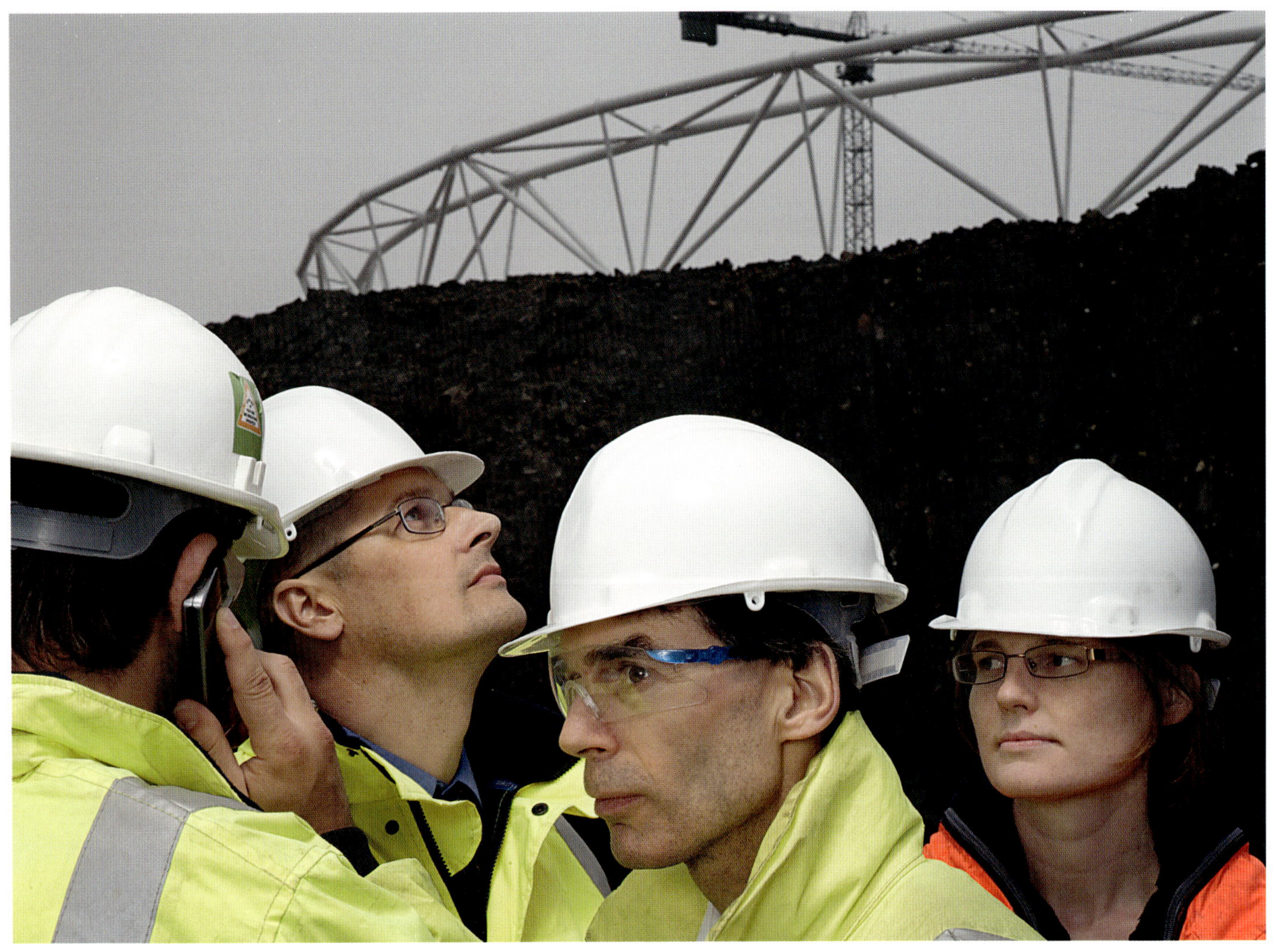

'Technically, Steve Deeble is a guru. He knows everything you need to know, down to the last detail.'

ANTONN RUSSEK

ANTONN RUSSEK, DAVID SKERRITT, STEPHEN DEEBLE AND CLARE STAVELEY

Photographed by Brian Griffin
5 October 2009,
Olympic Park, London

Antonn Russek, David Skerritt, Stephen Deeble and Clare Staveley (left to right) are civil engineers who worked with the Olympic Park Enabling Works, preparing the site for construction. Russek managed the Soil Treatment Centre and the soil-washing plants. Skerritt project-managed the Enabling Works in the south of the Park. Engineering Manager Deeble supervised the technical aspects of the project, including the innovative and sustainable techniques used to fulfil London's 'Green Games' targets. Staveley analysed soil and supervised the soil-washing plants.

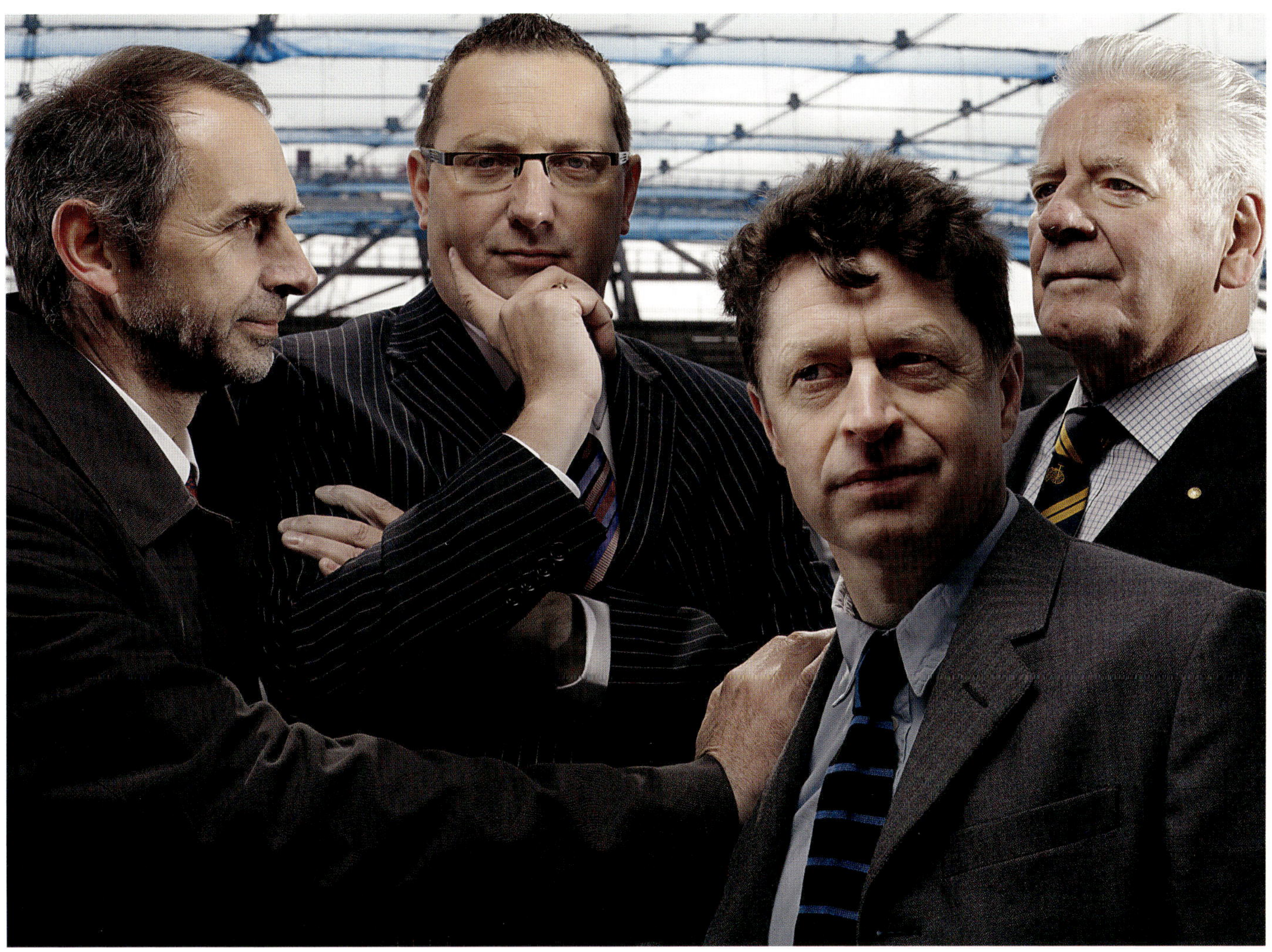

CHRIS WISE, DEAN GOODLIFFE, MIKE TAYLOR AND RON WEBB
Photographed by Brian Griffin
15 April 2010, Velodrome, Olympic Park, London

Chris Wise, Dean Goodliffe, Mike Taylor and Ron Webb (left to right) are responsible for the design and delivery of the Velodrome. Wise, founding director of Expedition Engineering, guided the structural engineering. ISG Divisional director Goodliffe was responsible for the construction of the venue, which includes one of the largest cable-net roofs in the UK. Taylor is an architect and a keen cyclist, who led the team responsible for the 2012 Velodrome and Legacy VeloPark. Former Australian cycling champion Webb has installed fifty-two tracks worldwide and came out of retirement, unable to resist the challenge to design a super-fast track.

'Building a track is like building a ship inside out.' **RON WEBB**

FAMILIES

The London 2012 Olympic and Paralympic Games bring together people from every walk of life – even from within the same family. The athletes, technicians and designers from these families are all supported by those close to them, sometimes even competing alongside their relations in the Games themselves. The collaborative, supportive spirit of their stories reveals the London 2012 Olympic and Paralympic Games to be a true team effort.

JONATHAN BROWNLEE AND ALISTAIR BROWNLEE WITH MALCOLM BROWN
Photographed by Finlay MacKay
24 November 2010, The Chevin, Yorkshire

Born and bred in Yorkshire, brothers Jonathan (left) and Alistair Brownlee (centre) are triathletes. They both attended university in Leeds and live on the edge of the Chevin and Ilkley moors, where they train. Alistair is ranked number one in the world, and is Britain's top triathlete. He competed in Beijing 2008 and was World Champion in 2009 and 2011. Jonathan, current World Under-23 Champion, finished second at senior level in the 2011 World Championships in Sydney and Madrid, behind his brother. Malcolm Brown (right) has been the Brownlees' running coach since 2004. A UK Athletics Association and voluntary coach for thirty years, Brown was a county track and cross-country runner.

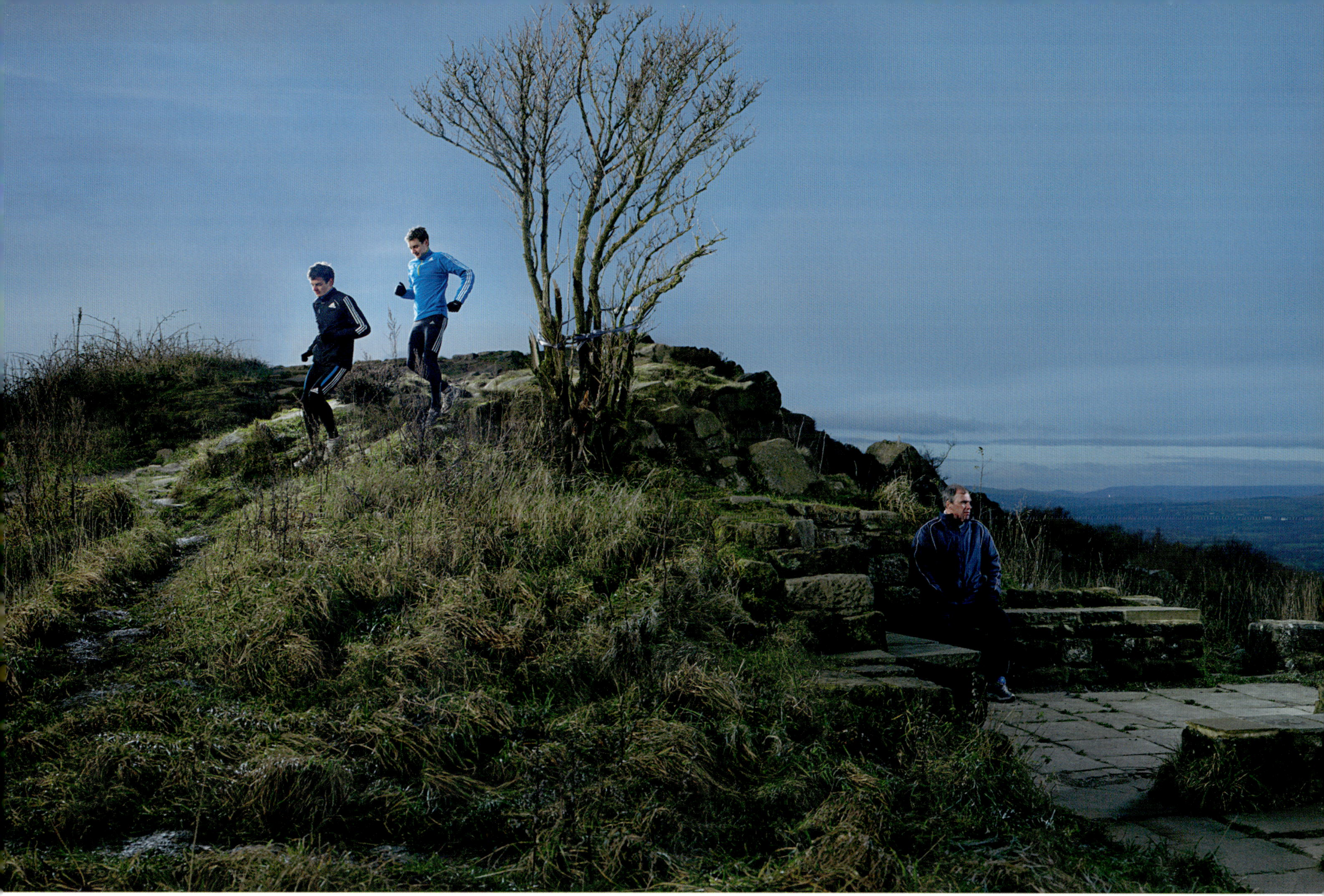

'The moors inspire them. They are fundamental in keeping them going, day after day, week after week.'
MALCOLM BROWN, COACH

MIKE KENNY, JASON KENNY AND MICK FEE
Photographed by Brian Griffin
24 February 2010,
Watson Steel Structures, Bolton

Two generations of the Bolton-based Kenny family have worked with Olympic Park suppliers Watson Steel Structures Ltd. Mike Kenny (left) joined the company as an operative after leaving college. Mick Fee (right), his brother-in-law, followed his father into steel manufacturing as an apprentice plater. Having won multiple world titles, Mike's son Jason (centre) was twenty years old when he emerged as an unexpected double medallist in track cycling in Beijing 2008, winning a gold medal in the team sprint, and silver behind Chris Hoy. In 2011 he won multiple medals, including individual gold at the Track Cycling World Championships and World Cup, and is a strong contender for a place on Team GB across all the sprint disciplines.

'This contract shows that the Olympics is not just for London and the south-east of England. There are opportunities for everyone in the UK.'
PETER EMERSON, MANAGING DIRECTOR WATSON STEEL STRUCTURES LTD

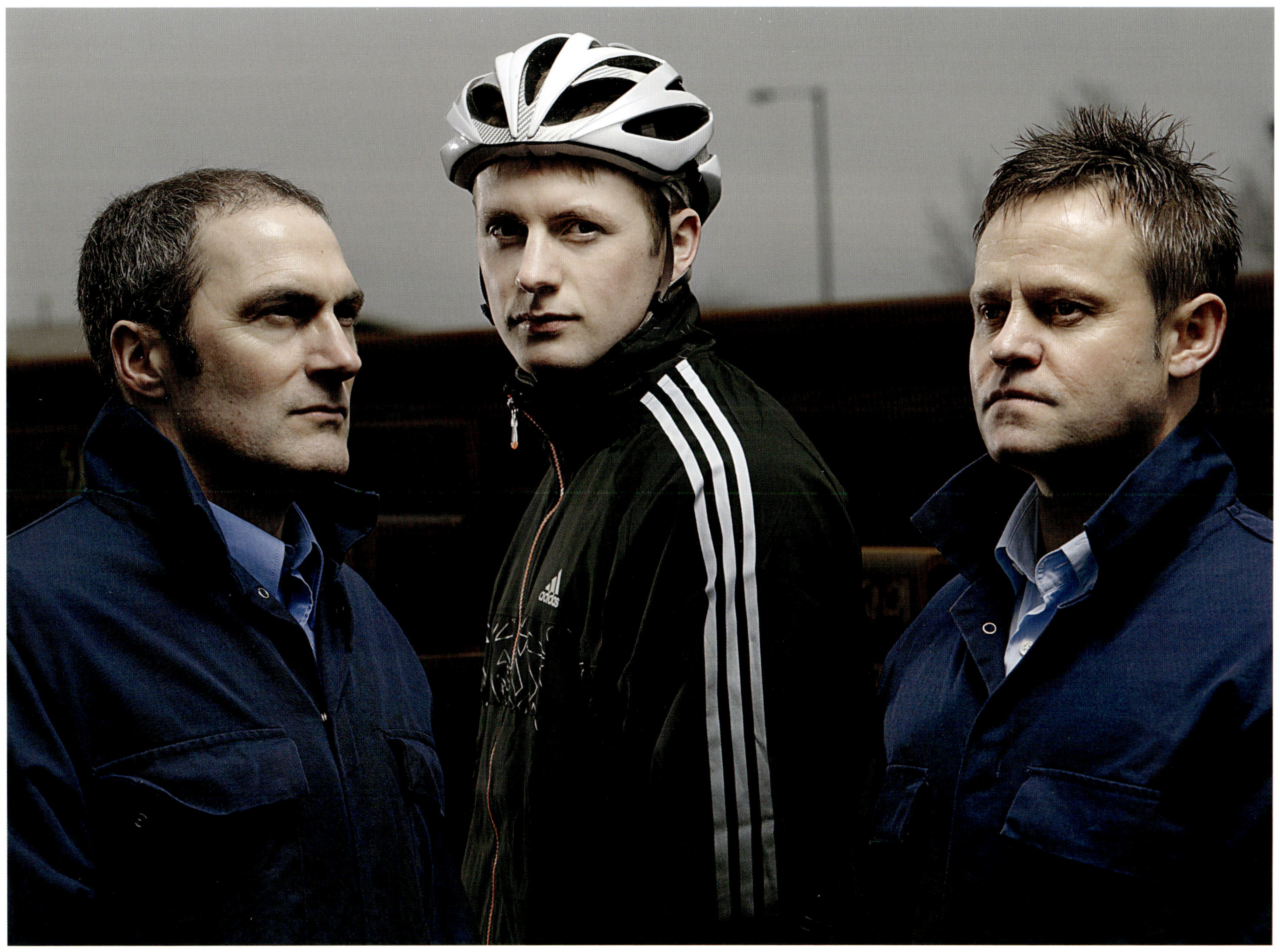
adidas

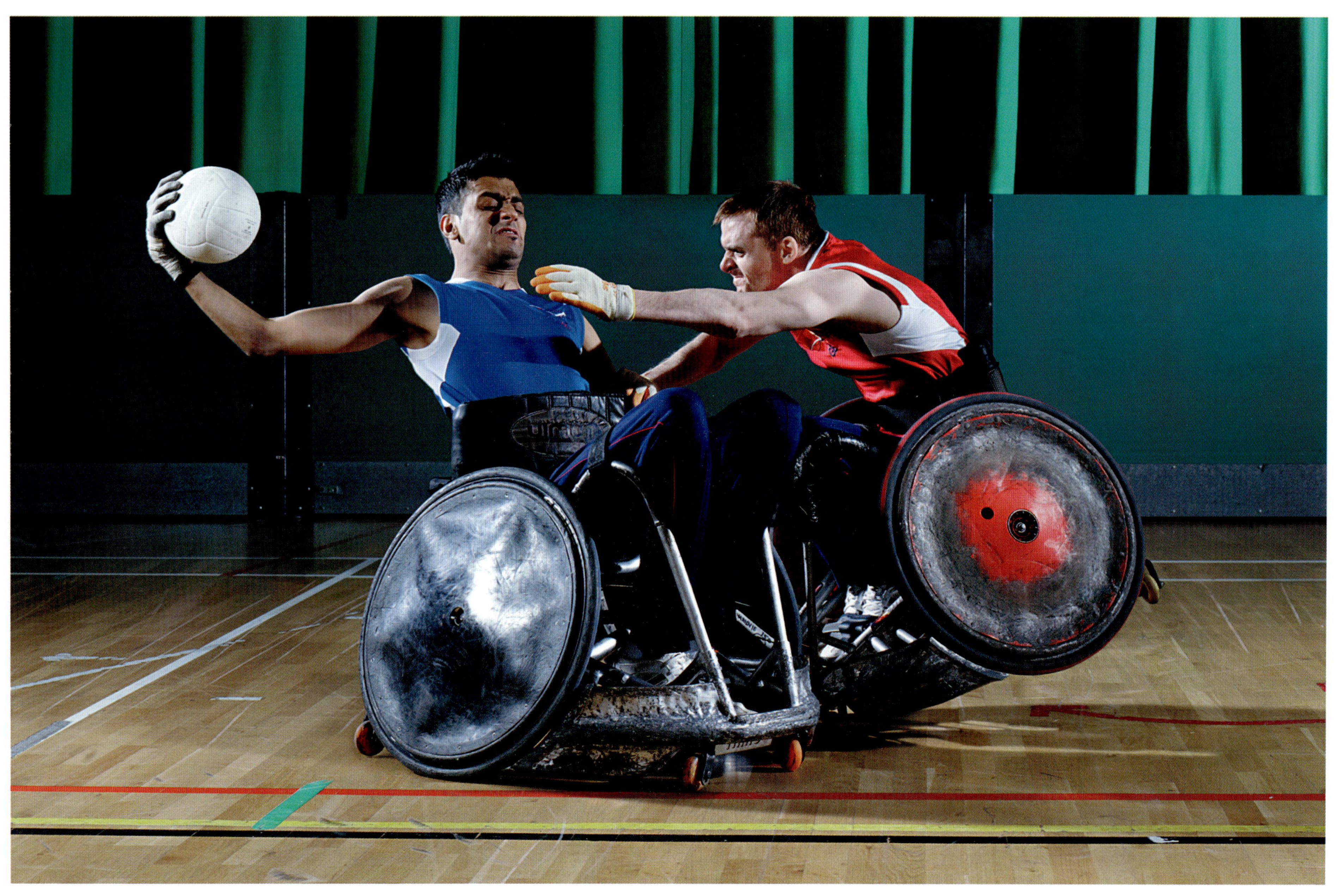

'We are athletes first, disabled second, and not just guys in chairs having a go.' **ANDY BARROW**

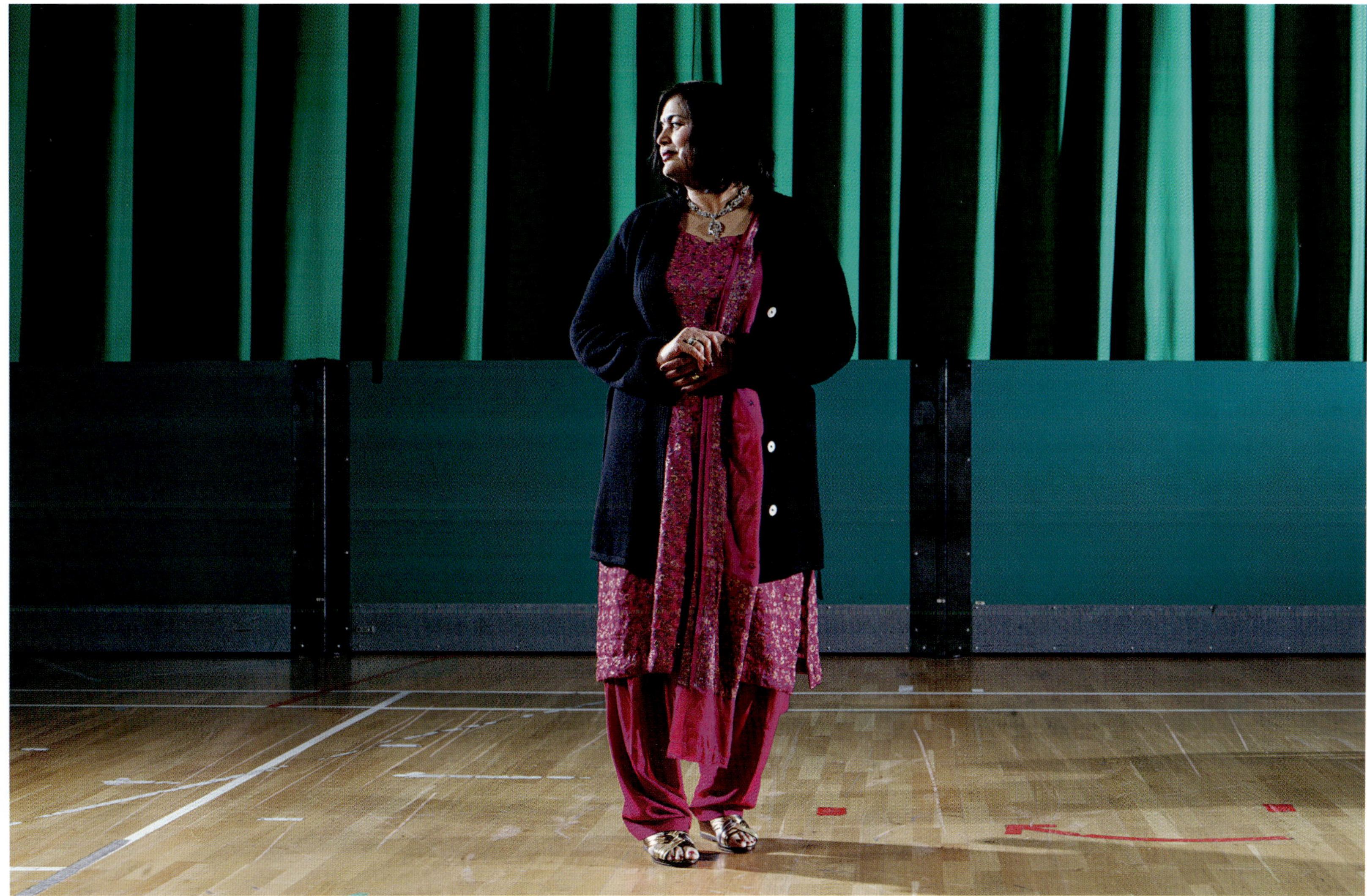

MANDIP SEHMI AND ANDY BARROW WITH JAGTAR SEHMI
Photographed by Finlay MacKay
8 March 2011, Stoke Mandeville, Buckinghamshire

Mandip Sehmi (left) and Andy Barrow play in the GB wheelchair rugby squad. Sehmi broke his neck in a car crash that left him paralysed from the chest down, and was introduced to wheelchair rugby during rehabilitation. He trains in London, and in 2011 competed in the US wheelchair rugby league, playing with Arizona team Phoenix Heat. Sehmi's mother, Jagtar Sehmi, was born in Punjab, India and moved to the UK in the 1970s. Barrow broke his neck during a game of rugby union at the age of seventeen, and took up wheelchair rugby. He has been a member of the national squad since 1999. As team captain, Barrow competed with Sehmi in the 2008 Beijing Paralympic Games.

MIKE DOBRISKEY AND LISA DOBRISKEY

Photographed by Brian Griffin
1 October 2009,
Olympic Park, London

Mike Dobriskey, a soil consultant, was a member of the soil survey and decontamination team for the Olympic Park. Lisa, Dobriskey's eldest daughter, began running competitively as a teenager. In 2006 she won a gold medal in the 1500m at the Commonwealth Games. She came fourth in the same event in Beijing 2008 and won a silver medal in the Athletics World Championships in 2009.

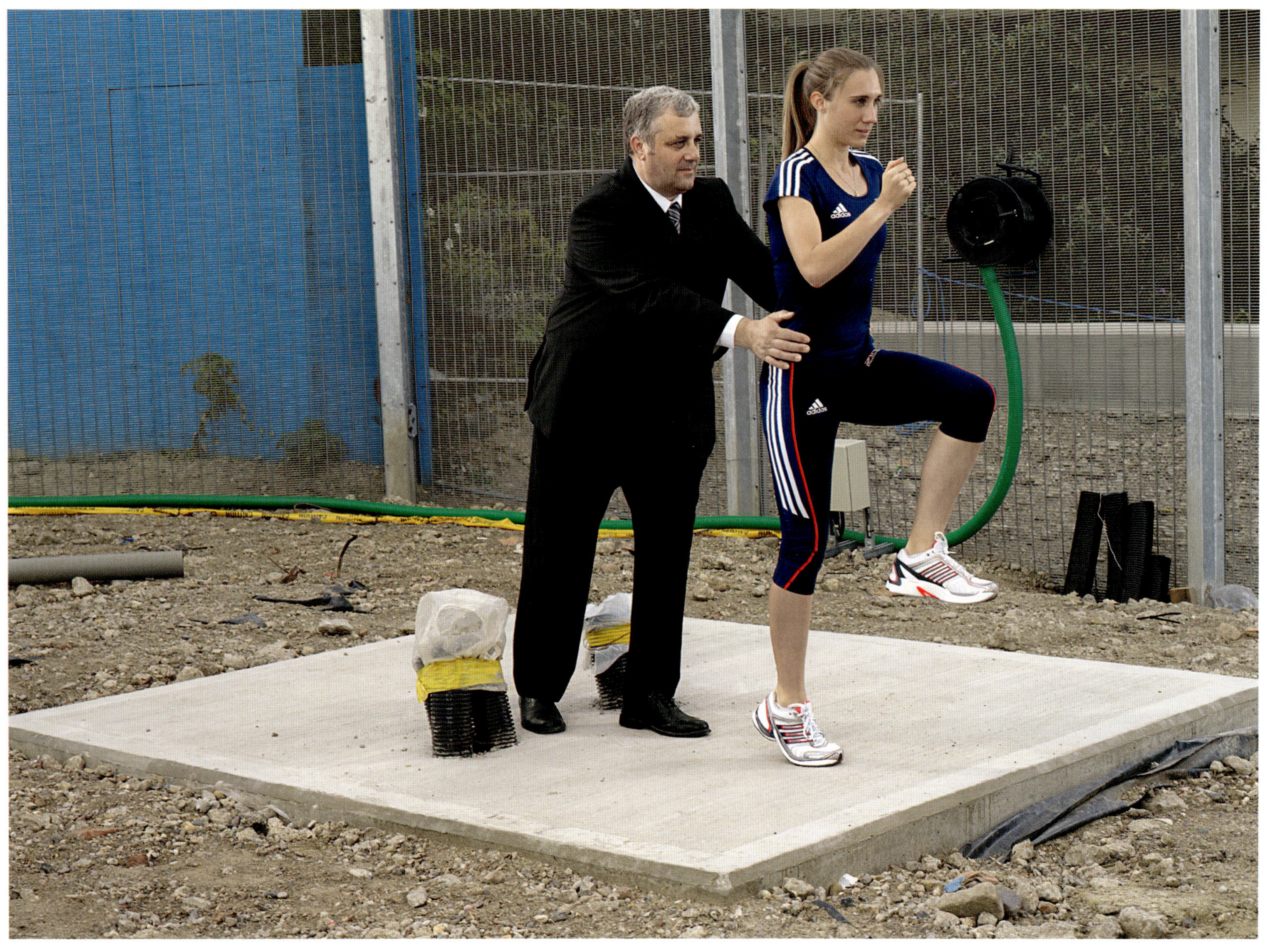

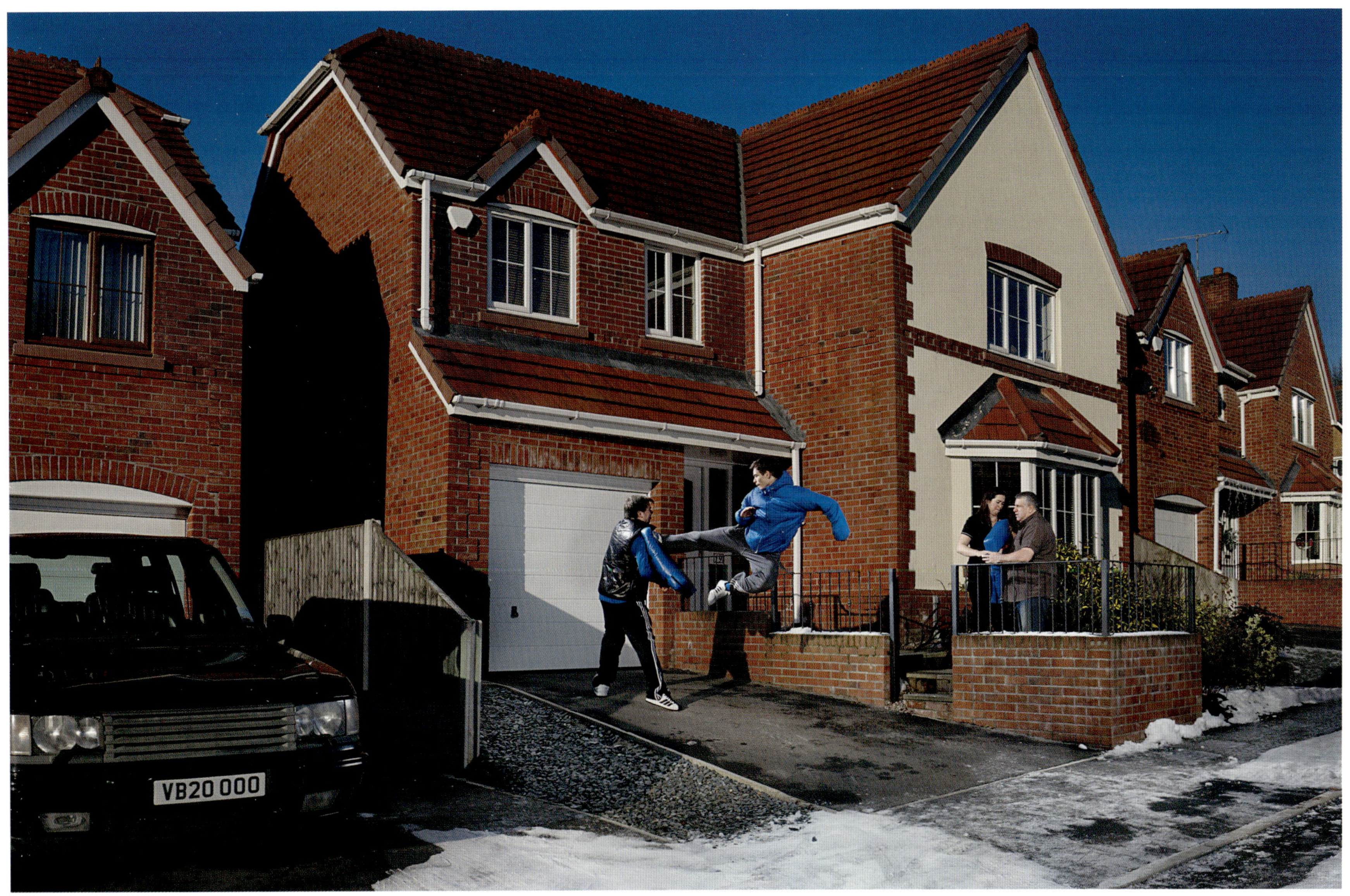

AARON COOK WITH LUKE COOK, CHRISTINE COOK AND NIGEL COOK

Photographed by Finlay MacKay
6 December 2010,
the Cook family home, Manchester

In 2010 Aaron Cook (second from left) became the first British man to be ranked world number one in taekwondo (under-80kg category), having taken up the sport at the age of five. He progressed to senior level in 2007 and became British Champion, a title he retains. To support his career, the Cook family left Dorset to move closer to the GB Taekwondo Academy in Manchester. Aaron reached the semi-finals at the Beijing 2008 Olympic Games, narrowly missing a medal. His brother Luke (far left), mother Christine and father Nigel each play a key role in his preparation for London 2012.

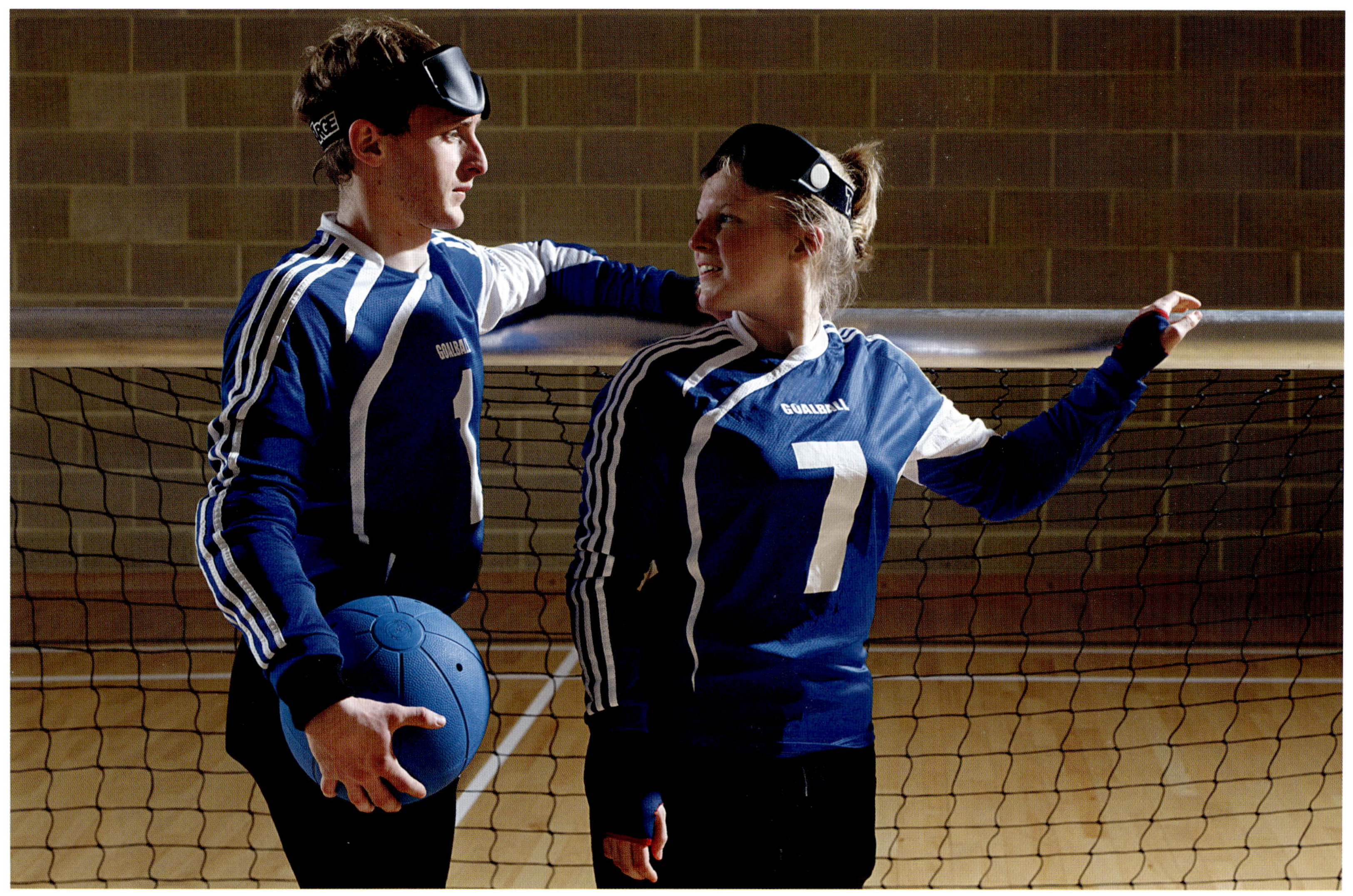

ANNA SHARKEY WITH MICHAEL SHARKEY
Photographed by Finlay MacKay
28 November 2010,
Bedford University

Anna Sharkey is a member of the GB Goalball Women's squad. She was introduced to the dedicated Paralympic sport at a 'have-a-go' day for the blind in 2001. She competed at junior international level a year after, and won gold as part of the senior GB team at the European Championships in 2009. Both Anna and her brother Michael have a congenital eye condition that causes partial sightedness. Michael is a member of the GB Goalball Men's squad and competes with his sister on the same team in domestic competitions. They are both physiotherapists.

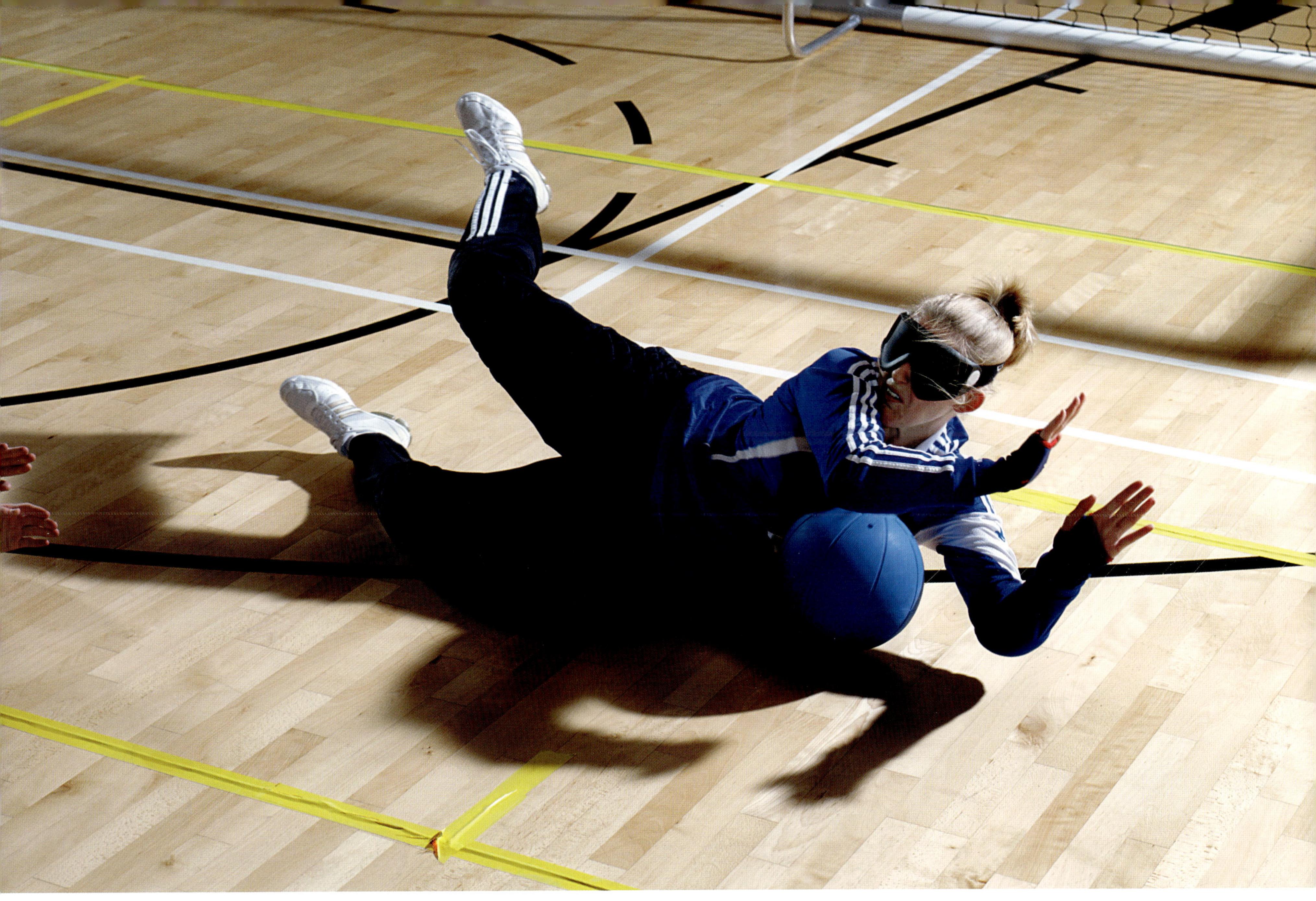

'We have been close growing up. I followed in his footsteps all the way.' **ANNA SHARKEY**

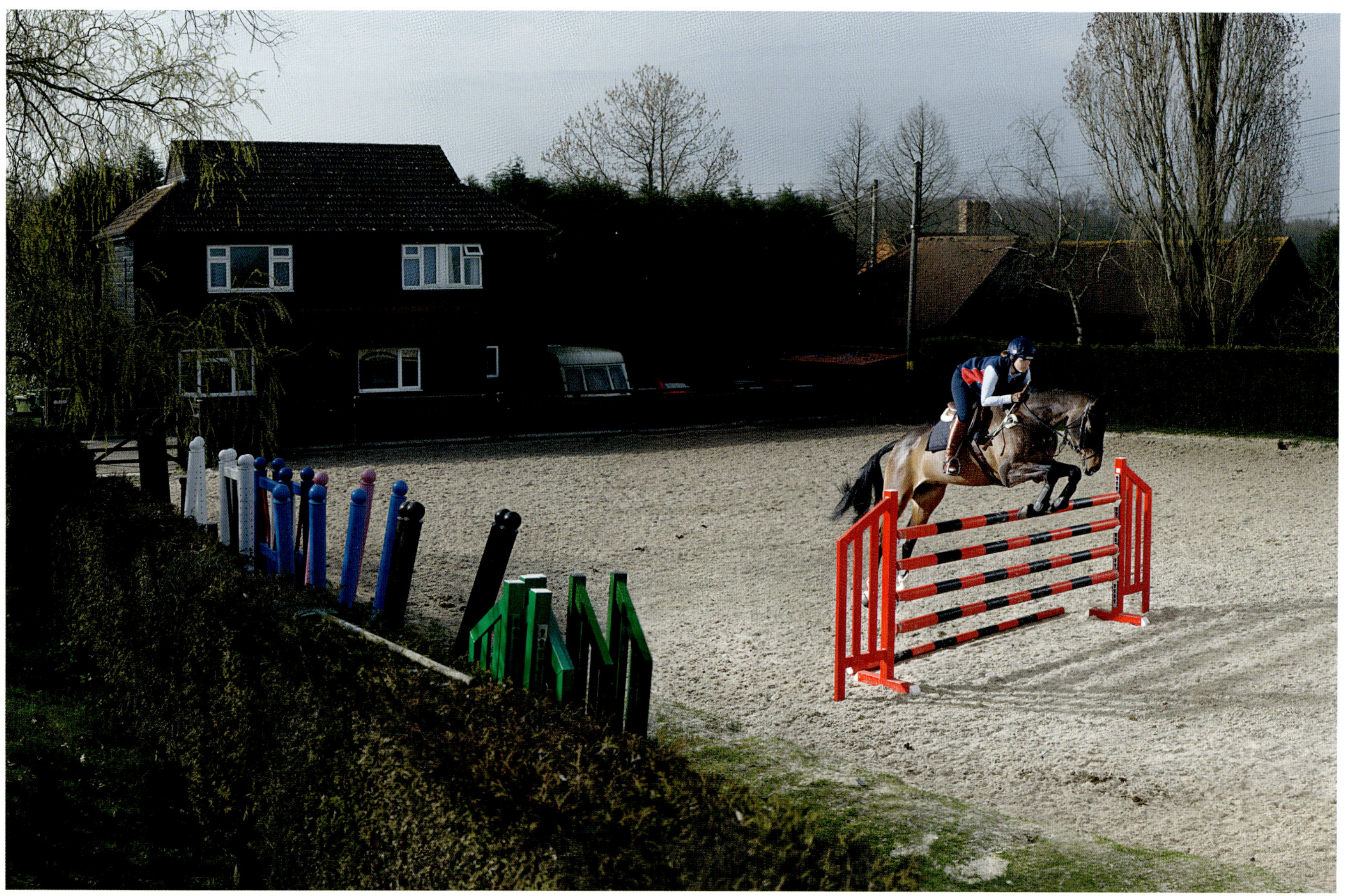

PIPPA FUNNELL WITH WILLIAM FUNNELL
Photographed by Finlay MacKay
15 March 2011, Dorking, Surrey

Pippa Funnell is a three-day event rider. She was a member of the medal-winning GB Olympic Eventing team in 2000 and 2004, when she also won an individual medal. Three-time Badminton winner Funnell is the only rider ever to win the Rolex Grand Slam, and was selected for the GB team again in 2010. With her husband William, an international show jumper, and Donal Barnwell, she set up the Billy Stud, now the largest producer of British-bred competition horses in the UK. She won bronze at the 2011 Olympic Test event on a horse bred at this stud.

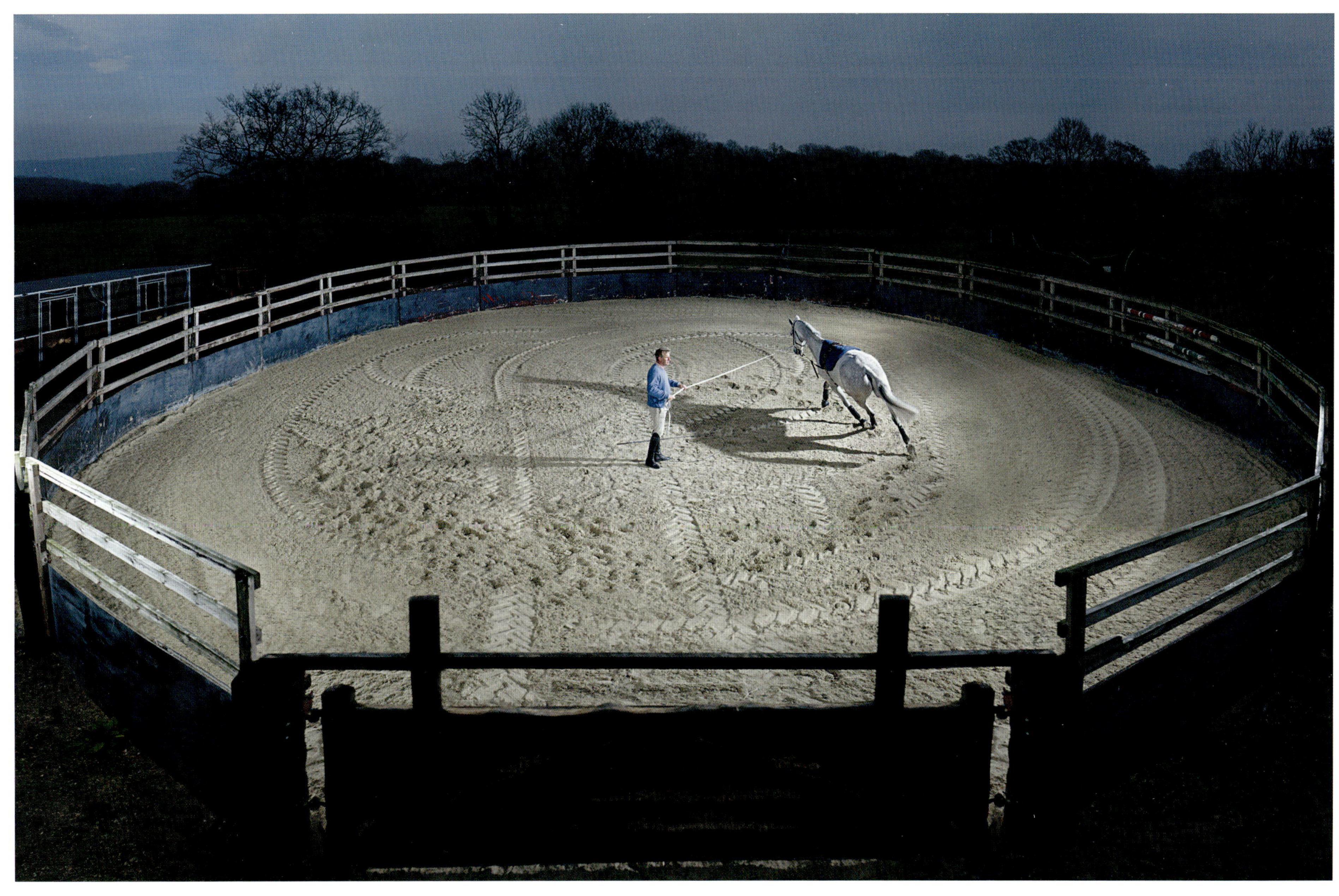

'We are both heavily involved in helping each other. Even though we are in different sports they run parallel to each other. Our dream is to bring horses on for the future, not just 2012.' **PIPPA FUNNELL**

CREATIVE THINKERS

The Olympic and Paralympic Games are about far more than just sport. The London 2012 Games will showcase the breathtaking creative talents of a wide range of extraordinary people from other fields, including those who had the original vision for the 2012 Games, those involved in creating and staging the ceremonies, and the director of the extensive and hugely varied Cultural Olympiad programme.

SIMON CLEGG AND DAVID LUCKES
Photographed by Brian Griffin
5 February 2010,
Wembley Stadium, London

Simon Clegg (left) joined the British Olympic Association in 1989, becoming its first Chief Executive in 1997. Luckes, a logistics expert and Olympic hockey player, produced the document (shown here) that assessed London's feasibility as a host city in 2000. Clegg led Team GB to success in Beijing 2008 and set the medal target for the London 2012 Olympic and Paralympic Games. He became Chief Executive of Ipswich Town Football Club in 2009. Luckes is Head of Sport Competition for the London Organising Committee of the Olympic and Paralympic Games (LOCOG).

'Sport alone was never going to win the argument. We needed to convince the Cabinet.' SIMON CLEGG

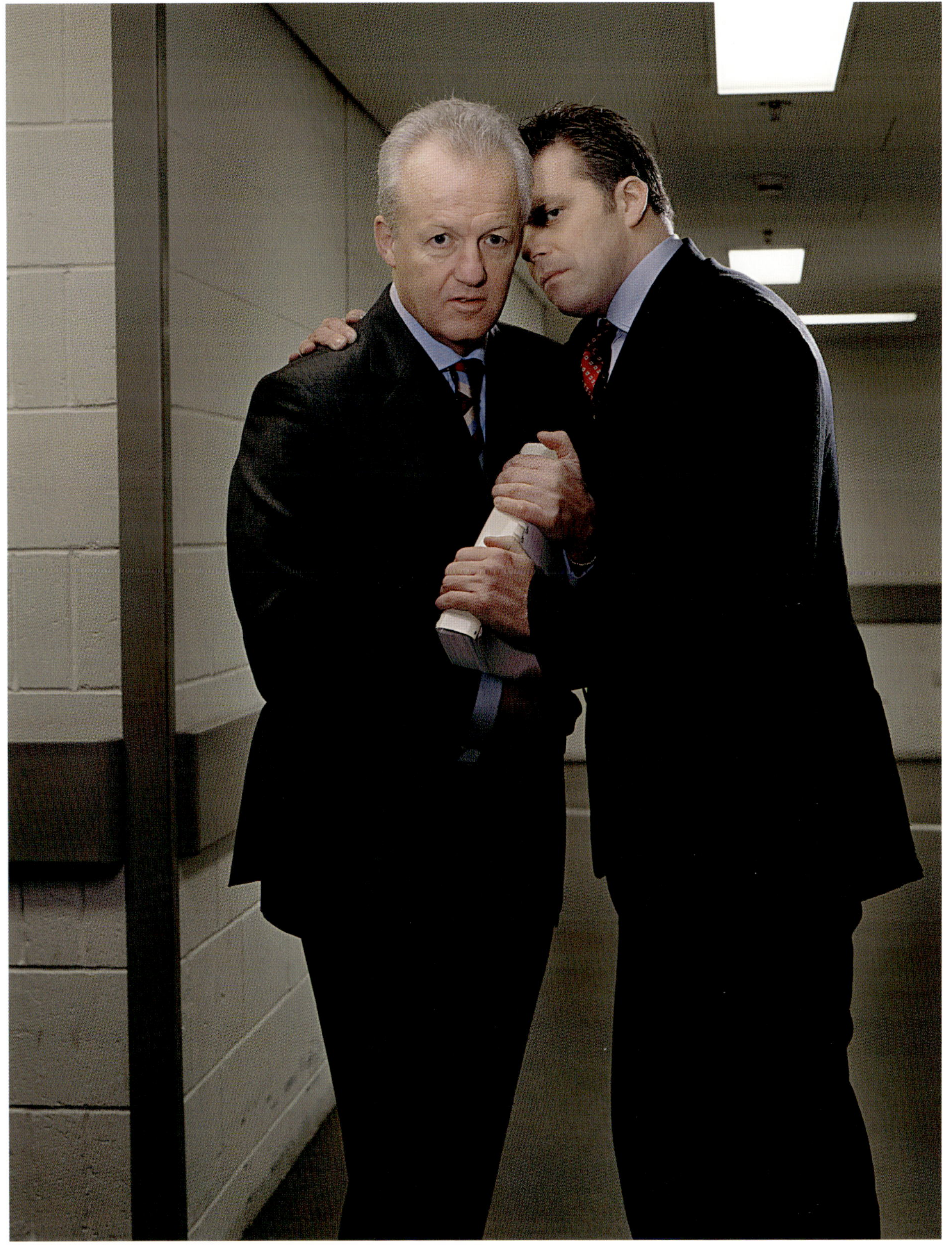

MARK TILDESLEY, DANNY BOYLE AND SUTTIRAT LARLARB

Photographed by Emma Hardy
14 April 2011, London

Mark Tildesley (left) trained in theatre design under Richard Negri at the Wimbledon School of Art. He was a co-founder of the Catch 22 Theatre Company (1987), where he directed, designed and performed. He has collaborated with Danny Boyle as a production designer on the films *28 Days Later*, *Millions* and *Sunshine*. Danny Boyle (centre), a director and producer, began his early career in theatre with the Joint Stock Theatre Company and the Royal Court, London. He has won numerous awards for his films, which include *Trainspotting*, *Slumdog Millionaire* and *127 Hours*. In 2010, Boyle was appointed Artistic Director of the London 2012 Olympic Games Opening Ceremony. Suttirat Larlarb and Mark Tildesley, long-term Boyle collaborators, are key members of his creative team for the Opening Ceremony, along with the writer Frank Cottrell Boyce. Suttirat Larlarb is a designer for film and theatre. She has been a member of Boyle's creative team since 2005, working with him on films including *Slumdog Millionaire*, for which she won a costume design award, and *127 Hours*, as both production and costume designer.

'There are very few directors who work the way Danny does. He breaks down the traditional boundaries. It's more like a think tank. With him we contribute to the story as opposed to decorating the story.' SUTTIRAT LARLARB

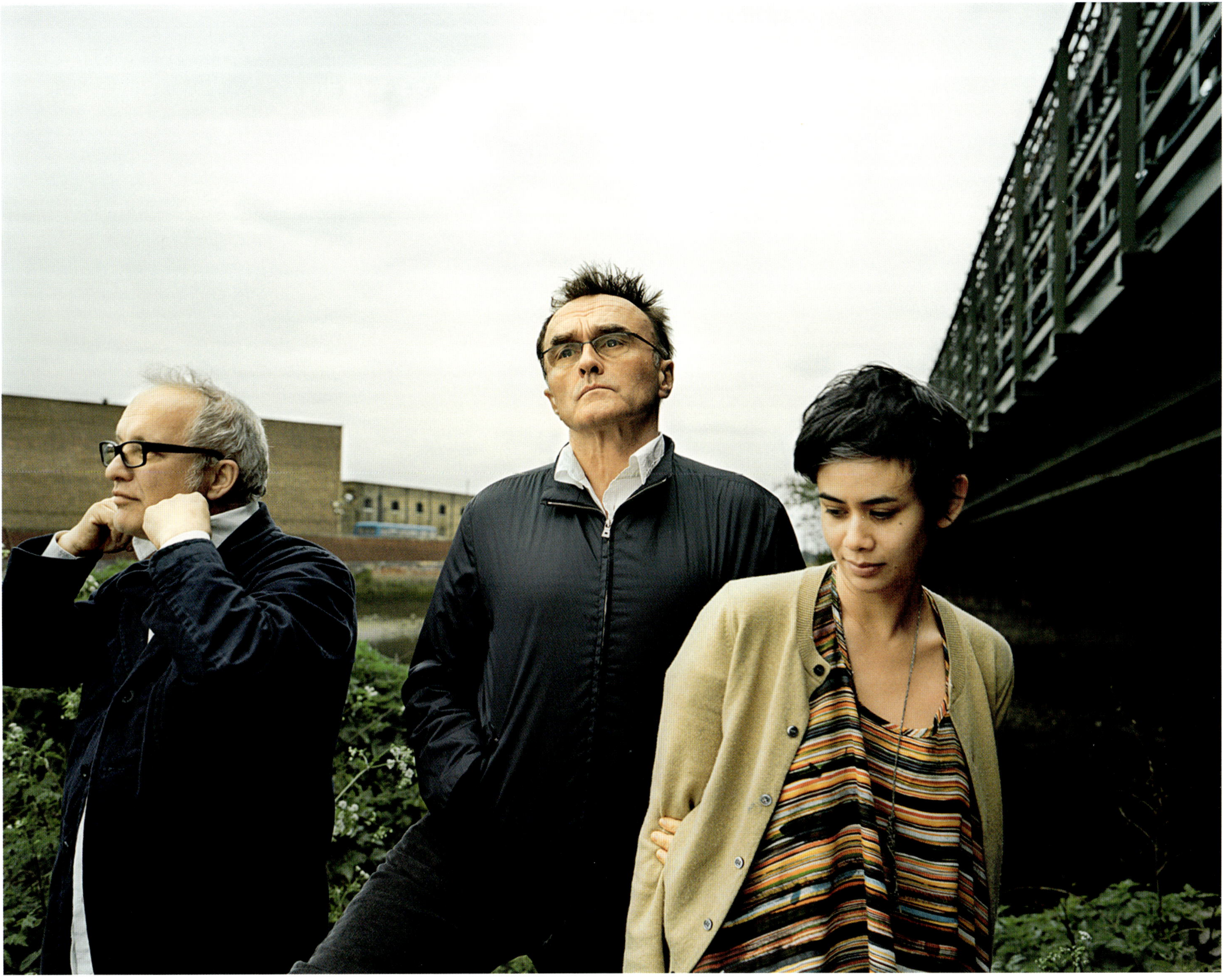

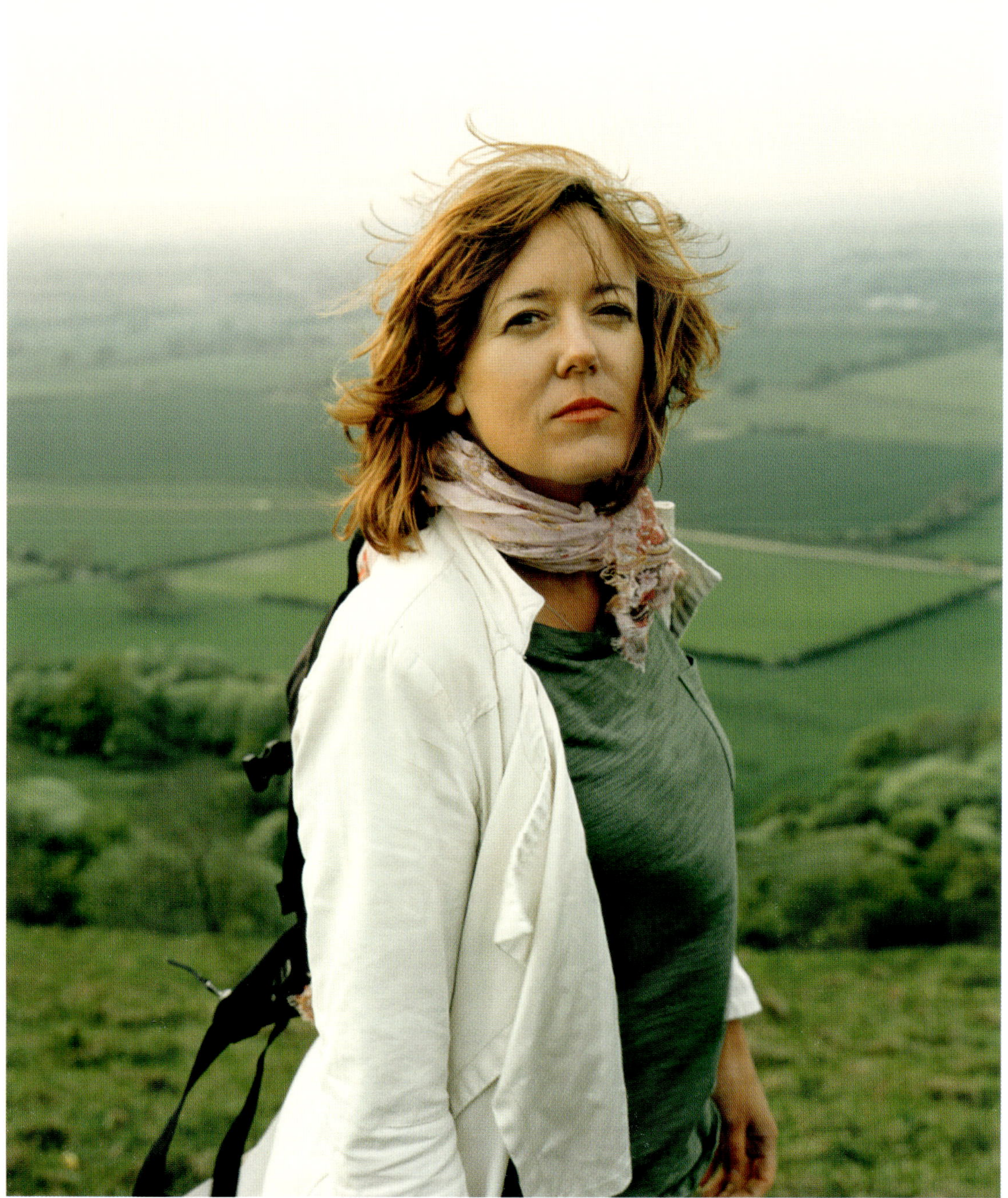

DEBORAH POULTON

Photographed by Emma Hardy
28 April 2011, West Sussex

Australian Deborah Poulton is Commissioning Editor for Channel 4, the host broadcaster for the London 2012 Paralympic Games. Poulton joined Channel 4 in 1998, and as Deputy Editor of Sport commissioned, acquired and licensed sport content, including the multi-award-winning coverage of Test cricket. The London 2012 Paralympic Games coverage is Channel 4's largest-ever commission, and Poulton aims to change the public's perception of disability and turn Paralympic athletes into household names.

'Our aim is to put the Paralympics on a par with the Olympics. It's a challenge.'
DEBORAH POULTON

CECIL BALMOND

Photographed by Jillian Edelstein
16 December 2011,
Balmond Studio, London

Sri Lankan-born Cecil Balmond is an internationally renowned designer, artist and writer. He founded his research-led practice, Balmond Studio, in 2010. He and sculptor Anish Kapoor won the Mayor of London's competition to build their proposed design, the ArcelorMittal Orbit, to commemorate the London 2012 Olympic and Paralympic Games.

'When you visit the Orbit you'll understand that it is an environment, not a viewing platform. Views are blocked and then revealed in a transforming narrative of space.' CECIL BALMOND

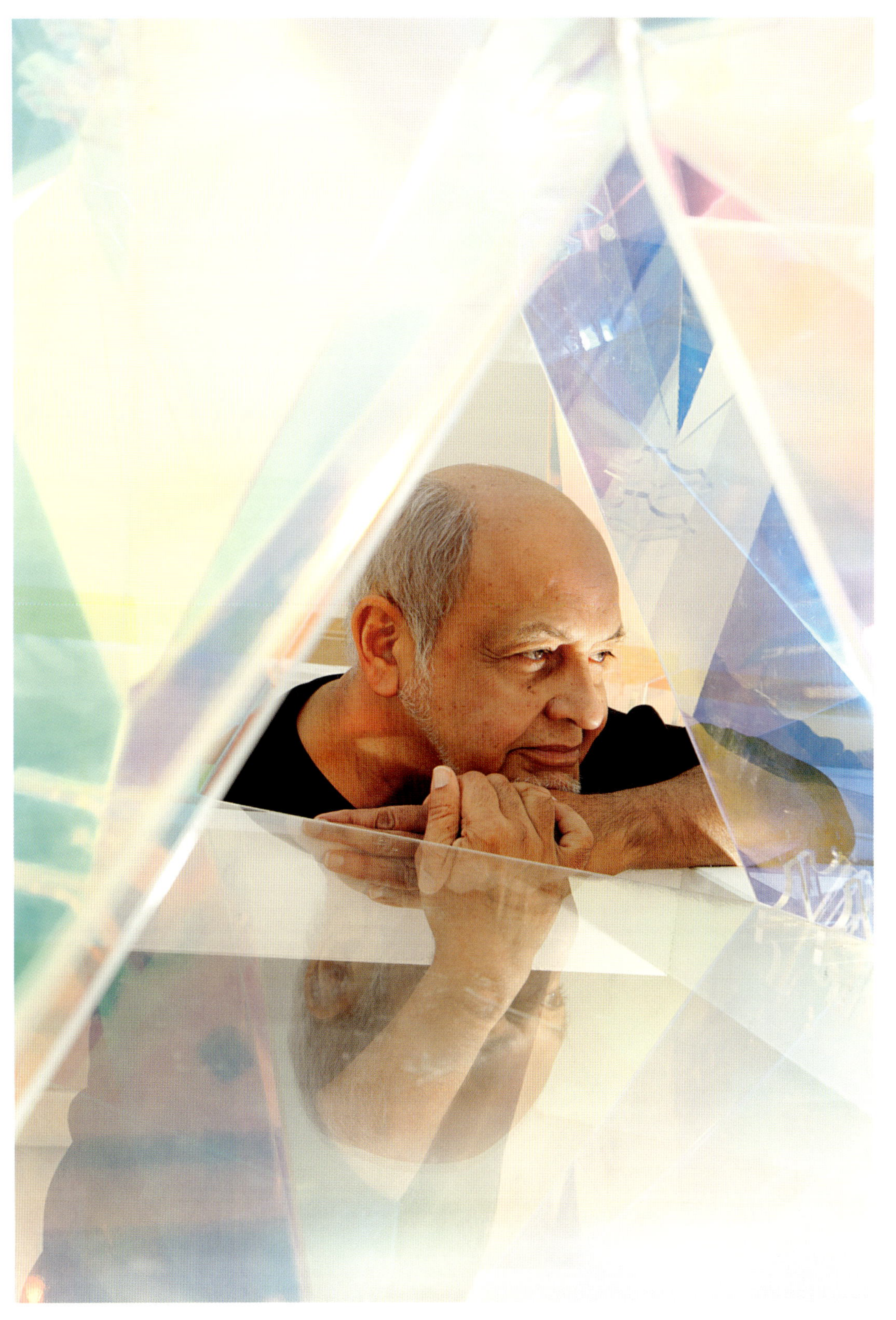

'One of the things we are really great at in this country is orchestral playing. We have great symphony orchestras here. So my take on it was to do symphonic versions of the anthems ...' **PHILIP SHEPPARD**

PHILIP SHEPPARD

Photographed by Jillian Edelstein
19 October 2011, Suffolk

Philip Sheppard is a composer, cellist and Professor at the Royal Academy of Music, specialising in film and television soundtracks, large-scale theatre and live events. After composing and producing the music for the handover to London in Beijing in 2008, Sheppard was commissioned to rescore the 205 national anthems that the London Philharmonic Orchestra have recorded for the London 2012 Olympic and Paralympic medal ceremonies. Sheppard has performed and recorded with such well-known names as Scott Walker, Juliette Binoche, Jarvis Cocker and David Bowie.

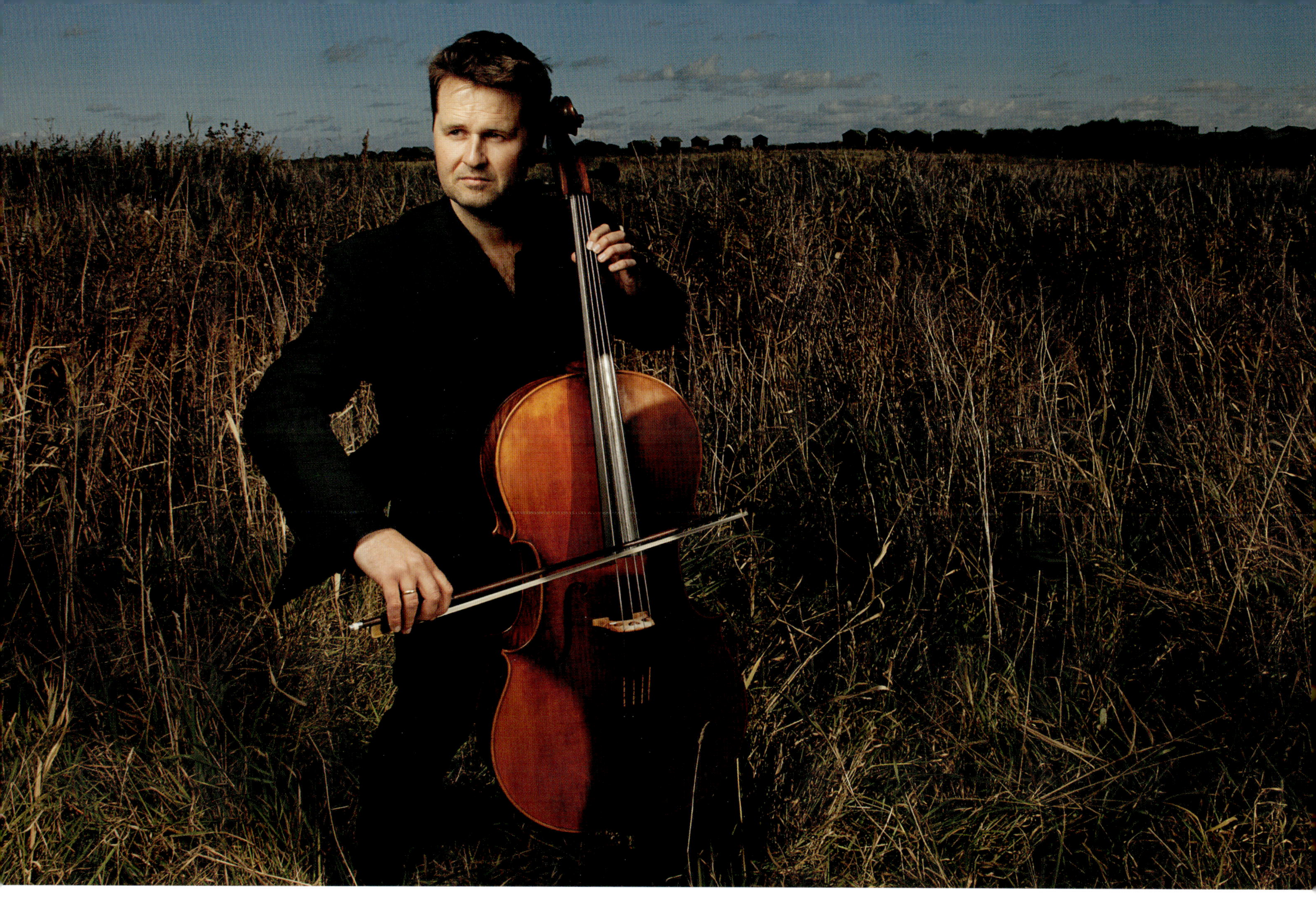

ADRIAN WARNER AND ROGER MOSEY

Photographed by Emma Hardy
19 April 2011, Serpentine, London

BBC London Olympics correspondent Adrian Warner (left) reports on all aspects of the London 2012 Olympic and Paralympic Games. He has written extensively about the history and politics of the Olympic movement and has covered every Olympic Games since 1988. Roger Mosey (right) is the Director of London 2012 for Olympic host nation broadcaster, the BBC. London 2012 will be the first-ever summer Olympic Games to stream every sport live, and Mosey leads the planning and delivery for this together with wider London 2012 and Cultural Olympiad coverage across all platforms.

'As the abdication was to radio and the Coronation to television, so the Olympics will be to digital Britain.'
ROGER MOSEY, BBC DIRECTOR OF LONDON 2012

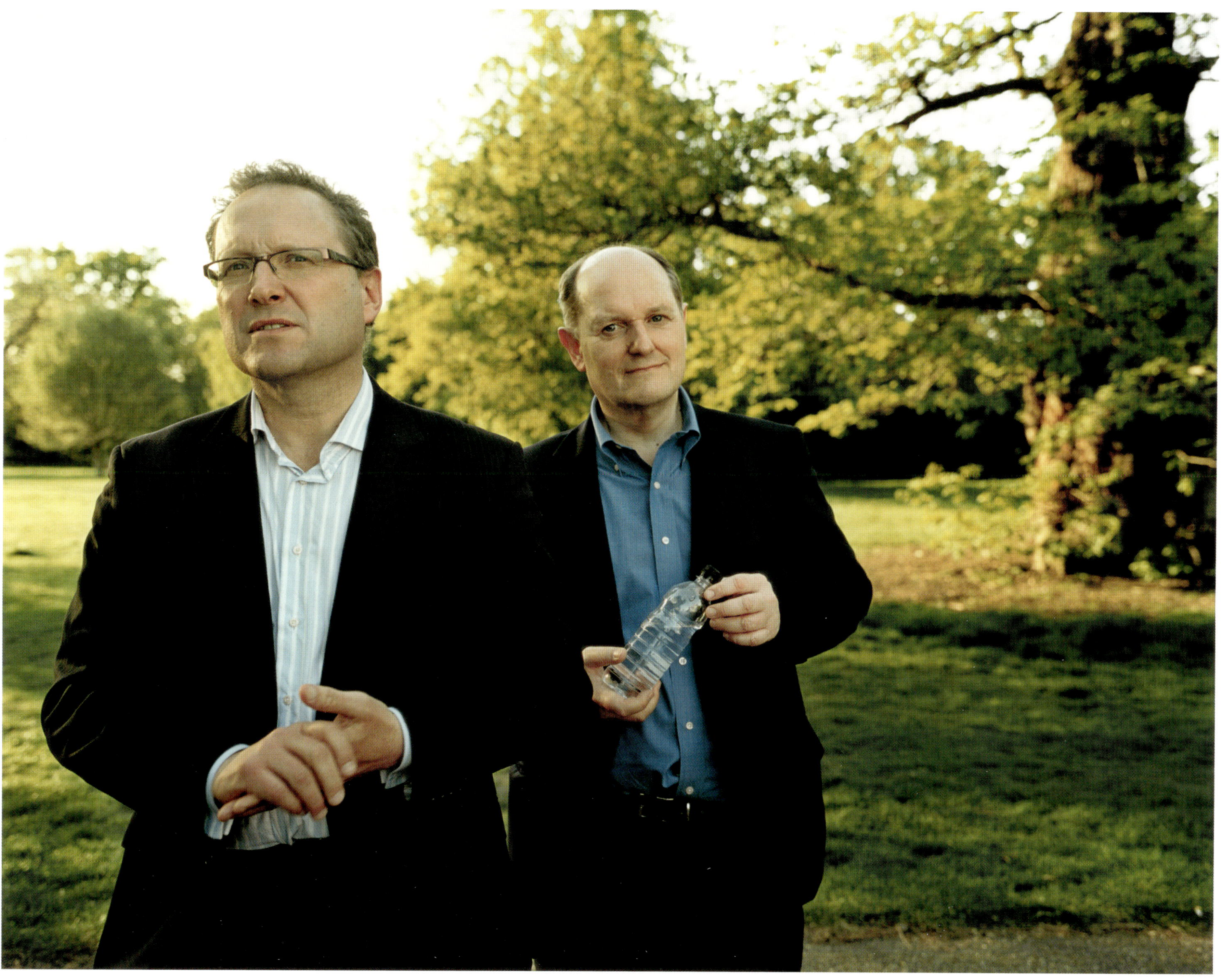

HAMISH HAMILTON

Photographed by Jillian Edelstein
30 October 2011,
Three Mills Studios, London

Hamish Hamilton is a Grammy- and BAFTA Award-nominated British television director, and is world renowned as a television creative. He is one of the four executive producers for the London 2012 ceremonies, responsible for the broadcasts and for ensuring that creative ideas are developed with their on-screen potential in mind. He trained at the BBC and then MTV, and has created and directed for the Brit Awards, the Super Bowl half-time show and the Academy Awards.

'Being in a room with Mark Fisher, Stephen Daldry, Danny Boyle and Catherine Ugwu is quite humbling. It is rare to be with such creative energy. We each have different perspectives on the same equation.'
HAMISH HAMILTON

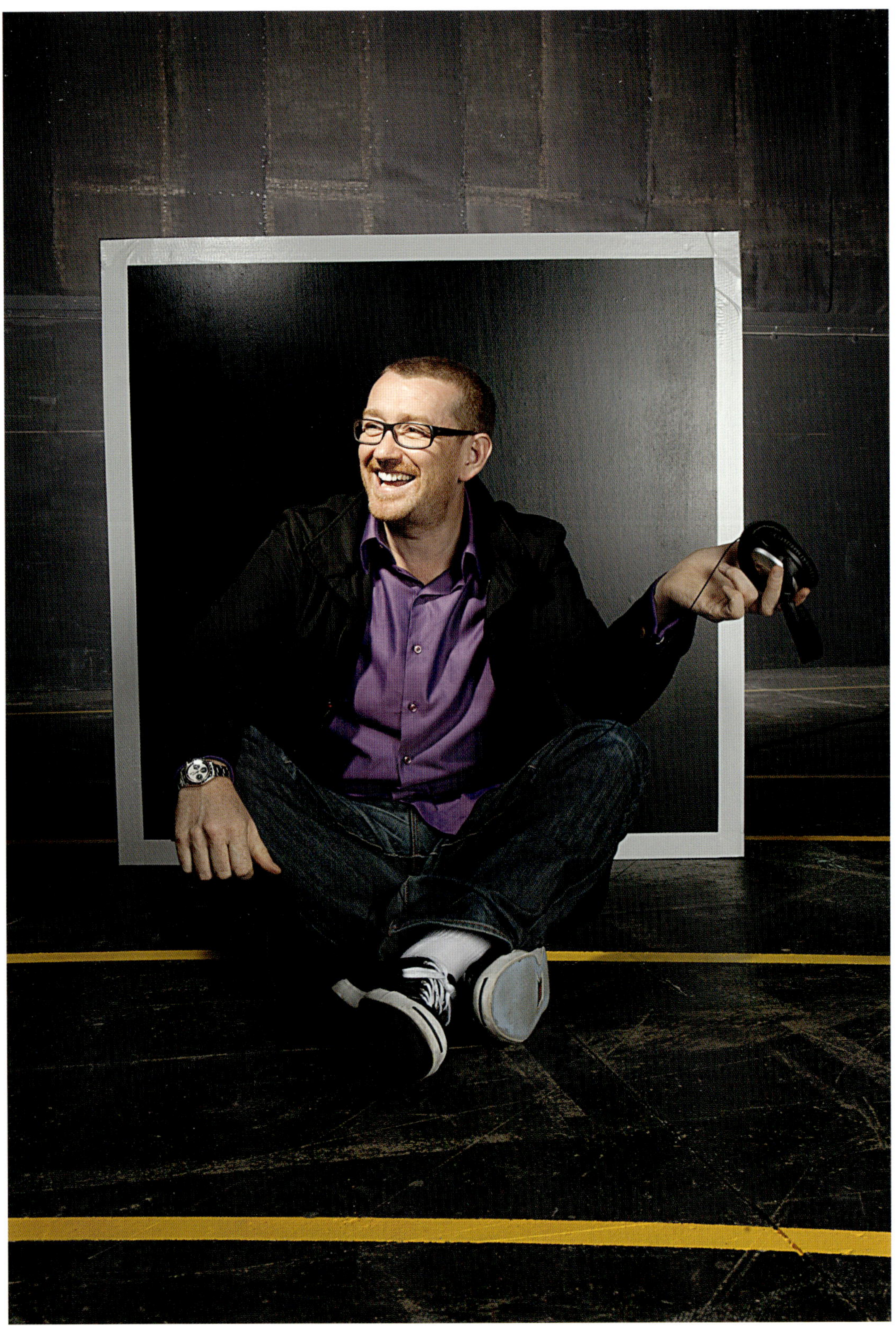

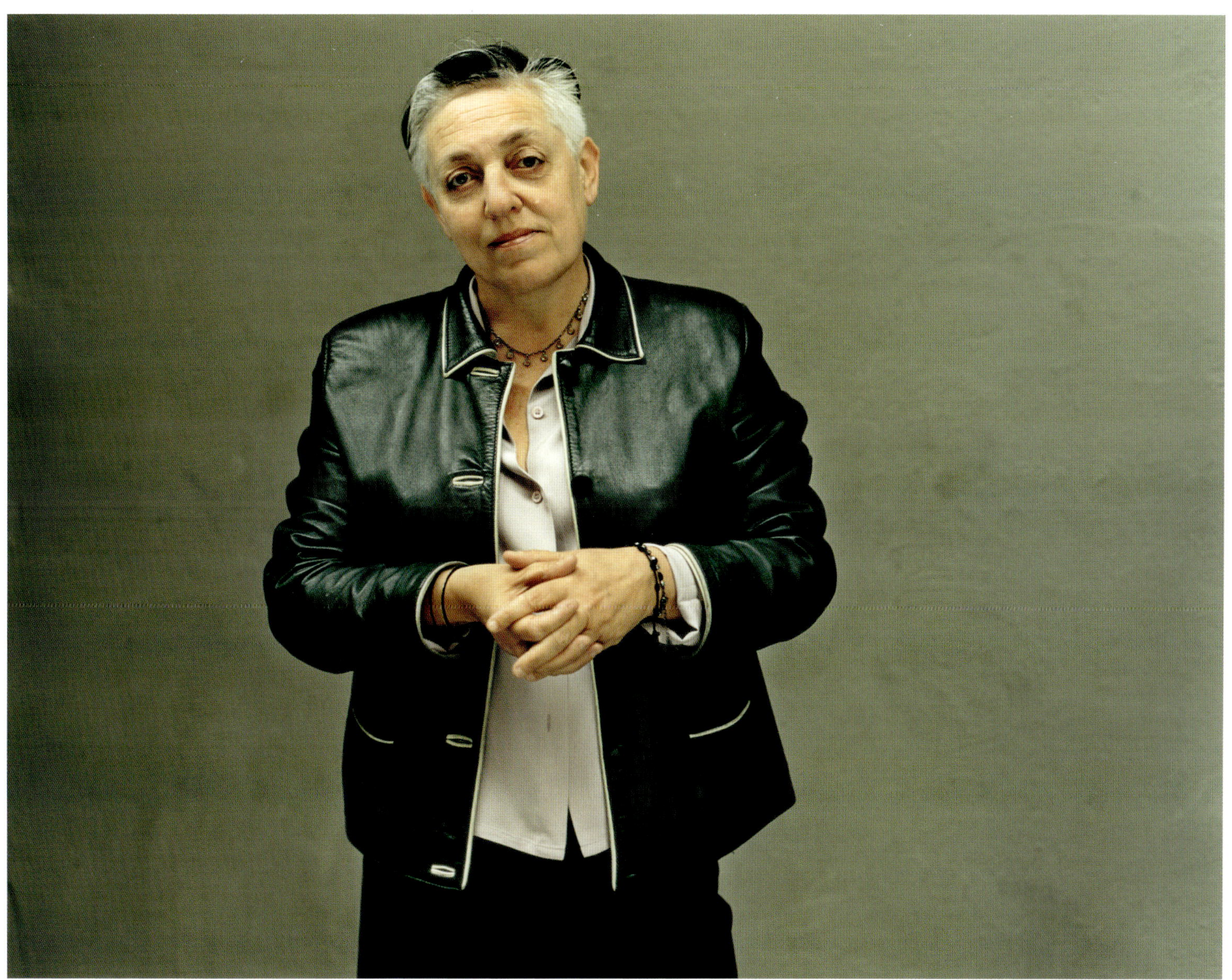

RUTH MACKENZIE
Photographed by Emma Hardy
29 April 2011, London

Ruth Mackenzie is the Director of the Cultural Olympiad. This four-year, UK-wide cultural programme culminates with a nationwide festival in summer 2012. It aims to give everyone the opportunity to celebrate the London 2012 Olympic and Paralympic Games through the arts. Mackenzie was Expert Adviser for the Department of Culture, Media and Sport and has also advised, among others, the Barbican Centre, BBC and Tate.

MICHAEL MORPURGO AND GREG NUGENT

Photographed by Emma Hardy
21 April 2011, Iddesleigh, Devon

Children's Laureate Michael Morpurgo (left) is the award-winning author of numerous books, including *War Horse*. Greg Nugent is the Marketing Director of London 2012, and commissioned Morpurgo to write the story of the London 2012 Olympic and Paralympic Games mascots, Wenlock and Mandeville. The mascots are named after the Shropshire town of Much Wenlock, which held a forerunner of the modern Olympic Games, and Stoke Mandeville Hospital in Buckinghamshire, which organised the Stoke Mandeville Games, the precursor of the Paralympic Games. While Marketing Director at Eurostar, Greg Nugent developed a pioneering partnership between brand and film as Executive Producer and funder of Shane Meadows' acclaimed film *Somers Town*.

'It's a journey and we're doing it together. It's developing – getting darker, more complex – and that's a good thing.'

MICHAEL MORPURGO, ON THE WENLOCK AND MANDEVILLE STORY

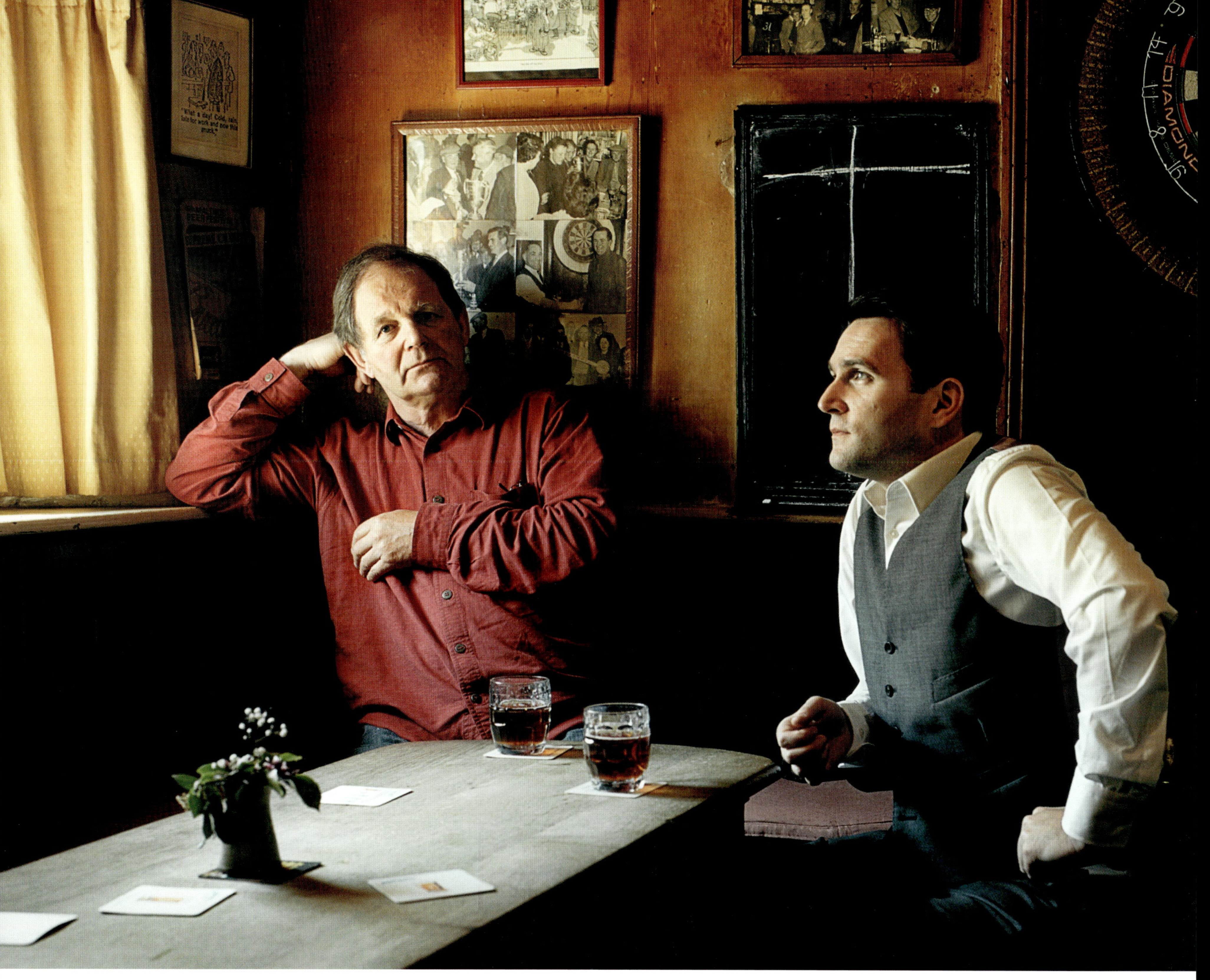
DIAMOND

FUTURE TALENT

The Olympic and Paralympic Games present a fantastic, once-in-a-lifetime opportunity for many young people to gain valuable experience, whether as a Young Ambassador, an apprentice on the Olympic Park, or a participant in the Young Leaders Programme. The Games will also showcase the incredible talents of a new generation of medal hopefuls, who are starting out in their senior athletic careers or defending their already hard-won titles.

JODIE WILLIAMS

Photographed by Nadav Kander
15 December 2011, London

Jodie Williams is recognised as 'the sort of athlete every country is waiting for' by UK athletics head coach Charles van Commenee. Following in the footsteps of her parents, both county-level sprinters, the eighteen-year-old joined her local athletics club at the age of thirteen. She holds three world junior and youth titles in the 100m and 200m, and is reigning World Junior Champion at 100m. Williams debuted at senior international level in 2011, coming fourth in the 60m with a personal best. She is currently studying for A-levels.

'Jodie asked how she could become an Olympic athlete after school sports day when she was seven years old. Her focus and competitive drive are amazing.'

CHRIS WILLIAMS, JODIE'S MOTHER

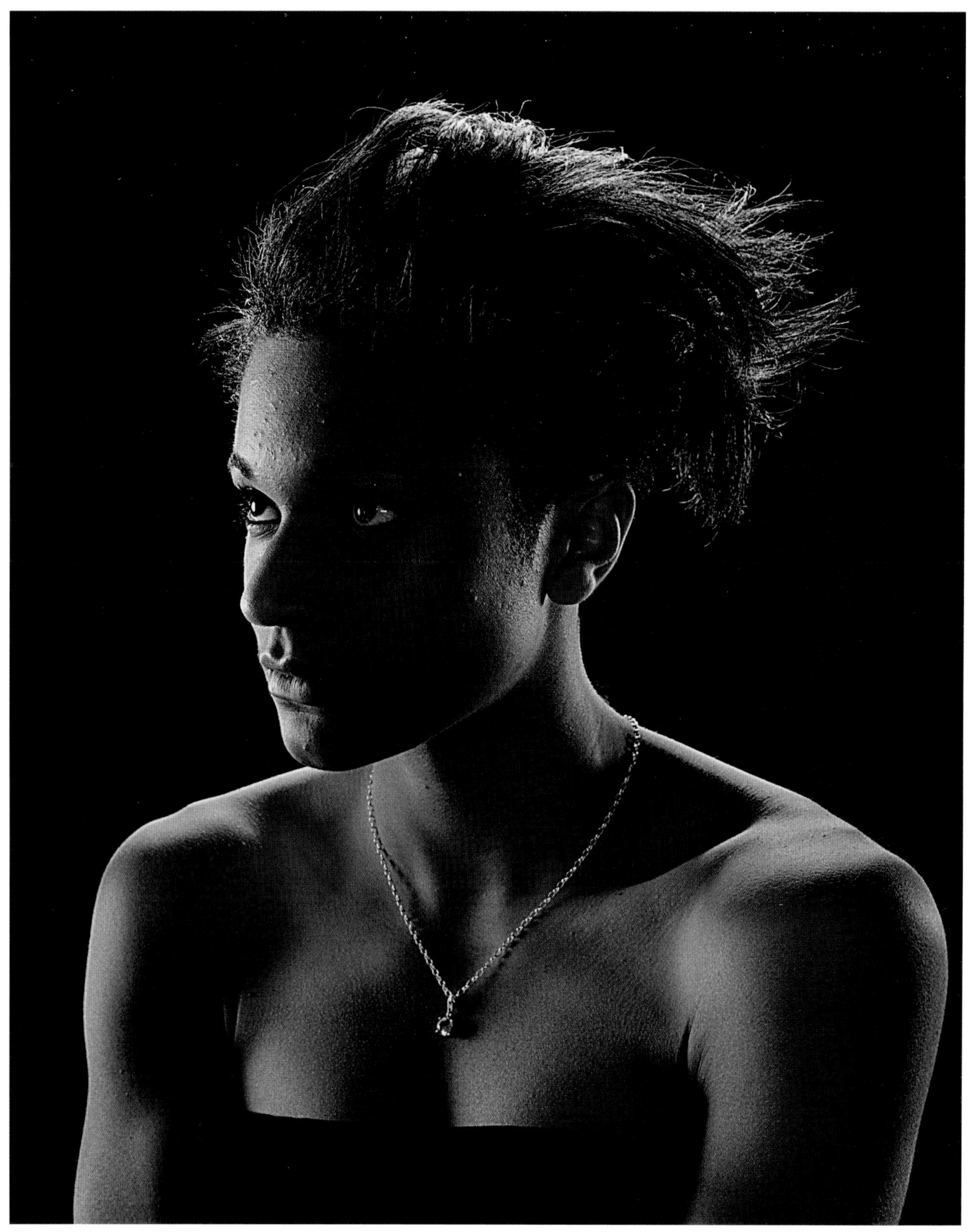

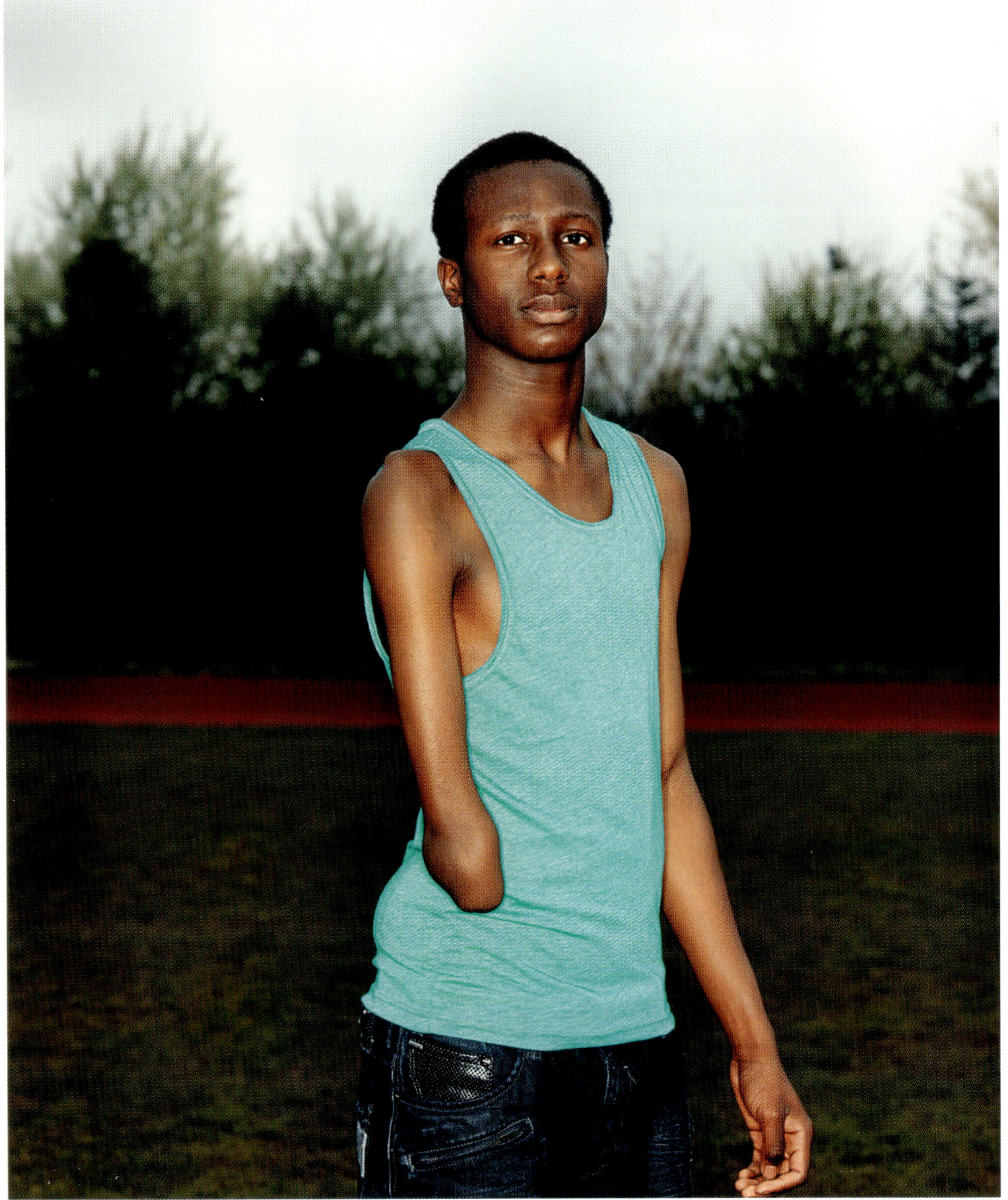

OLA ABIDOGUN

Photographed by Bettina von Zwehl
5 May 2010, Reebok Stadium, Bolton

Teenage sprinter Ola Abidogun made his international debut in 2009, and was invited to join the UK Athletics Association World Class Performance programme. In April 2011 he won 100m and 200m titles at the IWAS World Junior Championships for the second year running, and a month later marked his entry on the senior stage by winning gold and silver medals at the Paralympic World Cup. Bolton-based Abidogun started running at school, and now trains alongside able-bodied athletes at the Reebok Stadium.

'I admire Usain Bolt for his attitude … Most people expect sprinters to be very serious people on the line, but Usain Bolt tends to inject a bit of fun.'

OLA ABIDOGUN

SUSAN CABLE, GEORGE NOLAN, JAMIE NORRIS, NICOLA ZENI AND LIAM PADMORE

Photographed by Brian Griffin
5 February 2010,
Olympic Park, London

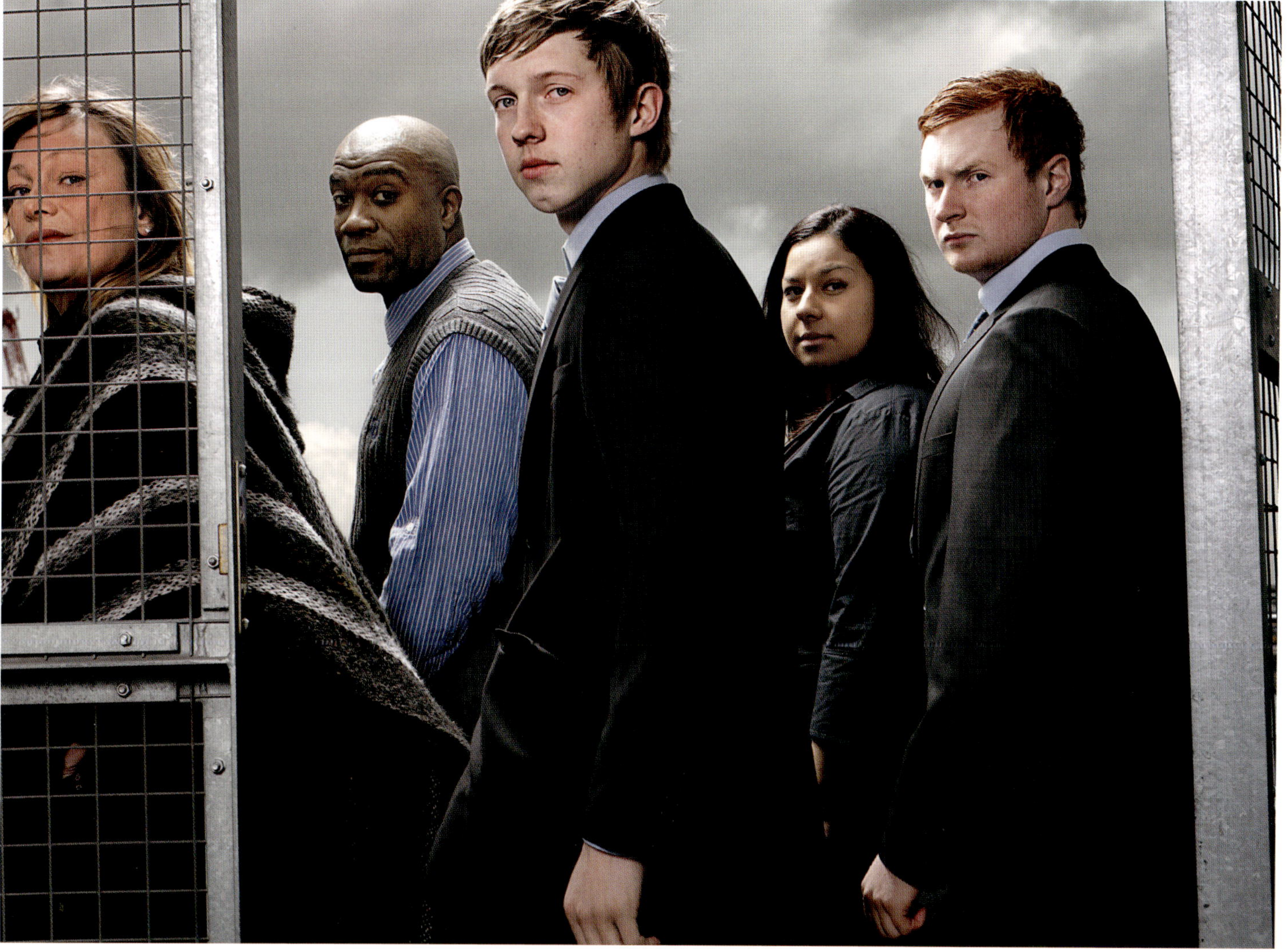

'Most jobs are sitting in offices, but there's a thrill to this. It's such an interesting job. You're underground, pushing tunnels through and building out timber in the shafts.' LIAM PADMORE

Susan Cable, George Nolan, Jamie Norris, Nicola Zeni and Liam Padmore (left to right) were apprentices on the Olympic Park. Cable, a resident of Tower Hamlets, joined the construction industry as an apprentice plumber on the Olympic Stadium. Newham resident Nolan had previously served as a gunner in the Royal Artillery and was unemployed when he joined the BeOnsite programme. Norris was an apprentice electrician working with the International Broadcast Centre suppliers. Zeni chose to join the construction industry as an apprentice electrician because she wanted a hands-on job. Newham-based Padmore was recruited through the Olympic Delivery Authority (ODA) as an apprentice technician.

KATIE MURPHY, GURPREET VIRDEE, SUTVEER KAUR AND ALEX LOUKOS

Photographed by Brian Griffin
17 September 2009,
Langdon School, London

Langdon School students Katie Murphy, Gurpreet Virdee, Sutveer Kaur and Alex Loukos (left to right) are four of the thirty young east Londoners who joined the delegation team in 2005 for the final stage of London's bid to host the 2012 Olympic and Paralympic Games. These Young Ambassadors represent both the communities that would benefit most from London 2012 and the ambition to inspire young people to take up sport. Kaur currently works for the London Organising Committee of the Olympic and Paralympic Games (LOCOG) as a Starting Blocks trainee. Loukos, now a design project manager, was inspired by his grandfather to take up boxing at Langdon School. Murphy joined Olympic suppliers Haydon M&E in London Docklands as a document controller, and Virdee is a university student.

'There were thirty of us, but we were representing all young Londoners. It was quite a responsibility.'

ALEX LOUKOS

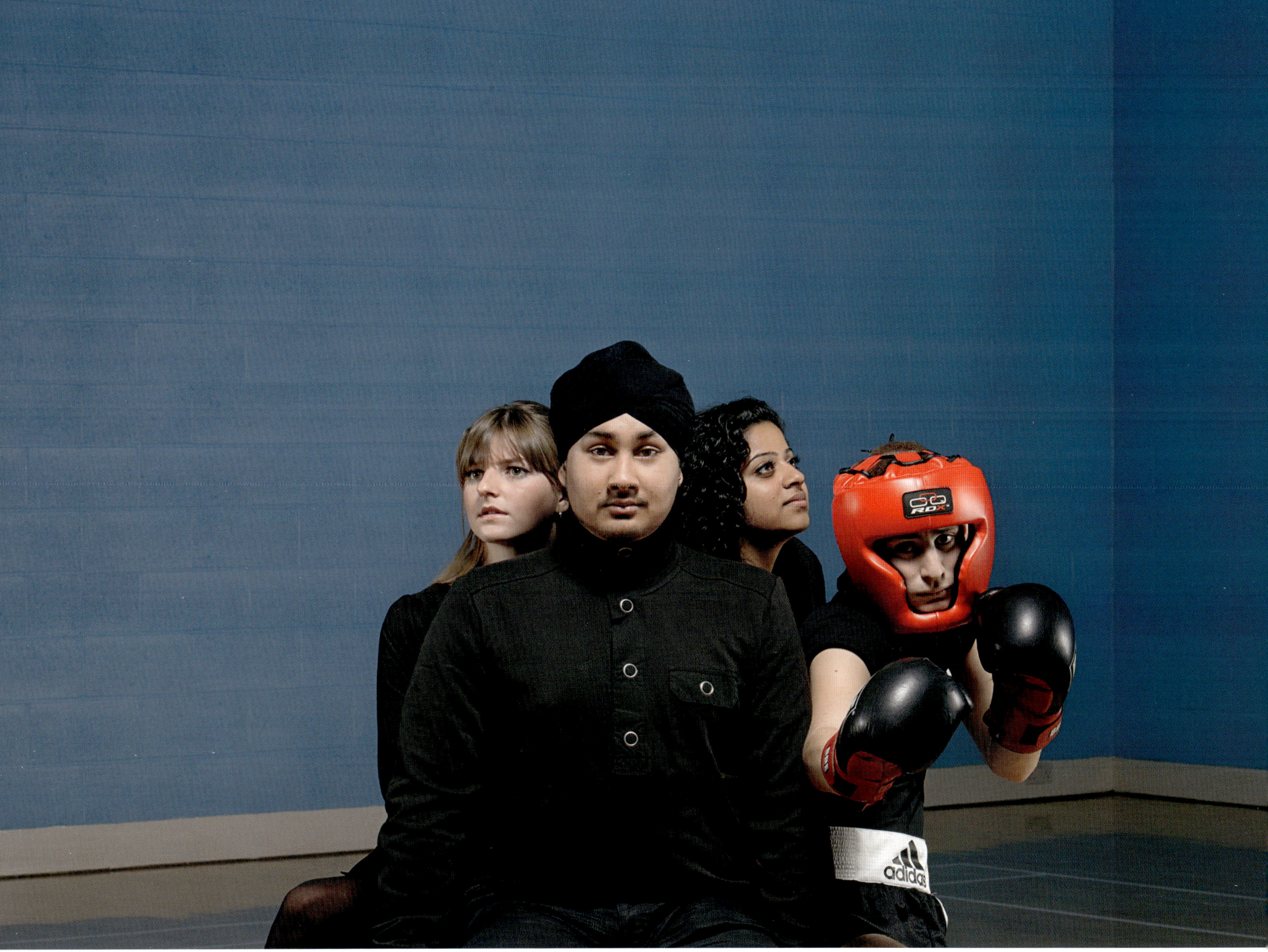
RDX
adidas

TOM DALEY

Photographed by Bettina von Zwehl
7 June 2010, Plymouth, Devon

Tom Daley became the UK's first individual world diving champion after winning the 10m platform event at the 2009 World Championships. Encouraged to swim when he was three years old by his father, Daley started diving at the age of seven. Three years later he was the under-18 National Champion, and at the age of fourteen was selected to represent Team GB at the Beijing 2008 Olympic Games. For London 2012 Daley hopes to compete in the individual 10m platform event and the synchronised diving events with his partner, Pete Waterfield.

'There have been lots of inspirational people in my life … people like the Olympic greats Sir Steve Redgrave and Dame Tanni Grey-Thompson – Olympic heroes.'
TOM DALEY

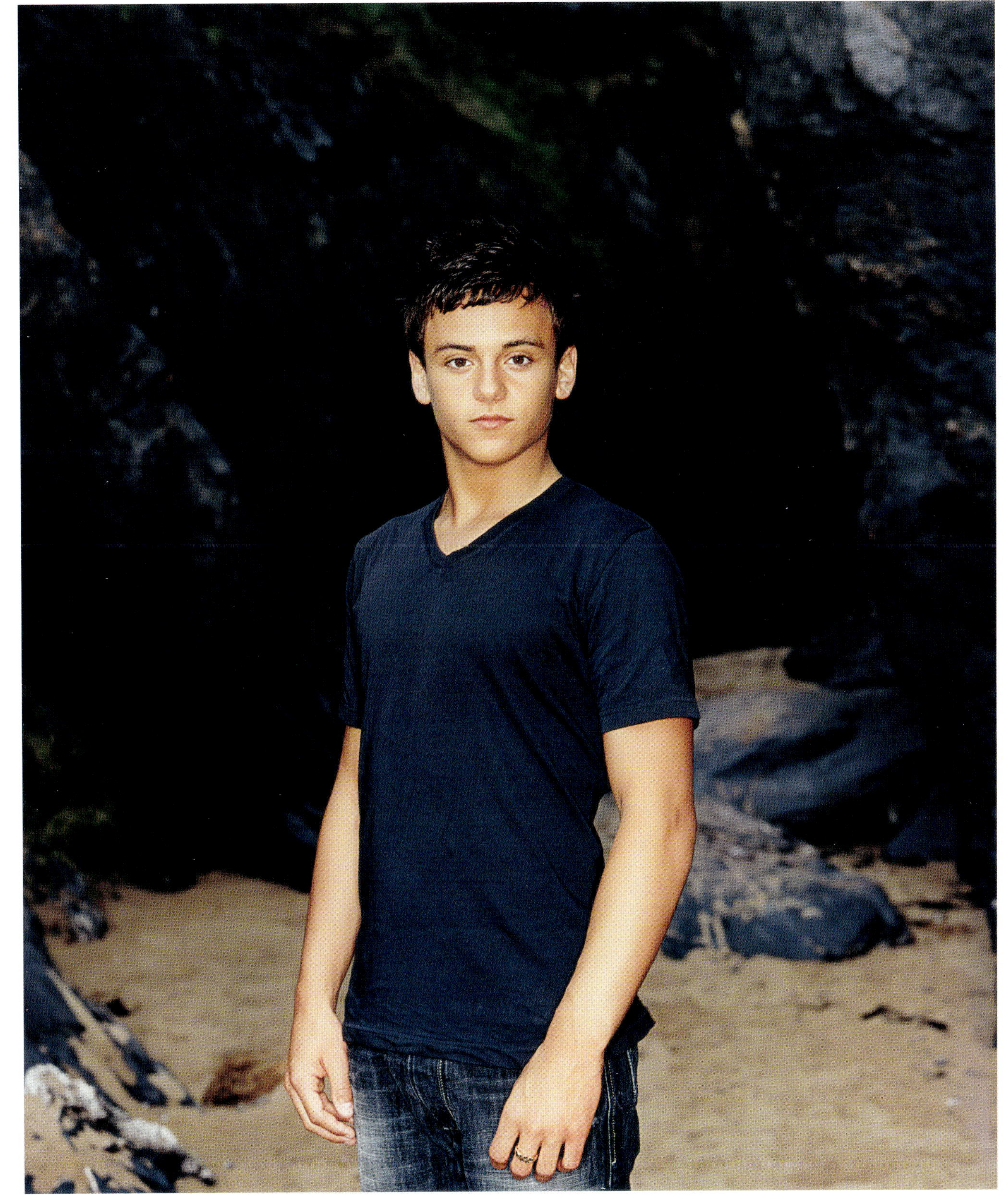

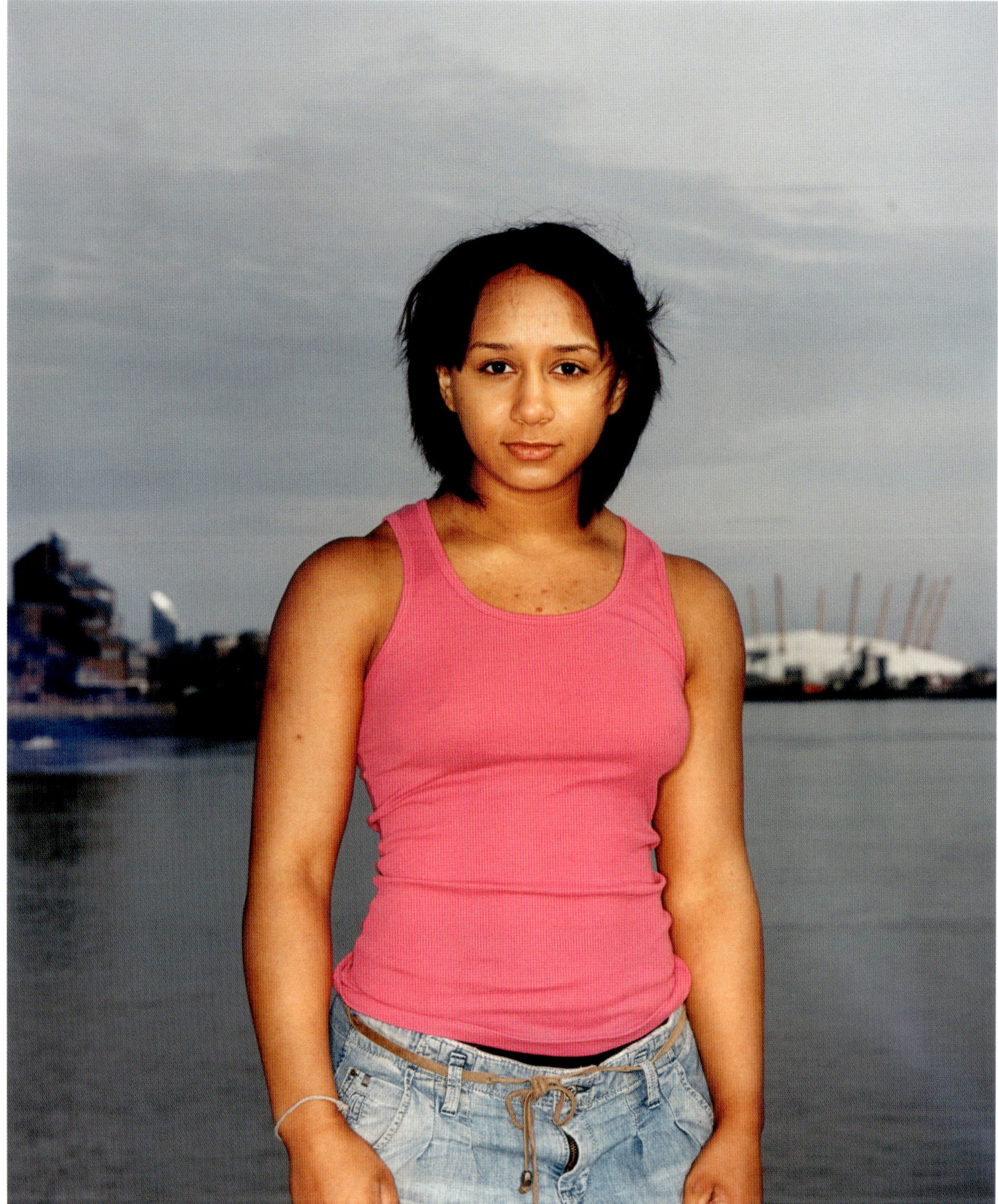

ZOE SMITH

Photographed by Bettina von Zwehl
10 April 2010, Greenwich, London

Greenwich-born teenager Zoe Smith started out as a gymnast, and now holds over 300 weightlifting records. In 2008 Smith was invited to Beijing as part of Britain's Olympic Ambition Programme, and was nominated the British Olympic Association's Athlete of the Year (Weightlifting). In 2010 she became the first-ever British woman to win a weightlifting medal at the Commonwealth Games, and went on to win silver at the World Youth Games a year later.

'Quite a lot of people stand out for me, like Kelly Holmes who worked for so many years to achieve the top of her game.'

ZOE SMITH

LAWRENCE OKOYE

Photographed by Nadav Kander
15 December 2011, London

Lawrence Okoye holds the British discus record of 67.63m and the world record for the longest throw by a teenager. A former rugby union player with London Irish, he switched to discus full time in 2010 and is ranked ninth in the world. Having won medals on the junior circuit, including gold at the U23 European Championships in 2011, he now competes at senior level.

'You know when you have done a good throw – you feel it immediately. It doesn't happen all the time. It's something you chase.'
LAWRENCE OKOYE

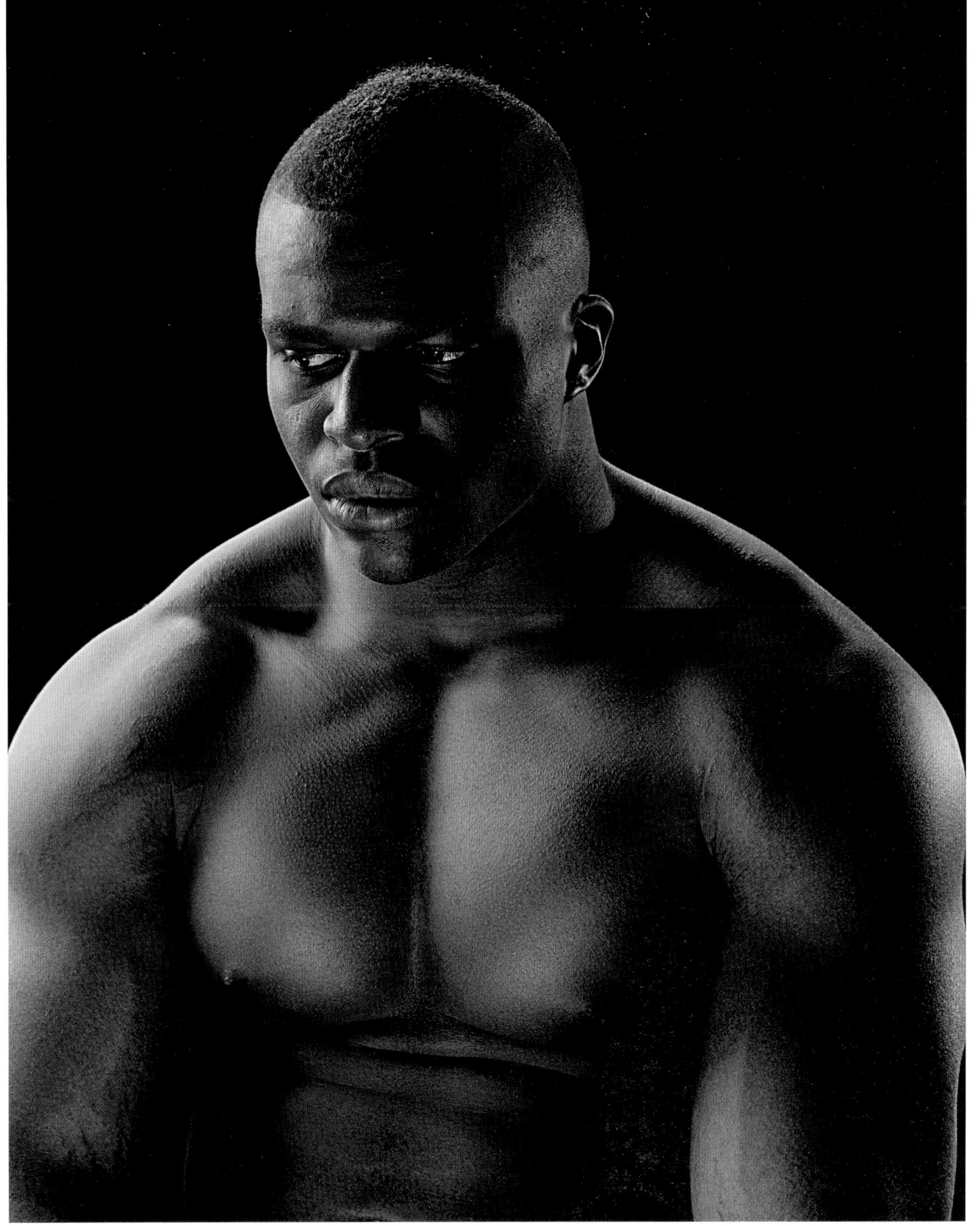

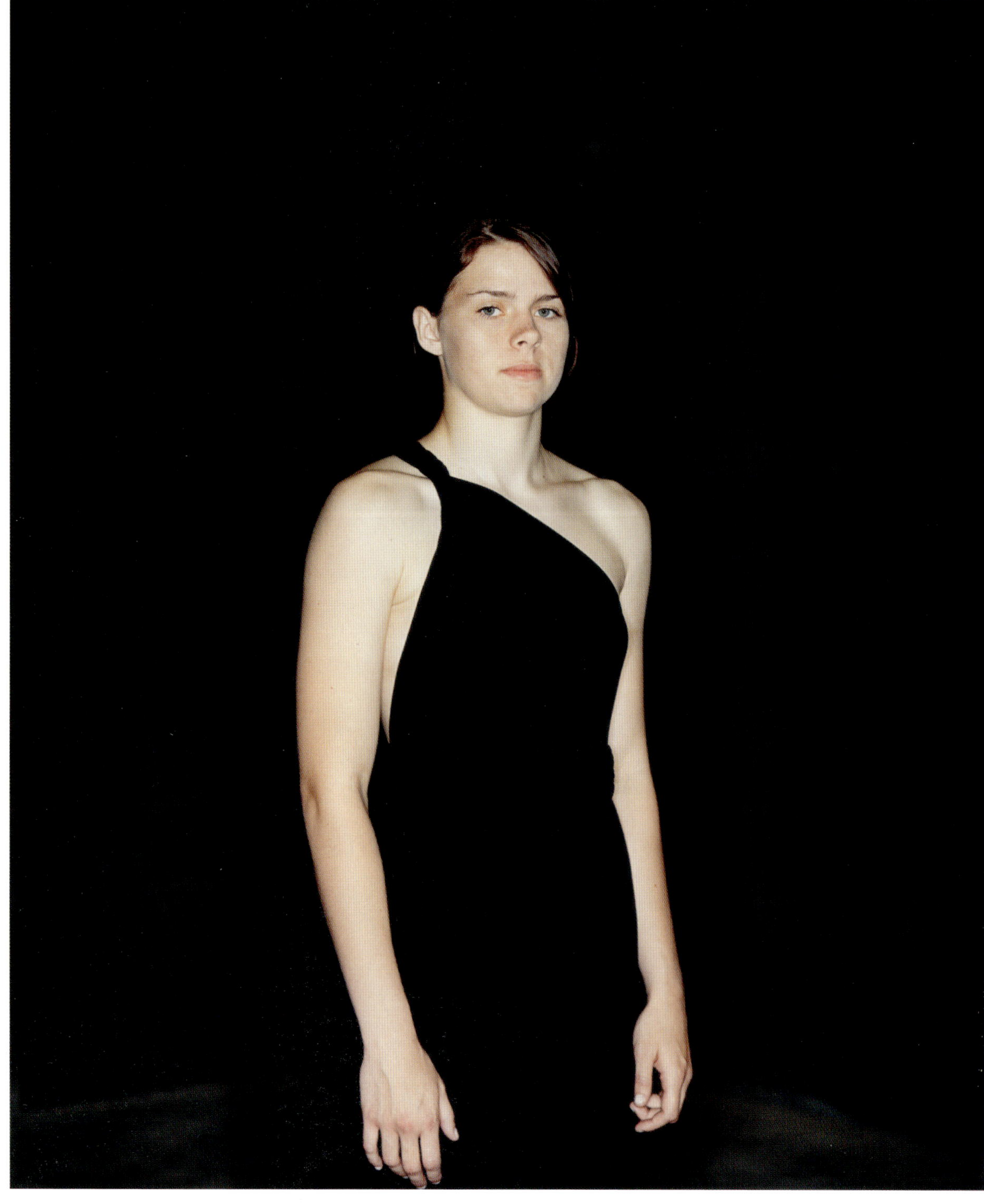

SAVANNAH MARSHALL

Photographed by Bettina von Zwehl
9 June 2010, ExCel, London

Savannah Marshall began boxing at the age of twelve. Undefeated at junior and senior level, she held both English and European middleweight titles. With the inclusion of women's boxing for the first time in the Olympic and Paralympic Games in 2012, Marshall is one of seven elite women boxers selected to receive funding and specialist training at the English Institute of Sport in Sheffield. Marshall won silver at the 2010 World Championships and gold at the London 2012 Olympic test event.

'My friends who I grew up with are supportive. I've got a friend who, if I ever wanted to take drugs or go out drinking, would probably slap me.'
SAVANNAH MARSHALL

NATHAN STEPHENS

Photographed by Bettina von Zwehl
18 May 2010, Barry Island, Wales

One of only two UK athletes to compete at both winter and summer Paralympic Games, Nathan Stephens was a member of Team GB's ice sledge hockey team in Turin 2006 and competed as a thrower in Beijing 2008. Despite losing both legs when playing on railway tracks at the age of nine, he continued with sport. His talent was recognised and he went on to win gold medals for the javelin, discus and shot put at junior and senior national level. He won a gold medal in javelin at the IPC World Athletics Championships in 2011.

'When I lost my legs, it was, "Right, what can we all still do together?" I still played football and rugby with my friends, sitting on the floor as goalkeeper and scooting myself around with a rugby ball in my hands.'

NATHAN STEPHENS

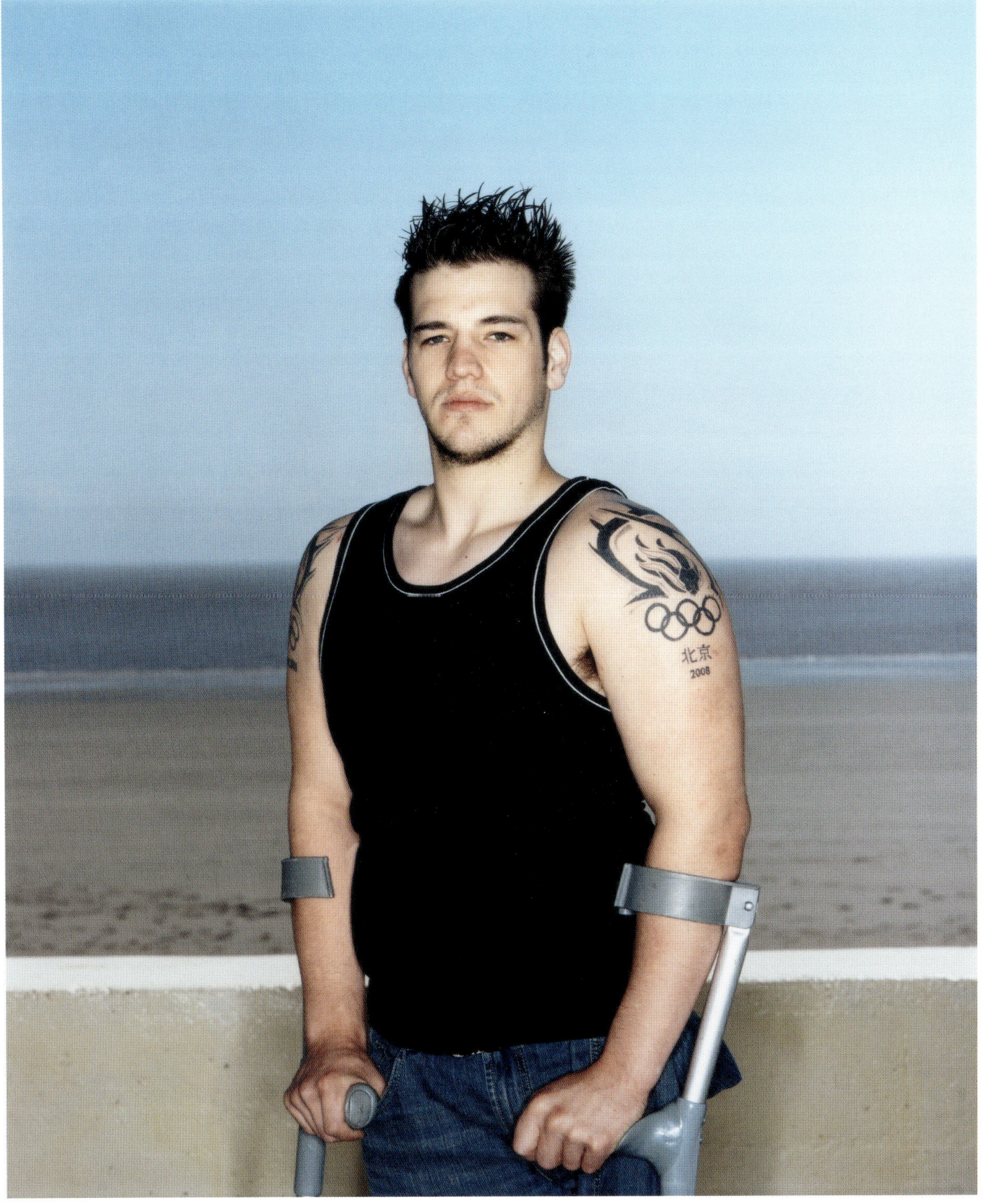

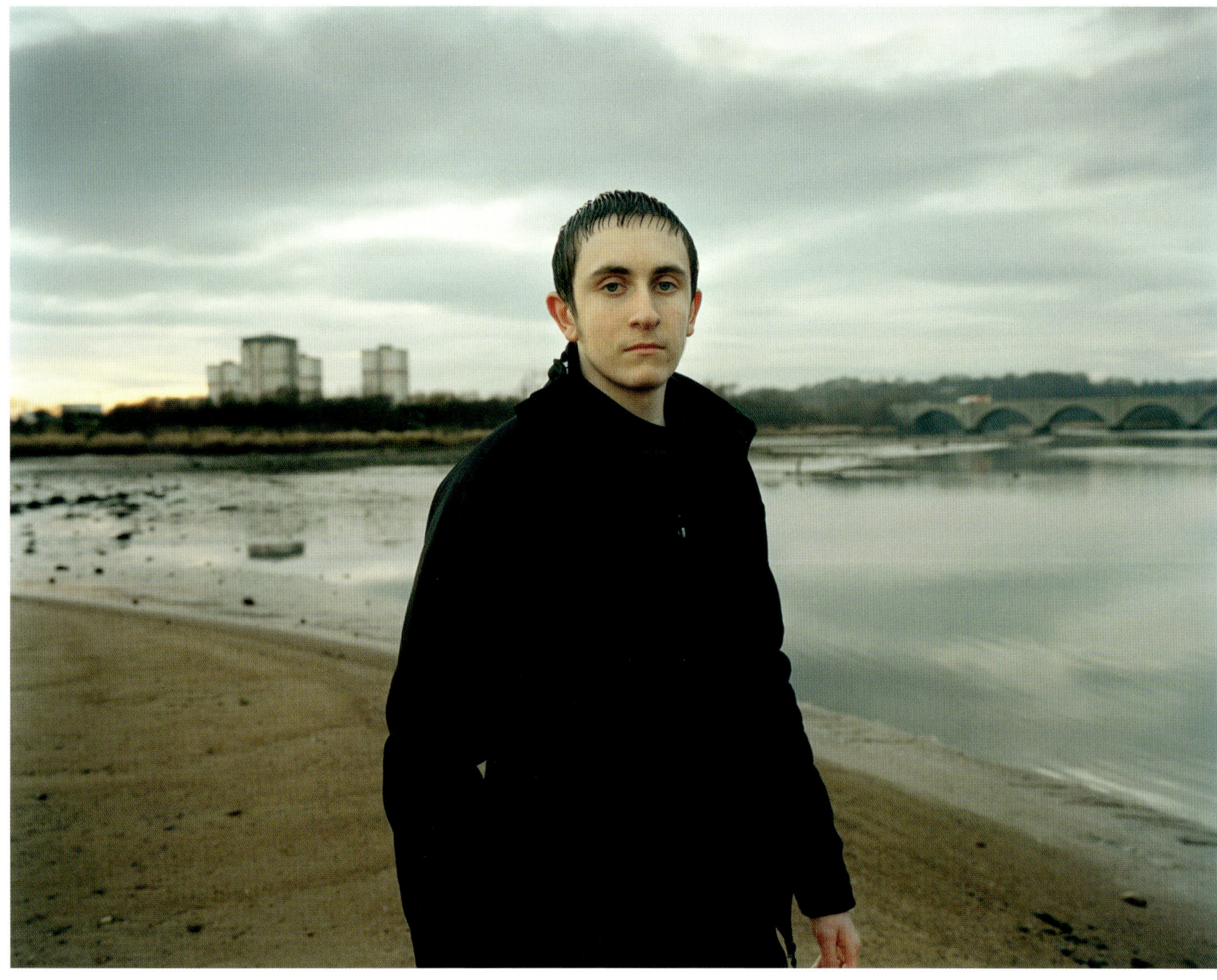

'Everything makes a difference, especially the Prince's Trust and the Young Leaders Programme.'

LEWIS BOWN

LEWIS BOWN
Photographed by Emma Hardy
2 March 2011, Aberdeen

Lewis Bown is a participant in the Young Leaders Programme. This volunteering scheme originates from a London 2012 Olympic and Paralympic Games bid commitment to give one hundred young people, who wouldn't otherwise have the opportunity, the chance to change their lives. Bown left school without qualifications but successfully completed a life skills course followed by a Prince's Trust Team programme in 2010, and will attend Aberdeen College in autumn 2012.

STEPHANIE FORBES

Photographed by Emma Hardy
2 March 2011, Aberdeen

Stephanie Forbes is a participant in the Young Leaders Programme. Forbes has cared for her younger brother since her early teens. Her father died several years ago, and Forbes has had to take over responsibility for the family in place of her mother. She has volunteered on various programmes, and her ambition is to join the Army.

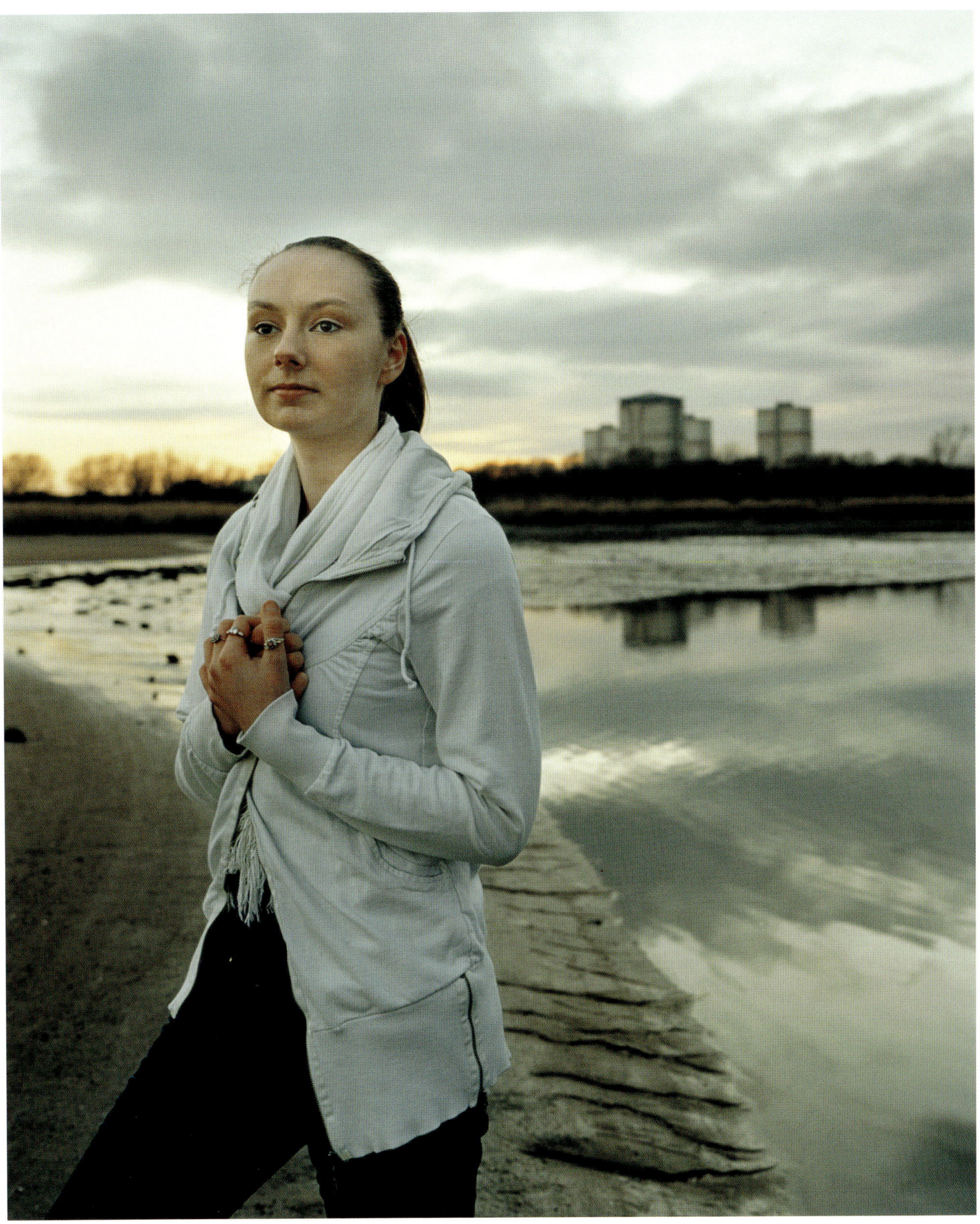

OLYMPIANS AND PARALYMPIANS

This group of elite athletes includes those who are returning to compete at the Olympic and Paralympic Games, as well as those inspirational individuals who have already experienced Olympic or Paralympic success and have chosen to give something back to the UK and to Team GB by acting as ambassadors for the London 2012 Games, sharing their invaluable experience with future generations.

REBECCA ADLINGTON
Photographed by Bettina von Zwehl
13 May 2011, Nottingham University

Rebecca Adlington's unexpected gold medals in the 400m and 800m freestyle events in Beijing 2008 made her the first British swimmer to win multiple gold medals at a single Olympic Games for a hundred years. She met her long-term coach, Bill Furniss, when she began competing in Nottingham at the age of ten. Winning double gold at the 2010 Commonwealth Games and gold at the 2011 World Championships were milestones on Adlington's continuing journey towards defending both her Olympic titles and her 800m Olympic record at the London 2012 Olympic Games.

'What inspired me was my two older sisters – they swam when I was little, and I wanted to be like them.'

REBECCA ADLINGTON

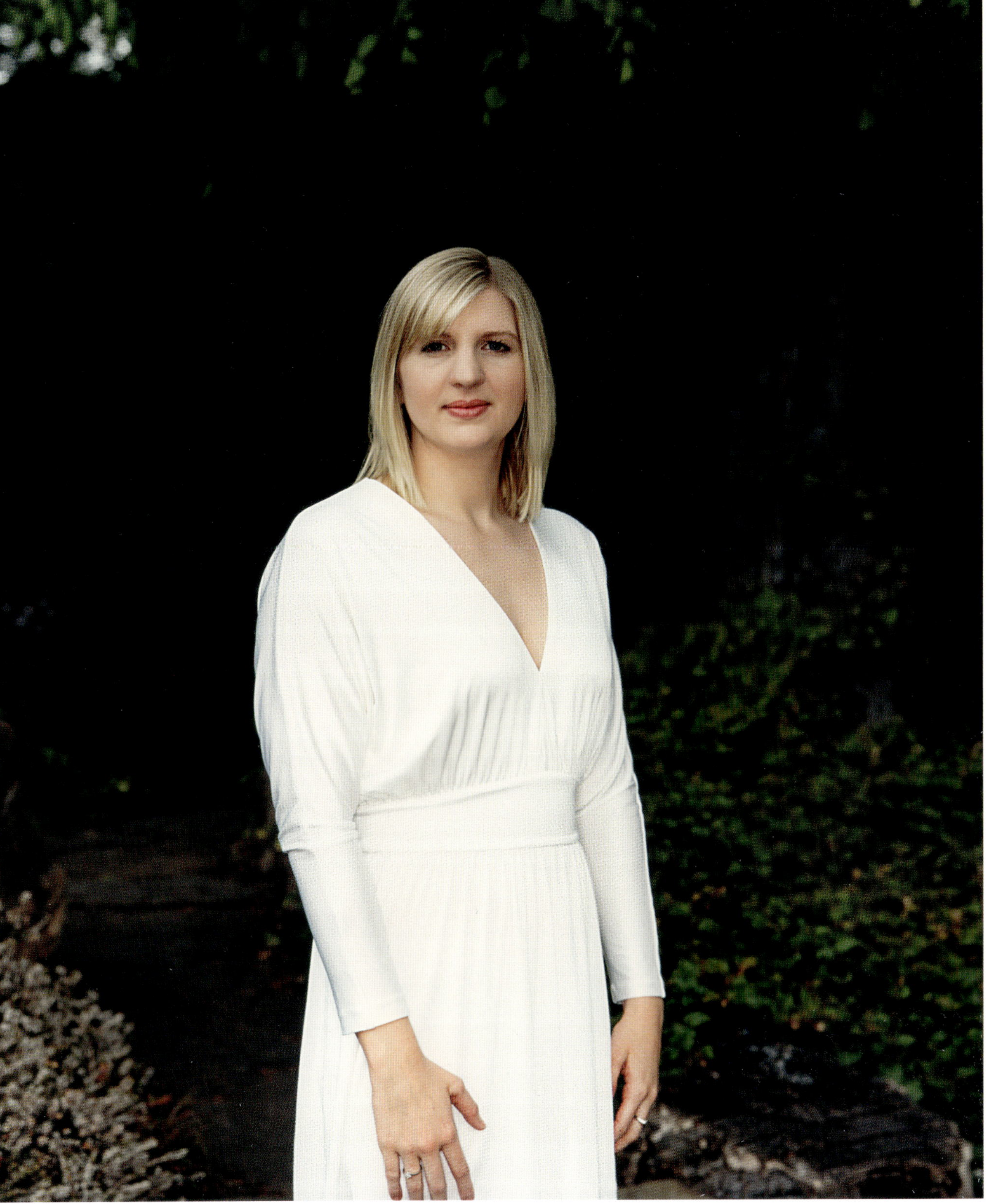

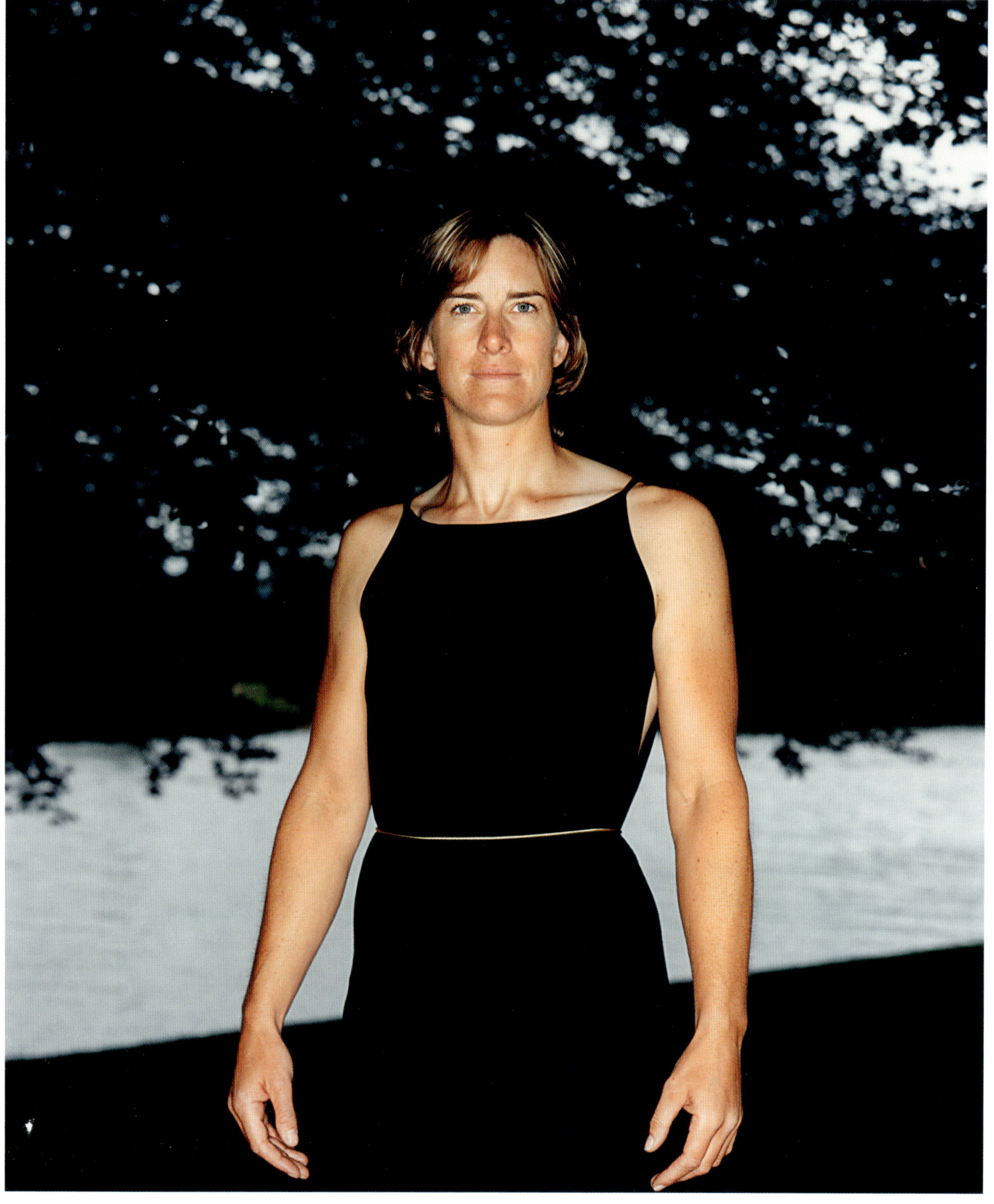

KATHERINE GRAINGER

Photographed by Bettina von Zwehl
31 May 2010, Bisham Abbey, Marlow

Katherine Grainger is Britain's most successful oarswoman, with six World Championship titles and three Olympic silver medals. She took up rowing in 1993, and competed internationally for the first time in 1997. At the finals of the first Rowing World Cup in 2010 she won gold in the double sculls with Anna Watkins, and an hour later won a second gold in the quadruple sculls. As well as aiming for gold at the London 2012 Olympic Games, Grainger is working towards a doctorate in homicide.

'The focus, the dedication, the life that they [the men's four: Steve Redgrave, Matthew Pinsent, James Cracknell and Tim Foster] were creating around them was really inspiring to see and be part of.'

KATHERINE GRAINGER

DENISE LEWIS AND JONATHAN EDWARDS

Photographed by Brian Griffin
29 September 2009, LOCOG offices, London

Denise Lewis, the West Bromwich track and field athlete, won the Olympic gold medal in the heptathlon in 2000. Jonathan Edwards is a triple jumper and former Olympic, Commonwealth, European and World Champion. He won an Olympic gold medal in 2000 and has held the world triple jump record since 1995. As London 2012 Ambassadors, Lewis and Edwards represented sport in the London 2012 bid team.

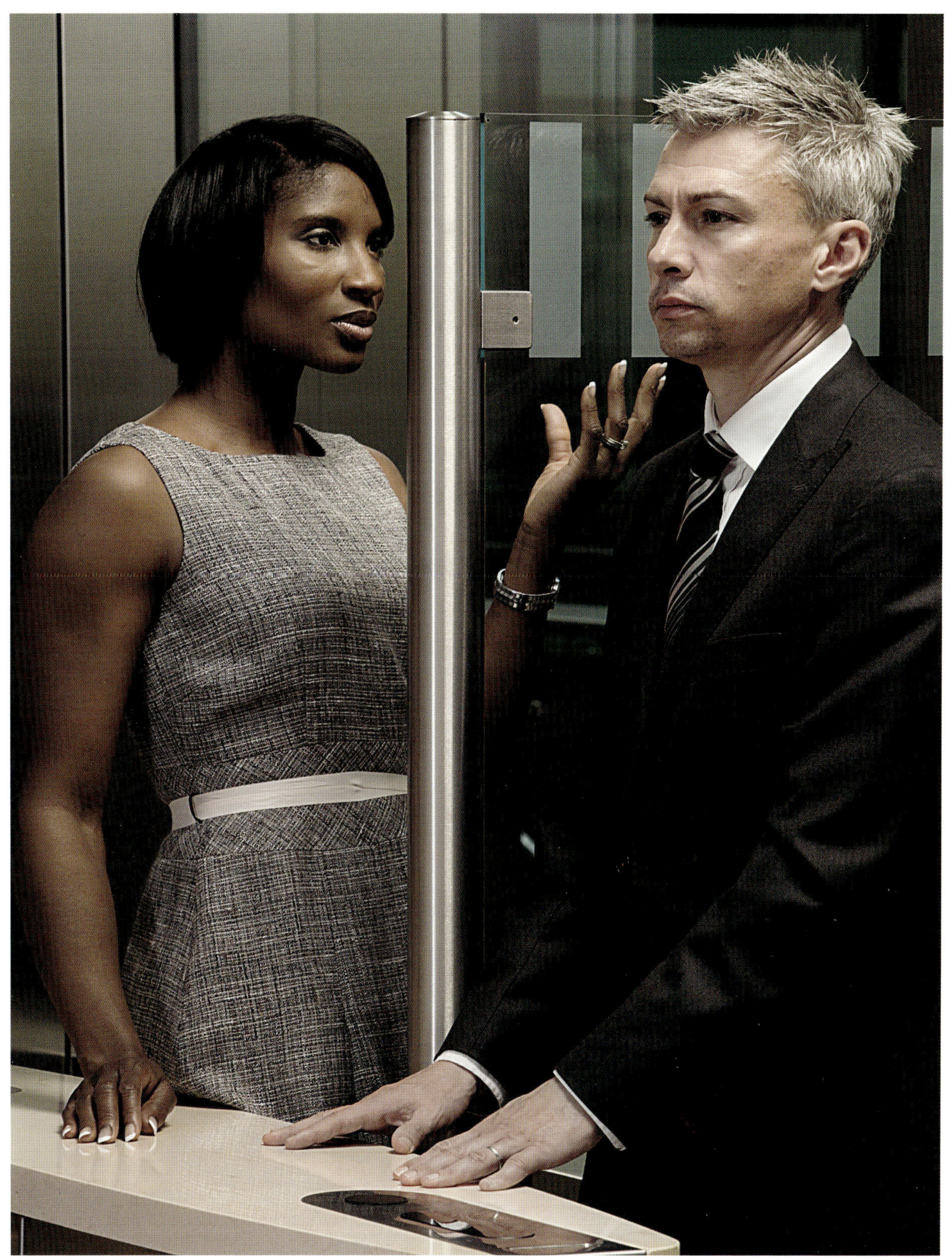

PHILLIPS IDOWU WITH ASTON MOORE

Photographed by Finlay MacKay
14 March 2011,
Birmingham High Performance
Centre, Birmingham

Phillips Idowu (right) was born and raised in east London and started triple jumping at school. He has held every major title, including World Champion, and won a silver medal at the Beijing 2008 Olympic Games. Idowu moved to Birmingham with his family in 2008 to train with UK Athletics coach Aston Moore (left), a Jamaican-born triple jumper who previously competed for Great Britain. Their training programme focuses on Idowu's determination to win an Olympic gold in his home city.

'You look at him. He's 6 foot 4, and he's 6 foot 4 all legs.'
ASTON MOORE

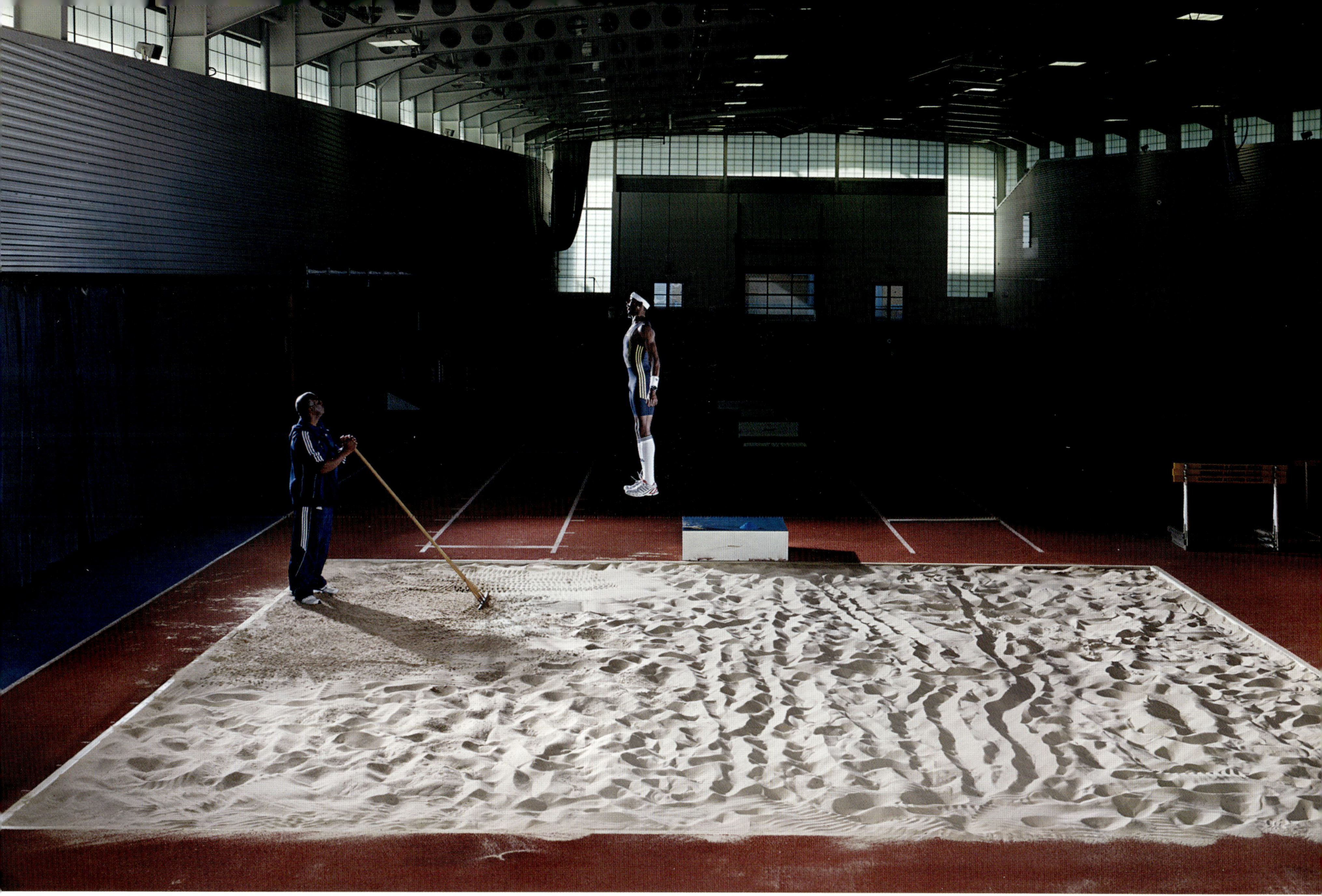

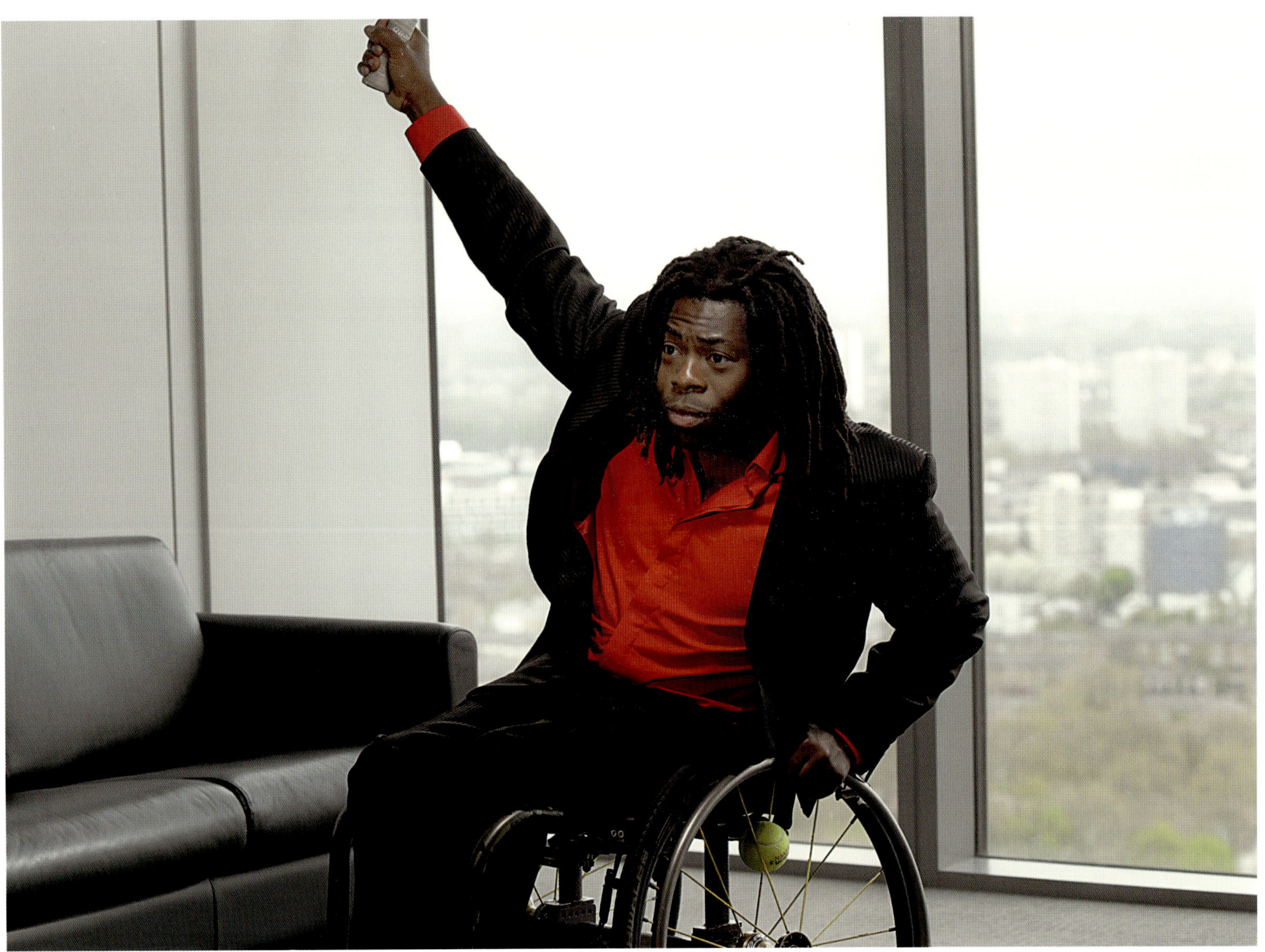

ADE ADEPITAN
Photographed by Brian Griffin
26 April 2010, LOCOG offices, London

Ade Adepitan was inspired to take up wheelchair basketball after watching coverage of the 1984 Olympic and Paralympic Games. As a member of Team GB he won a bronze medal in Athens 2004, and the following year won a gold medal at the inaugural Paralympic World Cup. As a London 2012 Ambassador he represented Paralympic sport to the International Olympic Committee. Adepitan switched sport from wheelchair basketball to tennis in 2007, competing at an elite level. He is the face of London 2012 for Channel 4's Paralympic coverage.

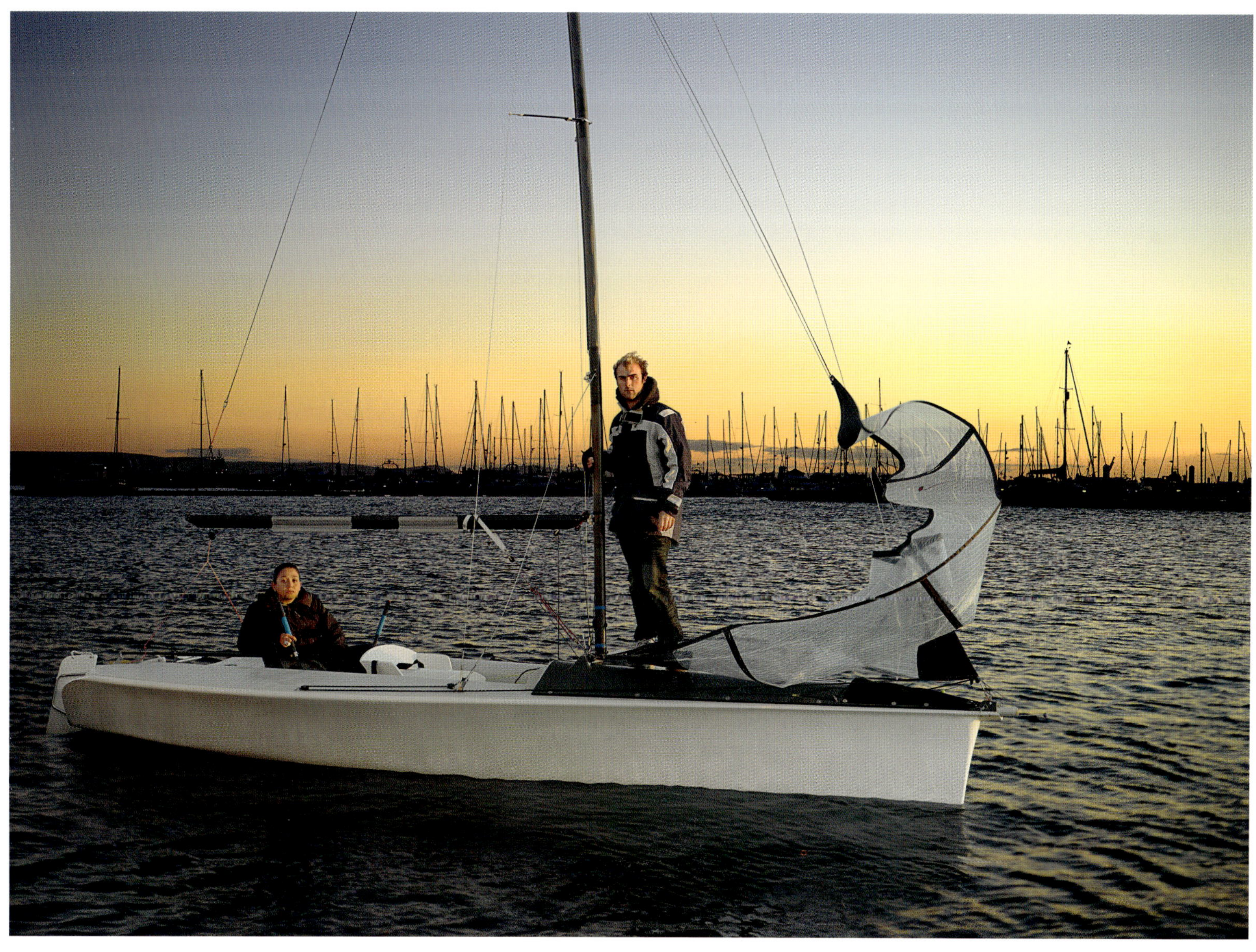

ALEXANDRA RICKHAM AND NIKI BIRRELL

Photographed by Anderson & Low
18 October 2011, Weymouth, Dorset

Four-time World Champions Alexandra Rickham and Niki Birrell will compete for ParalympicsGB at London 2012 in the SKUD 18 sailing class. Helm Rickham is a tetraplegic following a diving accident in 1995. She first sailed competitively as a student. Crew Niki Birrell was born with cerebral palsy. He began sailing at the age of nine and initially competed with his brother, joining the Paralympic Development Squad in 2007. He was teamed up with Rickham to compete at the Beijing Paralympic Games. Building on recent success, the duo's aim is to win gold on home waters.

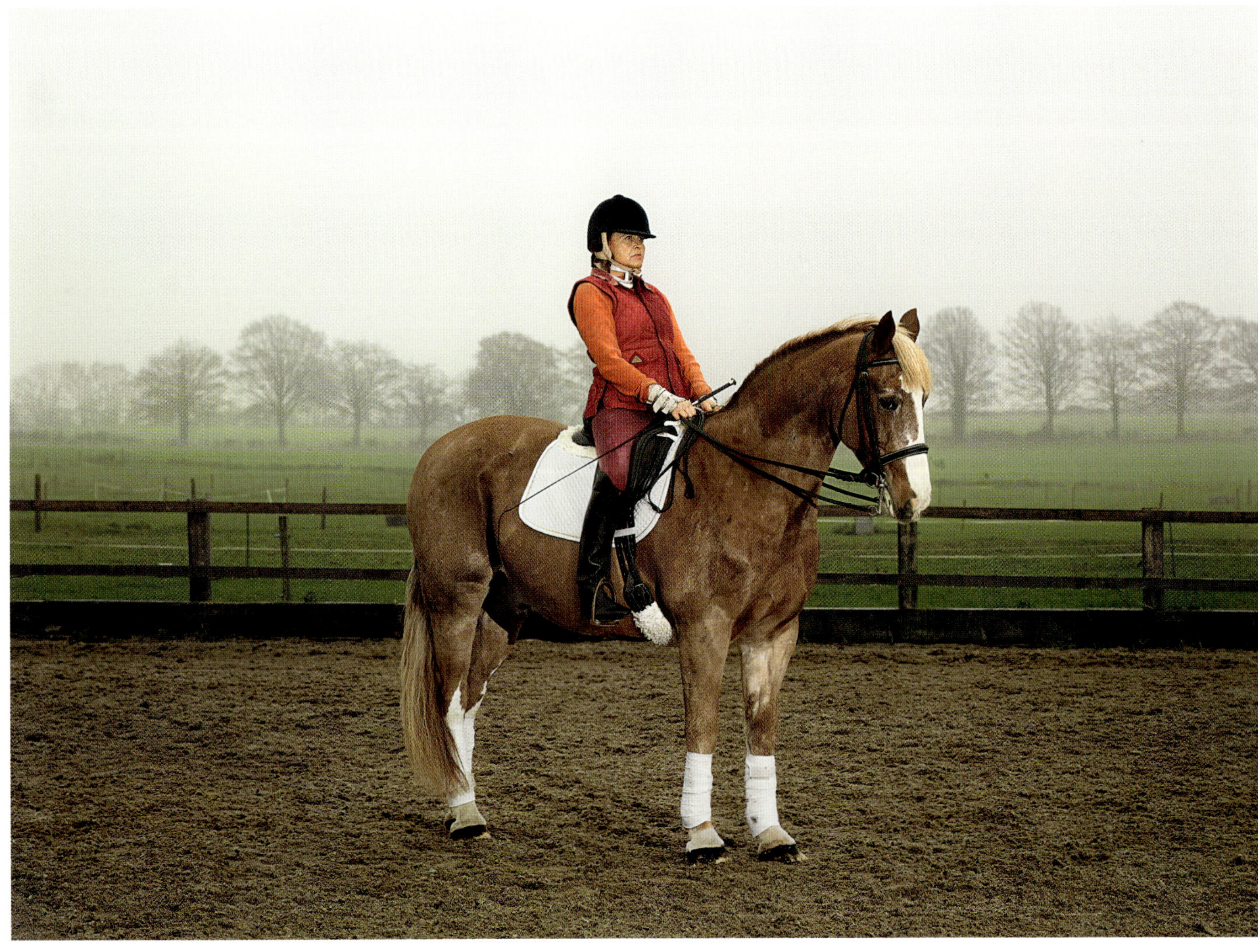

'To be part of a team, to not be quite so much of an individual as I could be when I was younger – that is what I would take from it.'

ANNE DUNHAM

ANNE DUNHAM

Photographed by Anderson & Low
7 November 2011,
Broad Hinton, Wiltshire

Paralympic equestrian Anne Dunham was diagnosed with multiple sclerosis at the age of twenty-seven, and has been a wheelchair user since she was thirty. Although she rode and worked in stables as a teenager, Dunham did not start competing until she was forty. She has since won team gold in four consecutive Paralympic Games, and her first individual gold in Beijing 2008, aged sixty. Her medals include team gold and individual silver and bronze at the 2010 World Equestrian Games. At the London 2012 Paralympic Games she will be aiming for a fifth gold medal in the team dressage event.

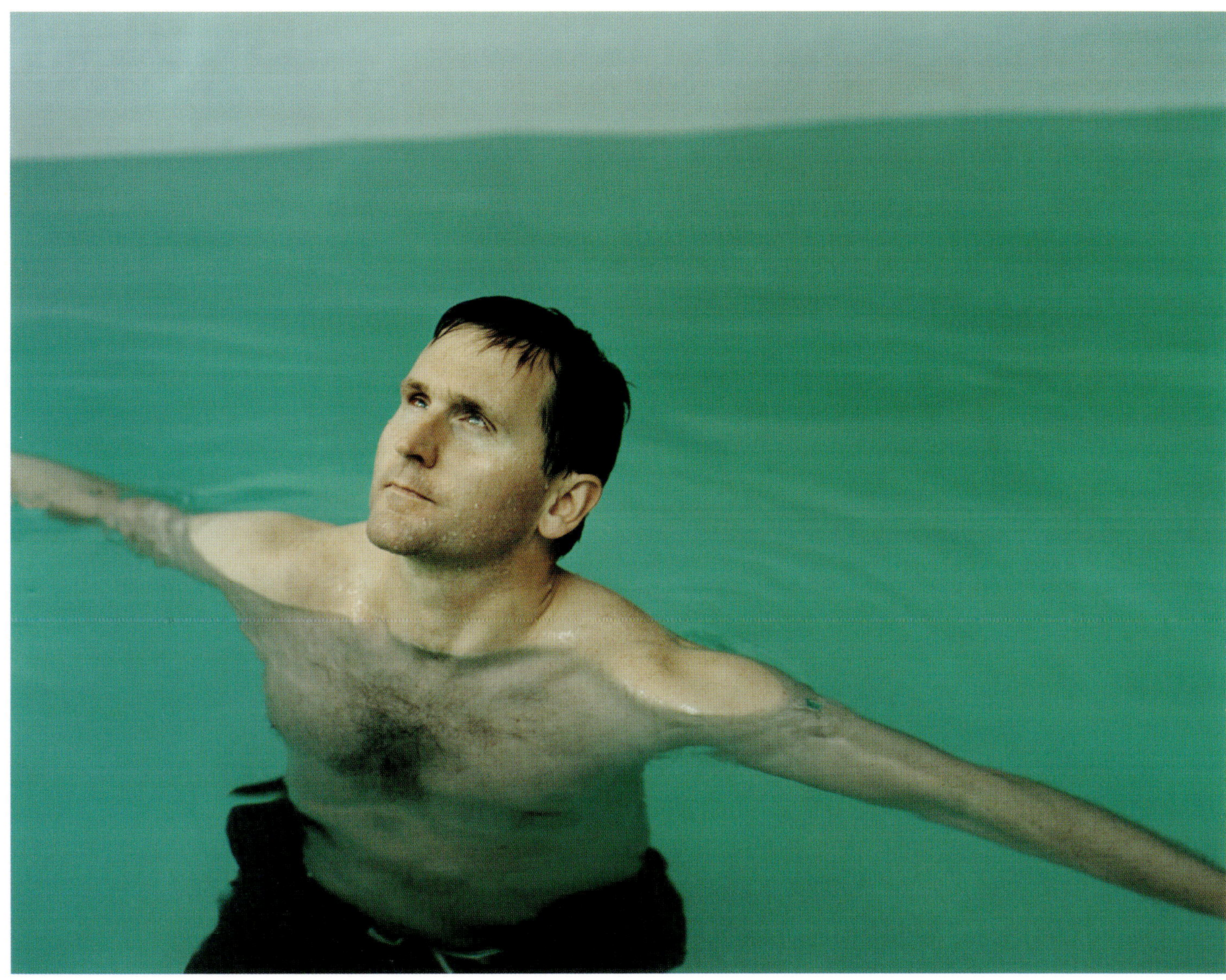

'To come from sport and meet people from every single background who are brilliant at what they do is incredible.'

CHRIS HOLMES

CHRIS HOLMES
Photographed by Emma Hardy
18 March 2011, London

As the London Organising Committee of the Olympic and Paralympic Games (LOCOG) Director of Paralympic Integration, Chris Holmes ensures that the London 2012 Olympic and Paralympic Games have equal status at every stage. Holmes lost his sight overnight at the age of fourteen and two years later competed in the first of four Paralympic Games (1988–2000). He became one of Britain's most successful Paralympic swimmers, winning an unequalled record of six gold medals at one event, and nine in total. A commercial lawyer, Holmes is also on the board of UK Sport.

KHALID YAFAI
WITH FRANK O'SULLIVAN

Photographed by Finlay MacKay
26 November 2010,
Birmingham City Boxing Club, Birmingham

Khalid Yafai (in red, sparring with Irfan Ali) has been a member of the GB Boxing team since he was sixteen, and is the first Englishman to win the World Cadet title (2005). He also competed in the Beijing 2008 Olympic Games. The son of Yemeni parents, Yafai joined his local boxing club, Birmingham City, where his talent was spotted by the founding coach, Frank O'Sullivan (left). In November 2011, Yafai lost his chance to compete at the London 2012 Olympic Games in a box-off against fellow Team GB flyweight Andrew Selby.

'It's very important that I train in a gym at home, where I was brought up. It's good to come back and show my face, especially to young kids who train here as well. They can look up to me and get to where I am one day.' **KHALID YAFAI**

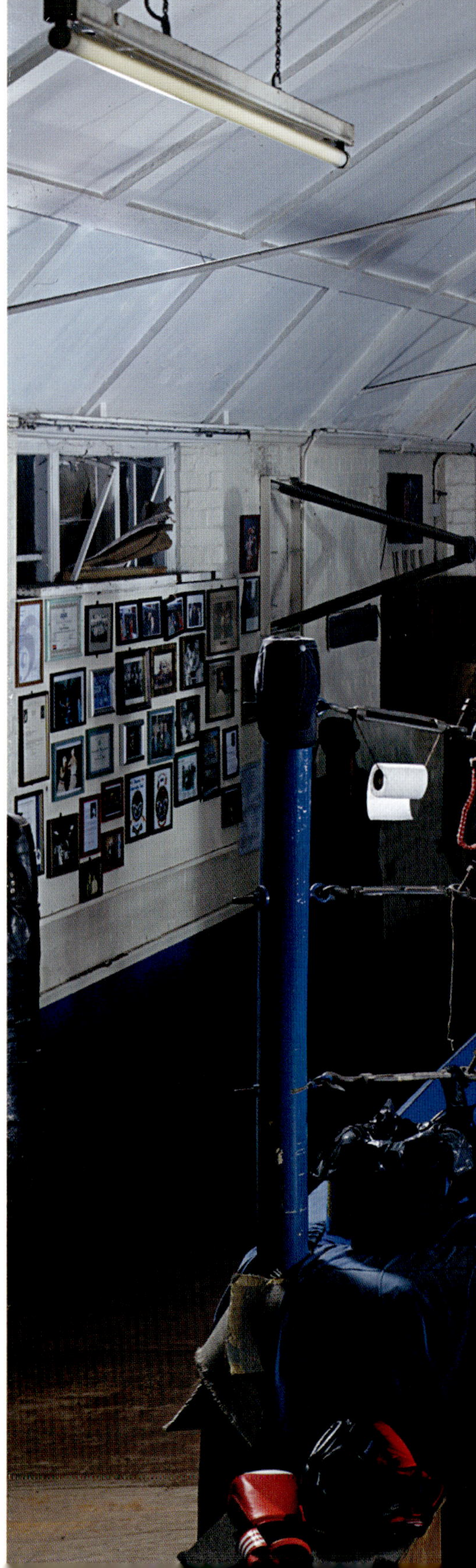

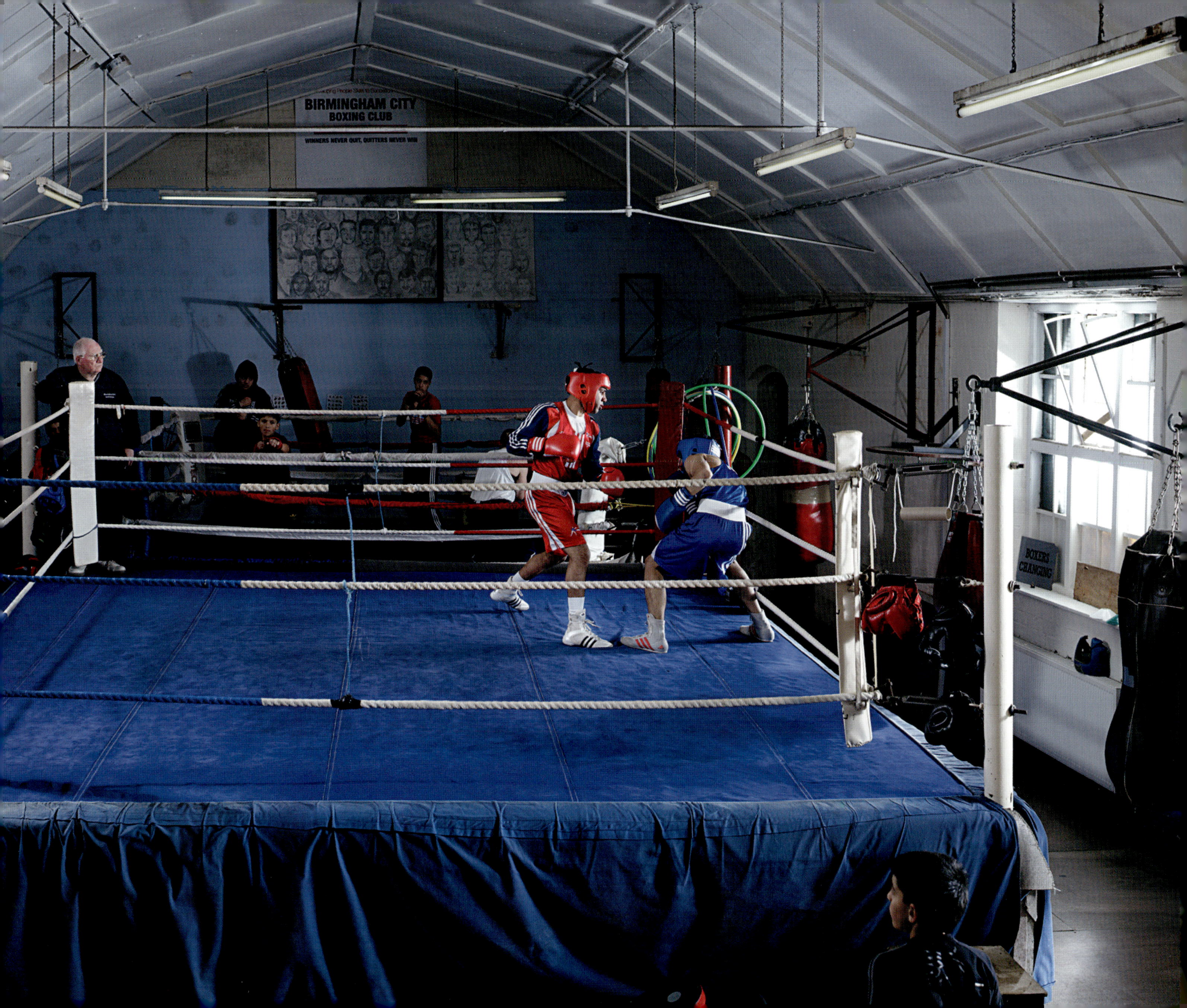
BIRMINGHAM CITY
BOXING CLUB
WINNERS NEVER QUIT, QUITTERS NEVER WIN
BOXERS
CHANGING

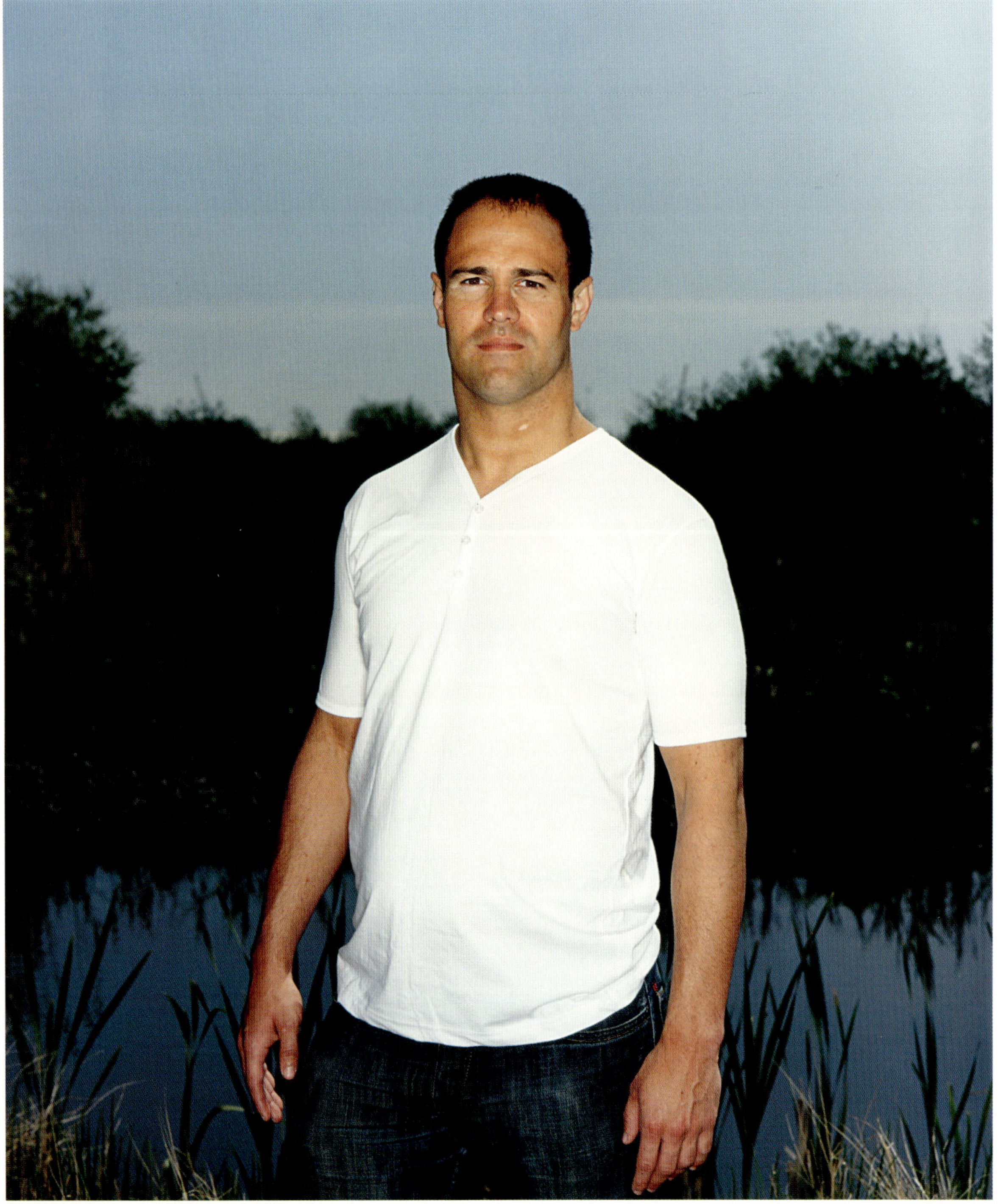

DAVID ROBERTS

Photographed by Bettina von Zwehl
18 May 2010, Cardiff, Wales

Welsh swimmer David Roberts is one of Britain's greatest Paralympians, with a total of eleven gold, four silver and one bronze medal in the last three Paralympic Games. Diagnosed with cerebral palsy at the age of eleven, Roberts started swimming at his local club as part of his physiotherapy programme. At London 2012 he aspires to become the UK's most successful Paralympian, overtaking Tanni Grey-Thompson's current record.

'My dad was my biggest inspiration and my biggest encouragement as well.'
DAVID ROBERTS

VICTORIA PENDLETON

Photographed by Bettina von Zwehl
7 July 2010, Wilmslow, Manchester

Victoria Pendleton was encouraged to cycle by her father, a national grass-track cycling champion, and rode her first grass-track race at the age of nine. After graduating she became a full-time track cyclist, and was selected to ride for Team GB in Athens 2004. She has since won gold medals in individual and team events. At Beijing 2008 Pendleton won a gold medal in the individual sprint event and in 2010 won the individual title at the World Track Cycling Championships for the fifth time. She will defend her title at the London 2012 Olympic Games.

'As a kid I always wanted to be really good at something. I always enjoyed sport, and my dad was successful and competitive. That's what I wanted to emulate. Cycling was an avenue.'
VICTORIA PENDLETON

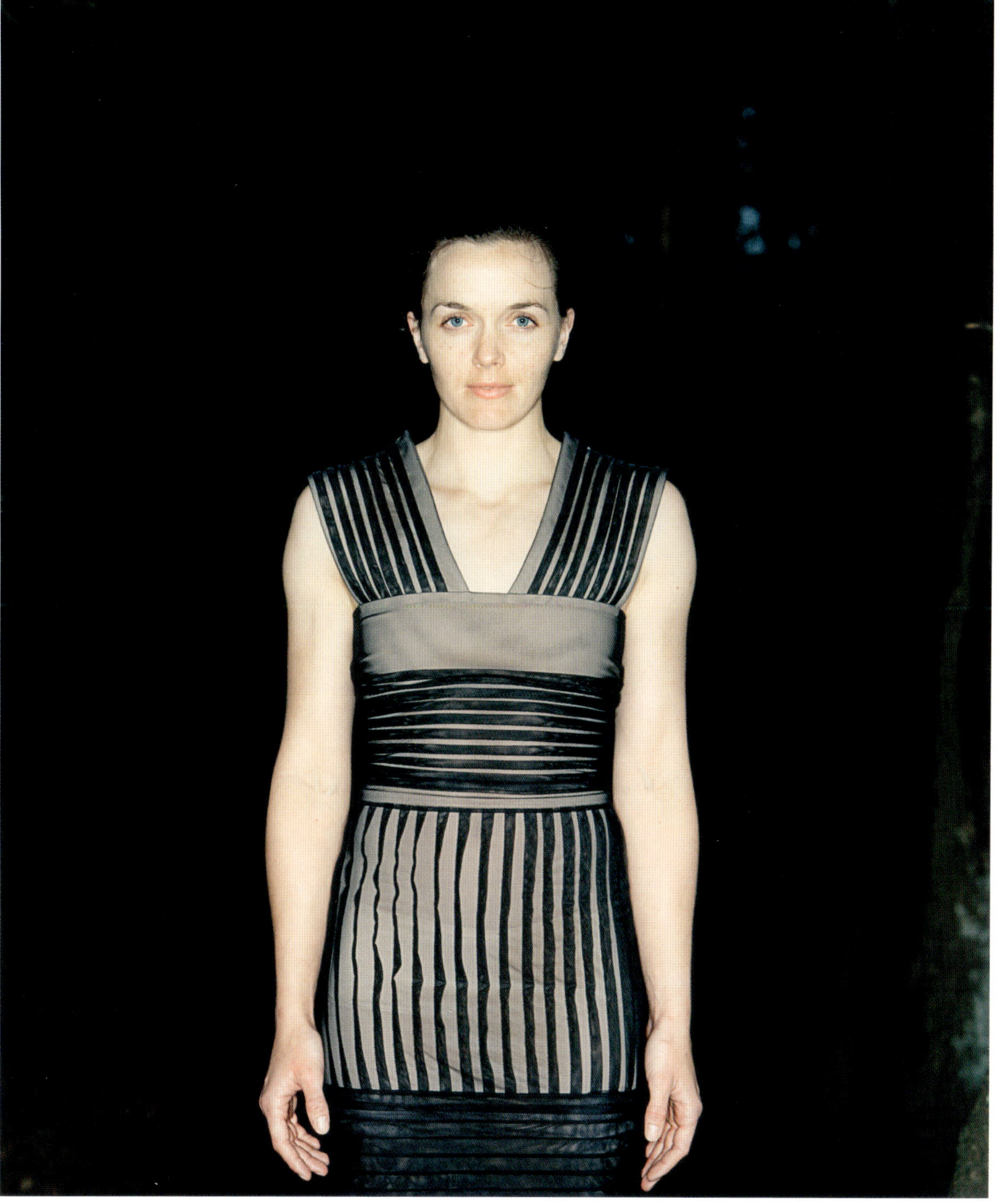

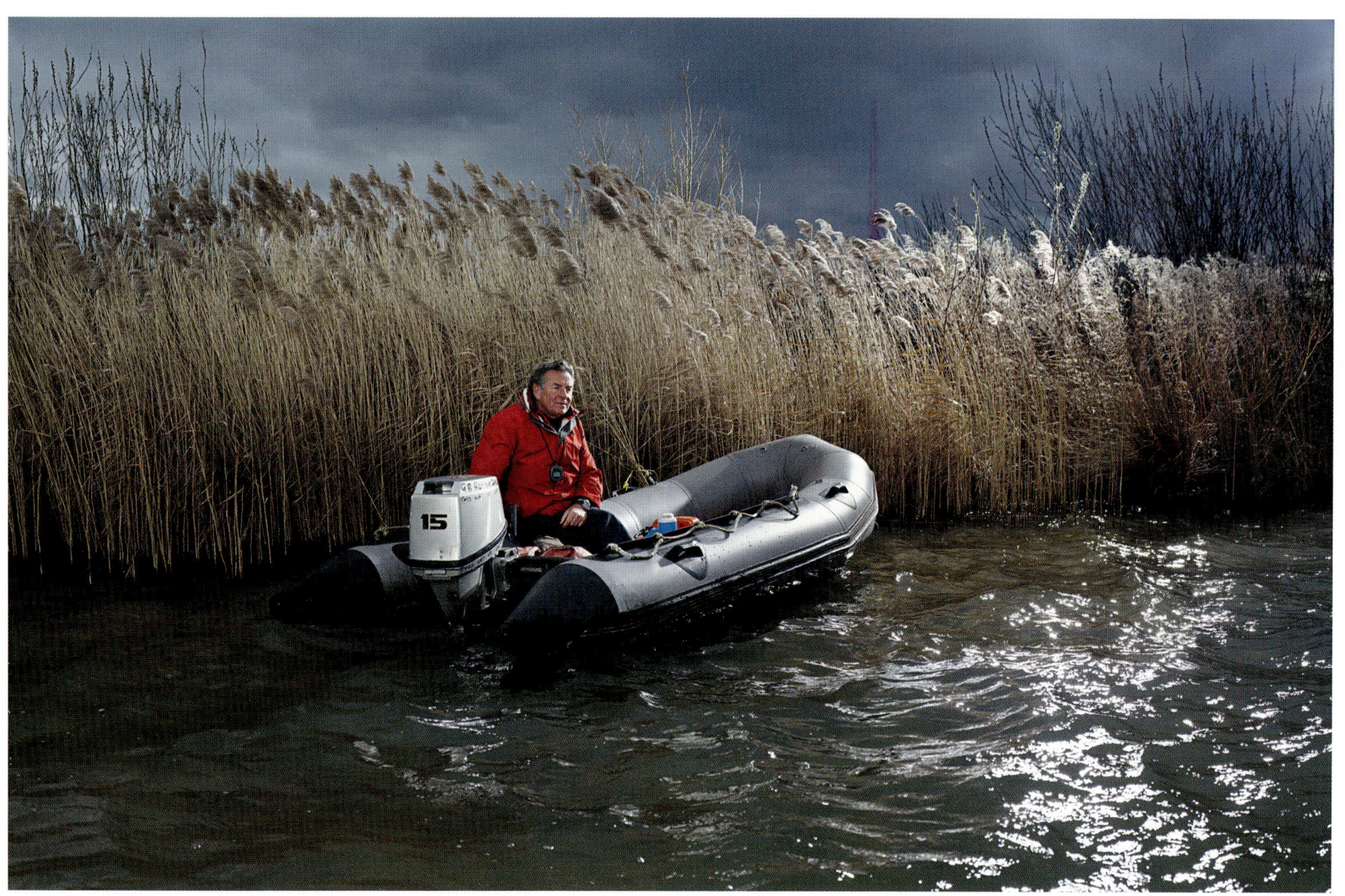

'Bringing together different characters and still motivating them to one point, when they can't escape because they are sitting behind one another … That is something fascinating for me.'

JÜRGEN GROBLER

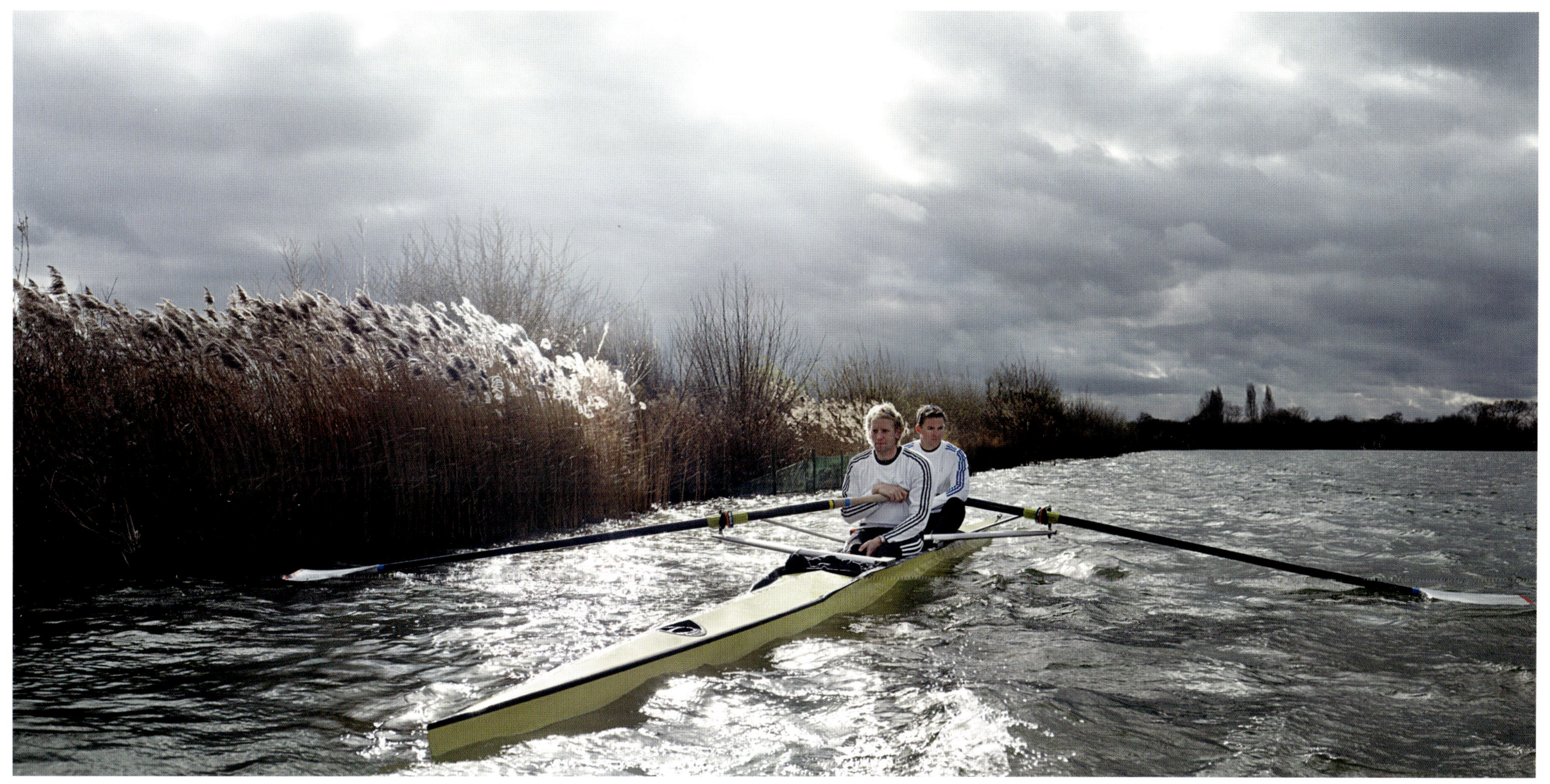

ANDY TRIGGS HODGE AND PETE REED WITH JÜRGEN GROBLER
Photographed by Finlay MacKay
9 March 2011, Redgrave-Pinsent Rowing Lake, Caversham

Andy Triggs Hodge and Pete Reed first rowed together in the winning Oxford Blue boat in the 2005 University Boat Race. Coached by Jürgen Grobler (opposite), they won Olympic gold in 2008 in the men's four with Steve Williams and Tom James. In 2009 they teamed up as a pair and have consistently won silver medals at the 2009, 2010 and 2011 World Championships. Grobler relocated to the UK from the former German Democratic Republic to take on the role of GB men's chief coach in 1992, and has personally coached gold medal crews in each of the subsequent five Olympic Games.

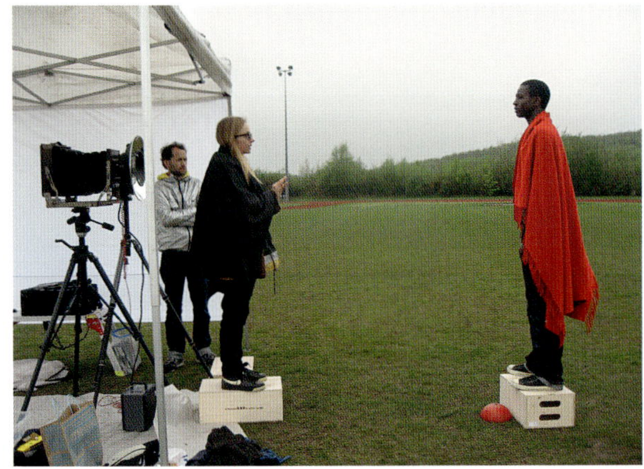
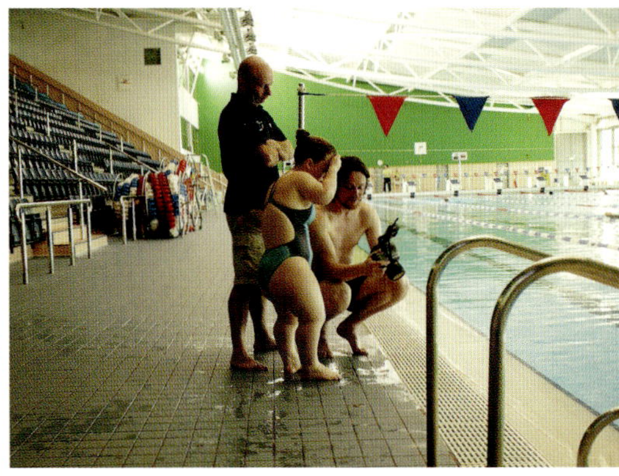
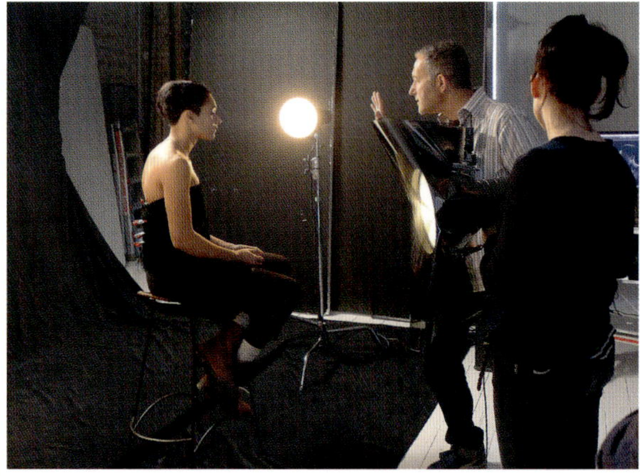
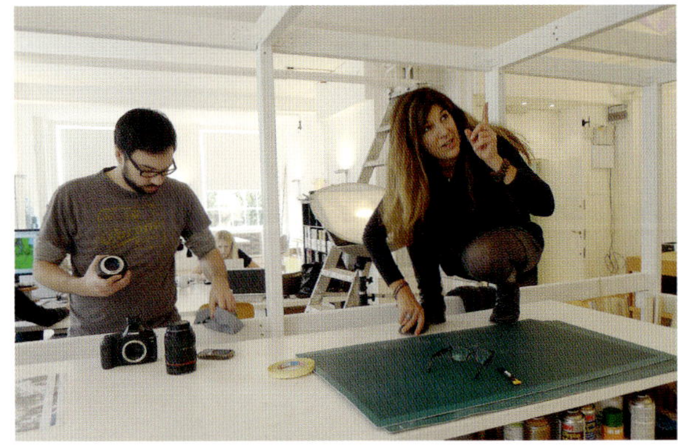
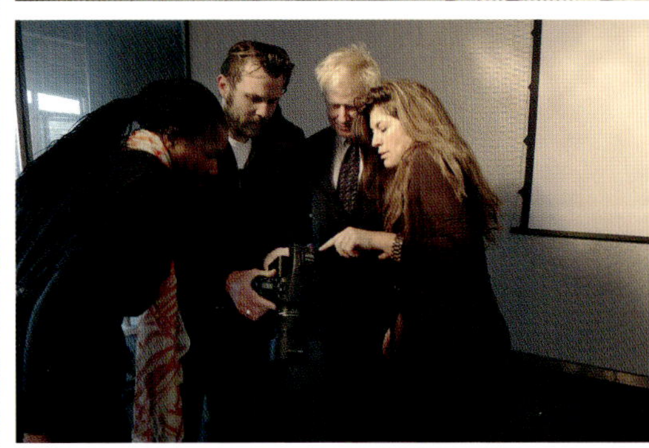
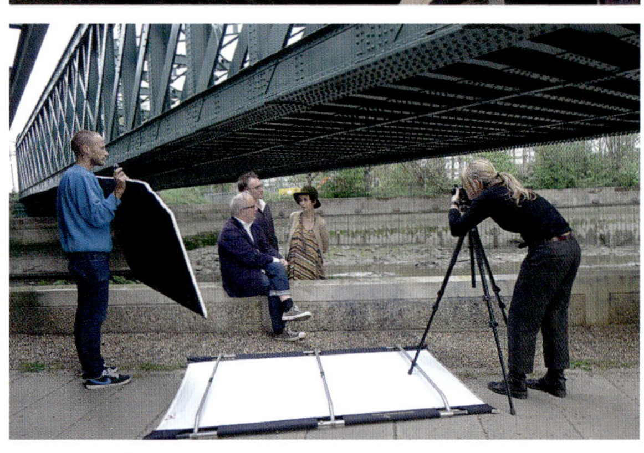
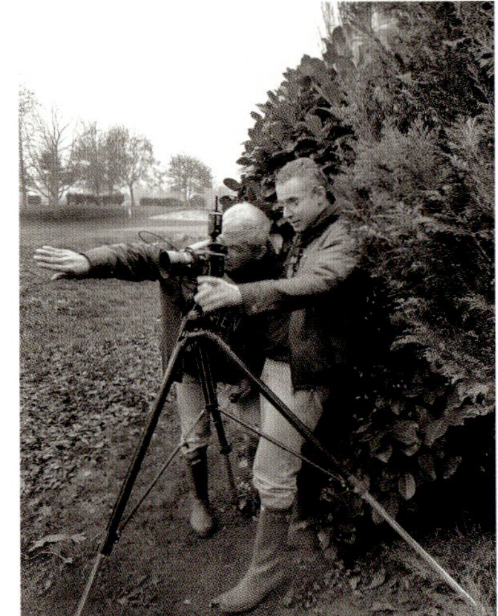
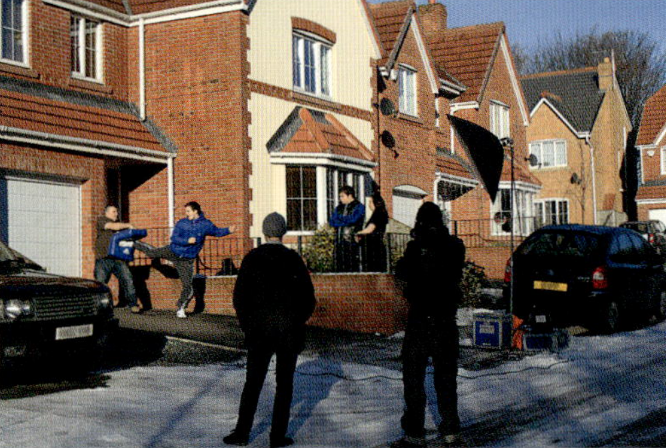
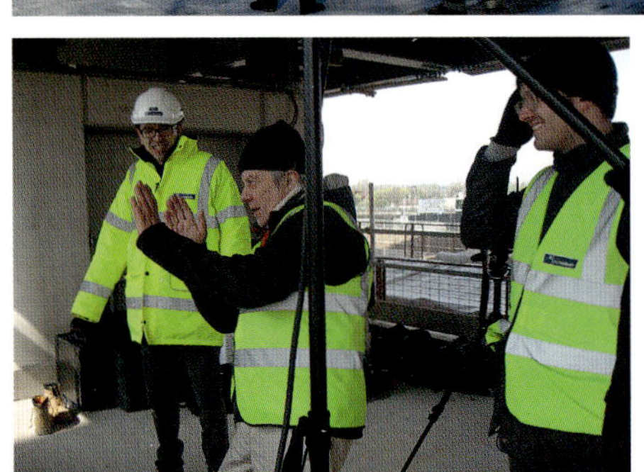
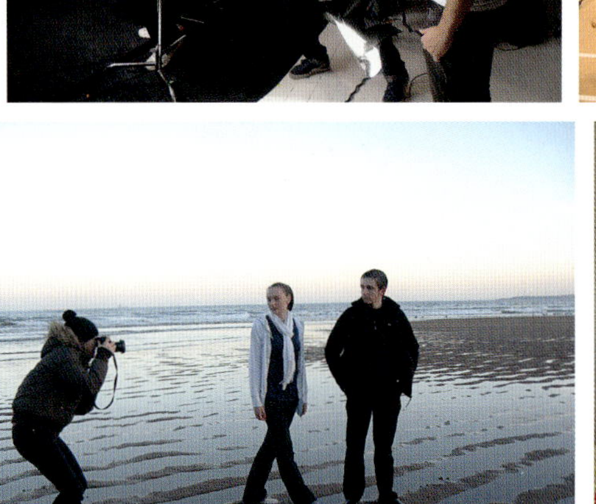
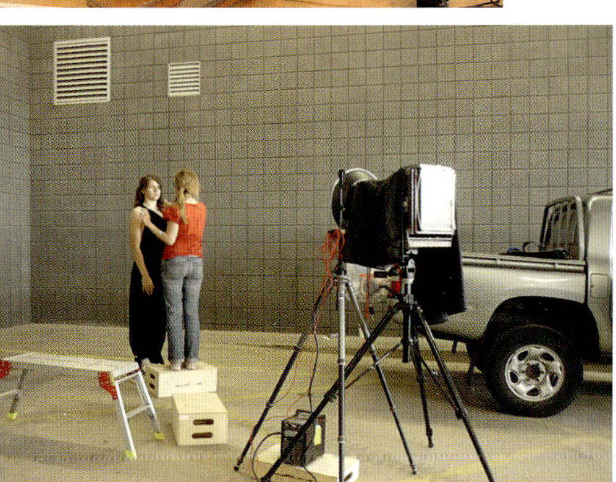

THE PHOTOGRAPHERS

ANDERSON & LOW

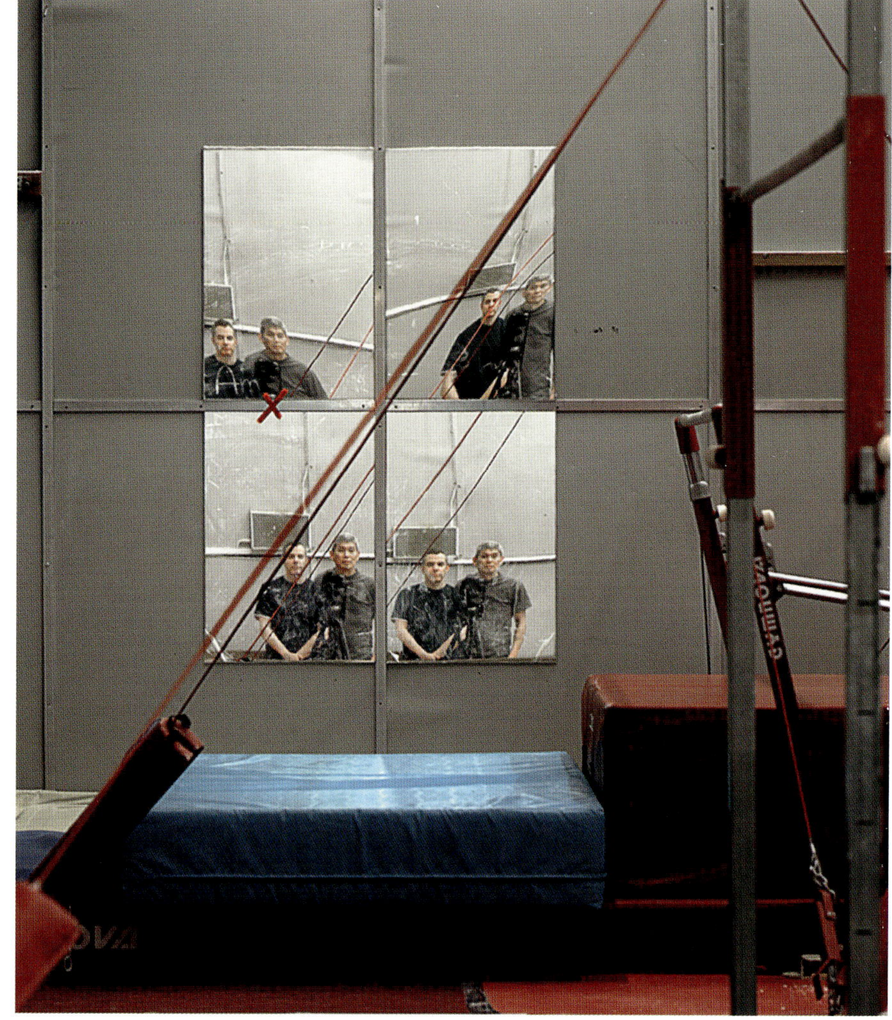

Born: Jonathan Anderson, 1961; Edwin Low, 1957
Recent projects: *The Athlete*, National Art Gallery of Malaysia (1998); *The Athlete* (to celebrate Sydney 2000 Olympic Games), National Portrait Gallery, Canberra (2000); *Contenders*, National Portrait Gallery, London (2002); *Athlete/Warrior*, museums and galleries throughout the USA and Europe (2005–8); *Champions* (to benefit the Elton John AIDS Foundation), National Portrait Gallery, London (2008–9); *Circus*, The Lowry (2010); *Manga Dreams*, Venice Biennale (2011), SCVA (2012), Maison Européenne de la Photographie (2012), Musée de la Civilisation (2012); *Family Intimacies*, National University of Singapore Museum (2012)
Publications: *Athletes* (2002), *Gymnasts* (2002), *Athlete/Warrior* (2005), *Chrysalis* (2007), *Champions* (2008), *Circus* (2008), *Manga Dreams* (2011), *Family Intimacies* (2012), *Endure – An Intimate Journey with the Chinese Gymnasts* (2012)

During their twenty-two years of collaboration, fine-art photography partnership Anderson & Low have created a unique body of work: their highly crafted photographic portraits explore the extraordinary physical endurance and emotional stamina of elite athletes.

Jonathan Anderson and Edwin Low's mutual interest in painting and sculpture provides the foundation for their investigations across a broad range of subjects, including architecture and the abstract possibilities of photography. They stress the importance of 'sculpting and subtly changing the light' in creating their images, and this masterful control of light and shadow, as well as painstaking attention to the final print and rigorous conceptual thinking, are the hallmarks of all their work.

Their groundbreaking project *Manga Dreams*, which was featured in the 2011 Venice Biennale, brings together portraiture, graphics, calligraphy and the visual language of cyber-culture. For their most recent work with athletes, *Endure – An Intimate Journey with the Chinese*

LEFT TO RIGHT
Anderson & Low self-portrait, after photographing Beth Tweddle
Michael Klim, from *Athletes*
Lu Liu Fang, Gymnast, China from *Endure*

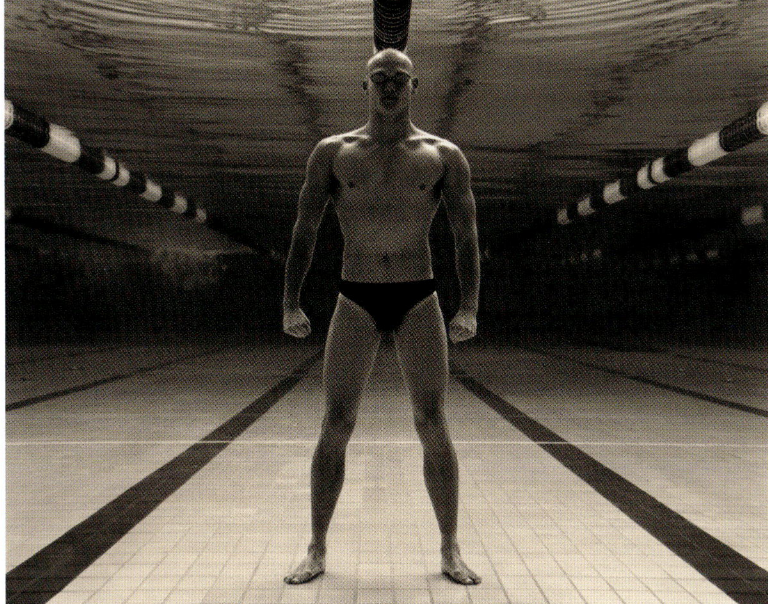

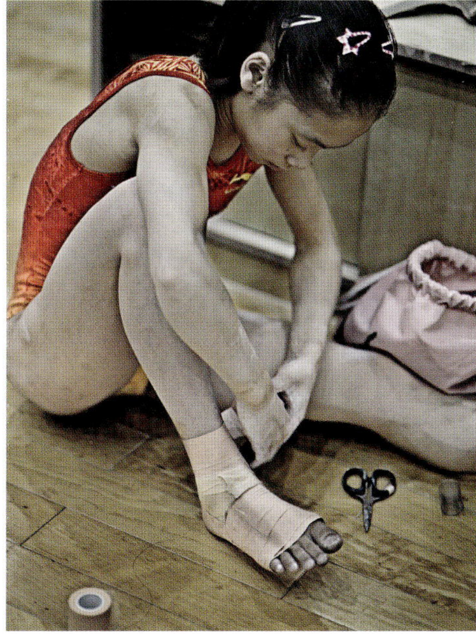

Gymnasts (2012), they developed a specific loose style and painterly palette for their sensitive documentation of a highly disciplined sport.

For their *Road to 2012* commission, the duo returned to a formal style and a naturalistic palette. By carefully selecting the locations and meticulously positioning their sitters, they created timeless tableaux that depict athletes as well as the support staff behind Olympic and Paralympic aspiration. Having been given access to some of the world's best training facilities, they have seen first-hand how the locations in which athletes train are integral to the pursuit of their dreams. With an eye for architectural and landscape details and a keen sense of narrative, the photographers skilfully used setting to enrich the personal stories in *Road to 2012*.

'Because of the nature of the *Road to 2012* commission, we had the opportunity to explore a certain formalism and painterly references in the imagery, partly because of the numbers of sitters involved for some of the pictures,' the duo explains. 'In our work, we have spent so long watching athletes in training facilities all over the world; it is the athletes' character – physical, mental, emotional – that interests us. They are so ordinary and so extraordinary at the same time. They are always slightly mysterious, and that is something magical to us.'

The inclusion of sports administrators in the *Road to 2012* commission reveals the collective spirit in which London is preparing to host the 2012 Olympic and Paralympic Games, and allowed the duo to explore new territory. 'We had not worked that often with administrators before, and it turned out to be quite special,' they add. 'In some cases there are just one or two people who have completely transformed a sport, so it was a great opportunity to put the record straight and acknowledge these contributions.'

In 2002, a National Portrait Gallery exhibition of Anderson & Low's images of Britain's most promising young athletes, *The Contenders*, celebrated the Commonwealth Games in Manchester. Six years later, *Champions*, a collection of their studio-based portraits of famous nude athletes to benefit the Elton John AIDS Foundation, was exhibited at the Gallery, including portraits of Venus Williams and Thierry Henry.

Anderson & Low's work is exhibited worldwide, and is in many museum and private collections.

JILLIAN EDELSTEIN

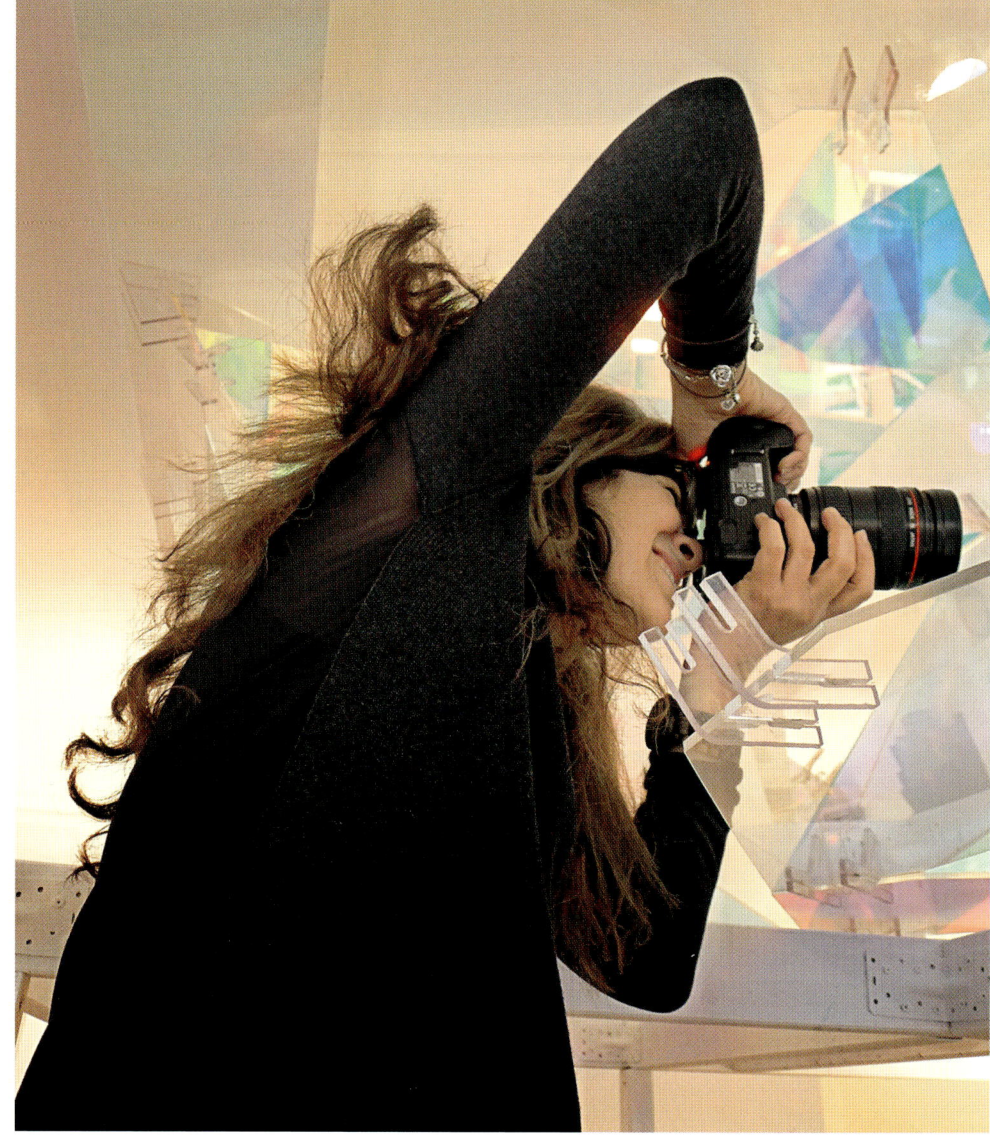

Born: Cape Town, 1957
Education: University of Cape Town; London College of Printing
Recent projects: *Intimate and Unseen*, Tom Blau Gallery (2005); *Jillian Edelstein: In Focus*, National Portrait Gallery (2009); *Truth & Lies*, Robben Island Museum (2009–10), also represented at Photo Off, KijK Galerie, Paris (2011) and at Dali International Photography Exhibition, Yunnan, west China (2011)
Publications: *Truth & Lies: Stories from the Truth and Reconciliation Commission in South Africa* (2002)

As a lifelong devotee of the arts, Jillian Edelstein has photographed leading performers in cinema, theatre, music and literature for more than twenty years. In 2009, a retrospective of her work was held at the National Portrait Gallery, featuring portraits of Damien Hirst, Bridget Riley and Daniel Day Lewis, while recent magazine assignments have included Jung Chang for *Vanity Fair* and Ralph Fiennes for *Intelligent Life*.

Naturally, the South African-born photographer was determined to bring a dash of theatricality to her *Road to 2012* contribution, which involved portraying those involved in Games-time and legacy pledges, from waterways specialists to the head of catering, cleaning and waste.

'On paper, it could have been such a staid subject,' admits Edelstein. 'I wanted the portraits to convey humour and vitality and give a sense of occasion. The Games are such a huge piece of theatre, and I wanted my photographs to have a bit of that, too.'

Conceiving each portrait as an 'epic and powerful production', Edelstein photographed transport bosses Peter Hendy and Graham Jones driving through London's unloved Blackwall Tunnel while it was closed to traffic at night. After a prolonged set-up and forty minutes draped over a car bonnet using medium-format lenses on a 35mm body, she emerged from the 'belly of the beast' with a cinematic vignette straight from a film noir or road movie. 'I'll never think of the Blackwall Tunnel in the same way again,' she says.

Central to Edelstein's working methods is a high degree of collaboration. If time permits, she researches and talks to her subject in advance of the shoot date to help fashion her ideas for the portrait. 'I may also ask the person to bring meaningful props or wear something specific which could add to making a graphic shape.'

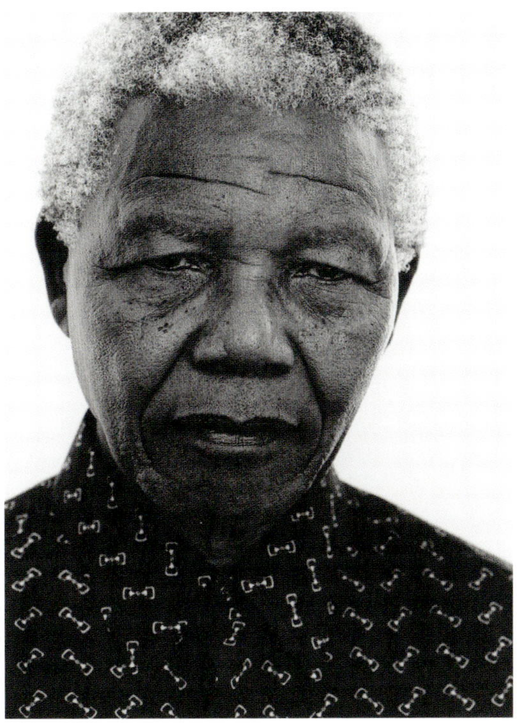

A conversation with composer Philip Sheppard, who recorded fresh arrangements of the world's 205 national anthems for the Games, revealed a mutual love of the Suffolk landscape with its links to Benjamin Britten. Within days, the pair were tramping about the marshes: Sheppard trying to prevent his cello from getting caked in mud; Edelstein fretting about the howling gale that threatened to collapse her lighting soft box.

'I control the sitting as much as I can and the rest I leave to chance, with the subject giving their ideas and offering up their contribution,' she explains. 'It is a two-way process and I am dependent on the other person. It is a bit like a dance, albeit a brief one.'

Some dances were shorter than others. Following months of negotiations with the London Mayor's office, Edelstein was finally allocated a mere ten minutes with Boris Johnson. 'It can be pretty nerve-racking trying to execute your vision with limited time, but in the past I have managed to make a portrait of Nelson Mandela in ten minutes and Tony Blair in seven. On those occasions you have to go into this tunnel-like zone. You just have to focus powerfully and be incredibly dogged until you get the shot.'

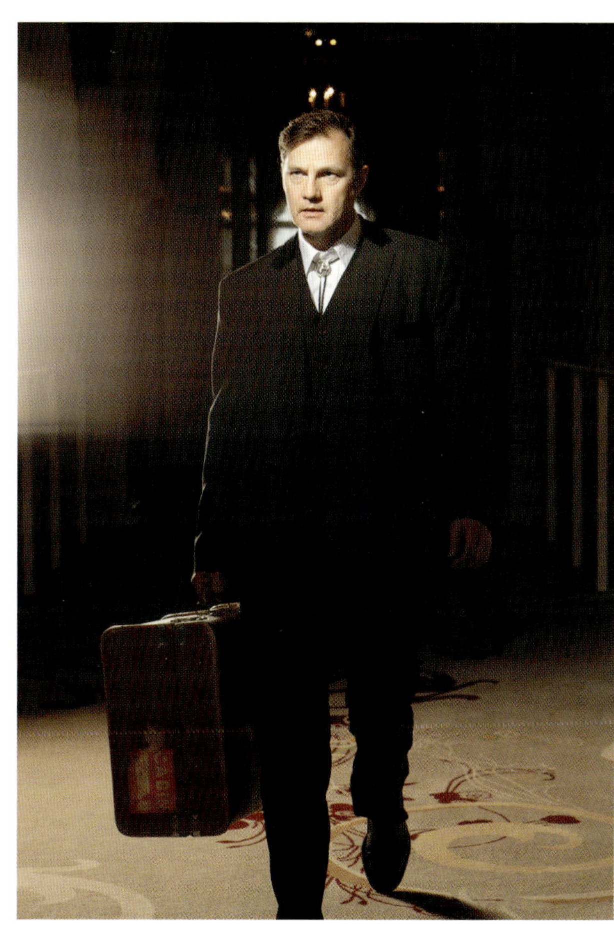

LEFT TO RIGHT
Jillian Edelstein photographing Cecil Balmond
Nelson Mandela, from *Truth & Lies*
David Morrissey, from *Hidden Gems*

KATHERINE GREEN

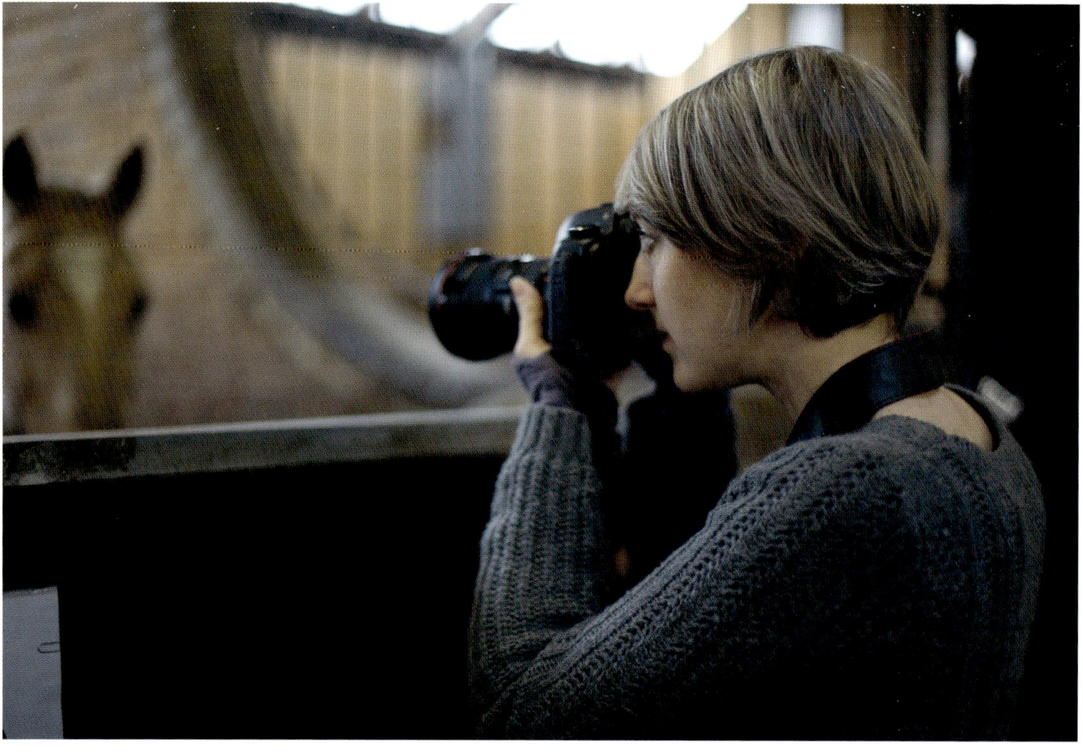

Born: East London, 1974
Education: Central Saint Martins, London; Surrey Institute of Art & Design
Recent projects: *Going to the Dogs*, Vestry House Museum (2009) and Light House (2010); *Inspired by Morris*, The William Morris Gallery (2010); *Taking Part*, Chestnuts House (2011); *1948 Olympians*, The Hat Factory, 20–21 Visual Arts, Rugby Art Gallery and Museum (2012)
Publications: *Wood Street, E17* (2007); *Last Days at the Dogs* (2009); *1948 Olympians* (2012)

Katherine Green's role in the *Road to 2012* project differed slightly from that of the other photographers. As a resident of Waltham Forest, one of the five Olympic host boroughs, she was ideally placed to capture the spirit and dedication of east London's sports communities, representing the local people whose lives have been, and will continue to be, affected by London 2012.

Working in the social documentary tradition, Green has rarely strayed beyond her immediate neighbourhood and has focused her lens almost entirely on the people and places she encounters on her own doorstep. 'I've always been inspired by photographers like Nigel Shafran, those people who don't necessarily look too far, but find something of beauty right under their nose,' says Green, whose previous projects include a series on the shops and small businesses in a Walthamstow street. 'I'm not unadventurous, but I find so much of interest in my own locality. I want to reflect the area and its people in a positive light.'

The aims and concerns of Green's personal work dovetailed neatly with the Gallery's proposal to create a visual record of grass-roots sports clubs located in the shadow of the Olympic Park but existing a world away from the Games' intense competition, corporate hospitality and chauffeur-driven dignitaries. 'The project was never about fame or stardom,' says Green. 'It's about celebrating the eighty-year-old table tennis player, or the disabled girl who keeps on taking part even when her prognosis has worsened. It's about giving a profile to the passionate people who run these groups.'

Green was commissioned to depict amateur enthusiasts participating in seven Olympic and Paralympic sports – boxing, table tennis, wheelchair athletics, equestrian sports, fencing, swimming and sailing – and taped her subjects' perspectives on 2012 as oral histories to accompany the portraits. By her own admission, she harboured negative feelings towards the Games before starting the series and expected a similar response

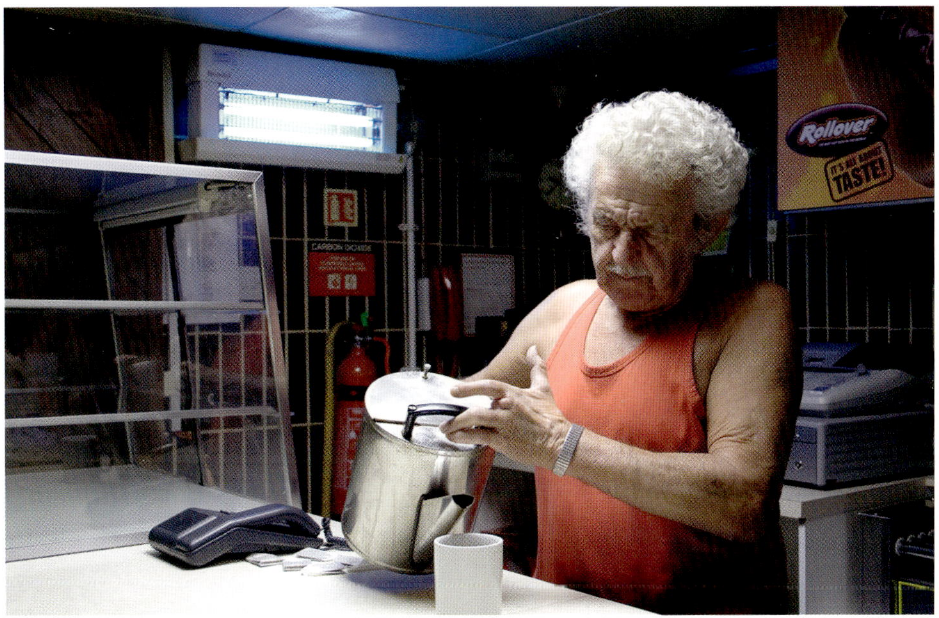

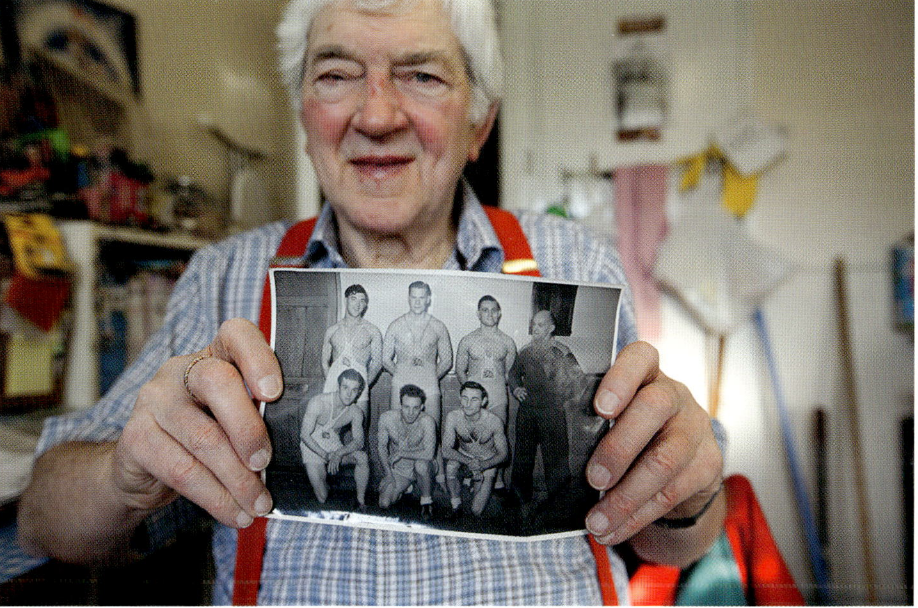

LEFT TO RIGHT
Katherine Green on location
John, cleaner, from *Going to the Dogs*
Edwin Bowey, wrestler, from *1948 Olympians*

from her sitters. 'I was anticipating that they would be aggrieved by not getting tickets, or would feel the same sense of isolation that I initially did. What I found was a real pride and excitement, especially from young people. Their expectations inspired me and made me rethink my cynicism.'

Green's remit took her to Docklands Sailing and Watersport Centre, situated between one of London's wealthiest areas and one of its poorest communities on the Isle of Dogs, where she witnessed 'kids from council estates out on the Thames sailing around these vast financial institutions'. She also visited Repton Boxing Club in Bethnal Green, which has a long tradition of producing champion prizefighters and is a former haunt of the Krays. 'Everyone was very welcoming, but I'd never experienced anywhere that was quite so masculine; you could smell the testosterone.'

Shooting with a handheld Canon 5D MkII, Green has a strong preference for natural light, though the 'horrible strip-lighting' in many of the sports halls necessitated the occasional use of flash. 'My equipment is pretty unobtrusive, which allows me to be quite quick and move around easily. It means people stay relaxed and don't get too self-conscious. That's important as I want to capture them acting as naturally as I can.'

BRIAN GRIFFIN

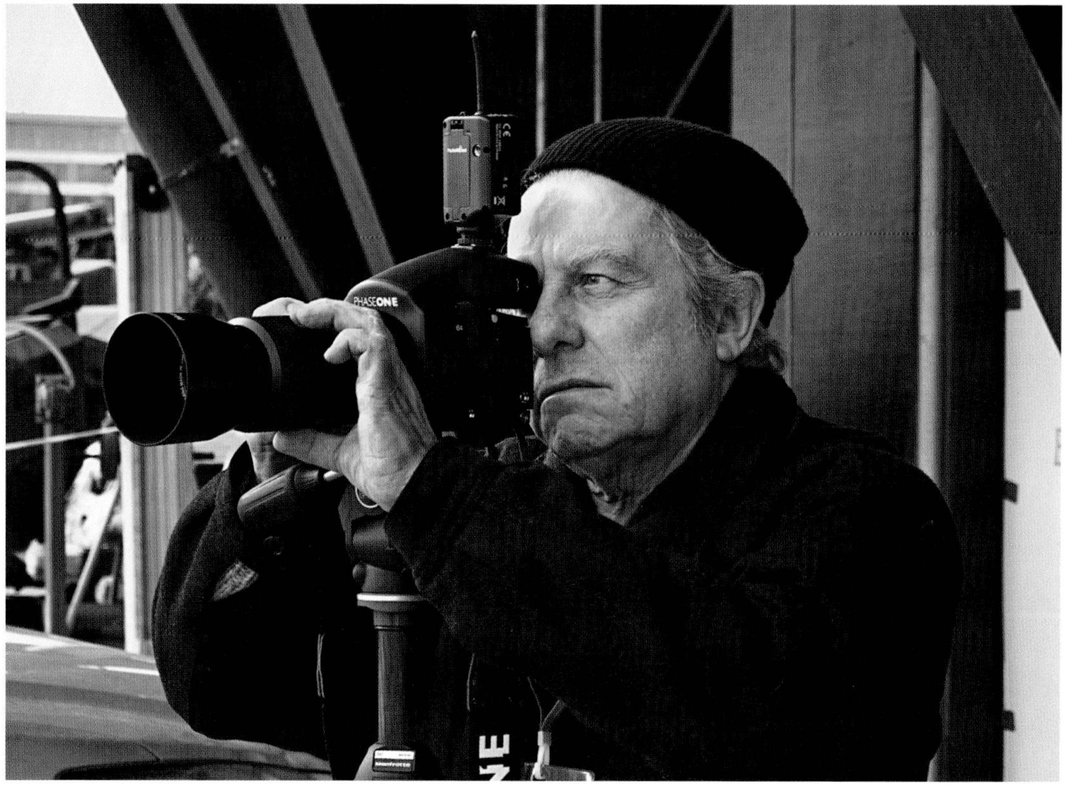

Born: Birmingham, 1948
Education: Halesowen Technical School; Manchester Polytechnic
Recent projects: *The Water People and St. Pancras* at Les Rencontres d'Arles (2009) and Birmingham (2010); *Face to Face, a retrospective*, Birmingham (2010); *The Black Country*, College des Bernadins, Paris (2010–11) and The New Art Gallery Walsall (2011); commissions for Marseille-Provence 2013 European Capital of Culture (2011–13), new Library of Birmingham (2012–13) and City of Derby (2012–13)
Publications: *Influences* (2005); *The Water People* (2006); *Team* (2007); *Face to Face* (2010)

With his wealth of experience in documenting the British workforce, Brian Griffin was an obvious candidate to launch *Road to 2012* by photographing the leaders and behind-the-scenes people charged with carrying out the London Olympics bid and delivery. Beginning as a staff photographer on *Management Today* in the 1970s, Griffin injected a quirky humour into the then lifeless world of corporate imagery, and he has continued to chronicle both boardroom and building site, notably through his acclaimed 1980s series detailing the construction of the Broadgate development in the City of London, and his record of the high-speed rail link to St Pancras in 2007.

'When I started out, the business sector was the most boring side of photography,' he recalls. 'Then Margaret Thatcher came to power and business became sexy. All of a sudden I was part of the most dynamic side of photography; I was the most famous photographer in the executive arena. If you wanted men in suits, I was your man.'

Tasked with creating several group portraits for *Road to 2012*, Griffin took inspiration from a variety of sources. His image of the Olympic Delivery Authority leadership team makes playful reference to wartime film posters. Elsewhere, he turned to the Old Masters, crowding his subjects in Rembrandt-like clusters or finding inspiration in the National Maritime Museum to light the group portrait of the Olympic Delivery Team, the work he describes as 'the closest I came to a painting'.

'I always spend as long as possible observing the gestures and mannerisms of my sitters, then using them in the portrait,' he explains. 'I'm naturally perceptive. I don't have a car, so I travel everywhere on foot or by Tube, watching people all the time. I keep a visual dictionary in my head.'

Shooting digitally with a Phase One camera, Griffin used a telephoto lens in

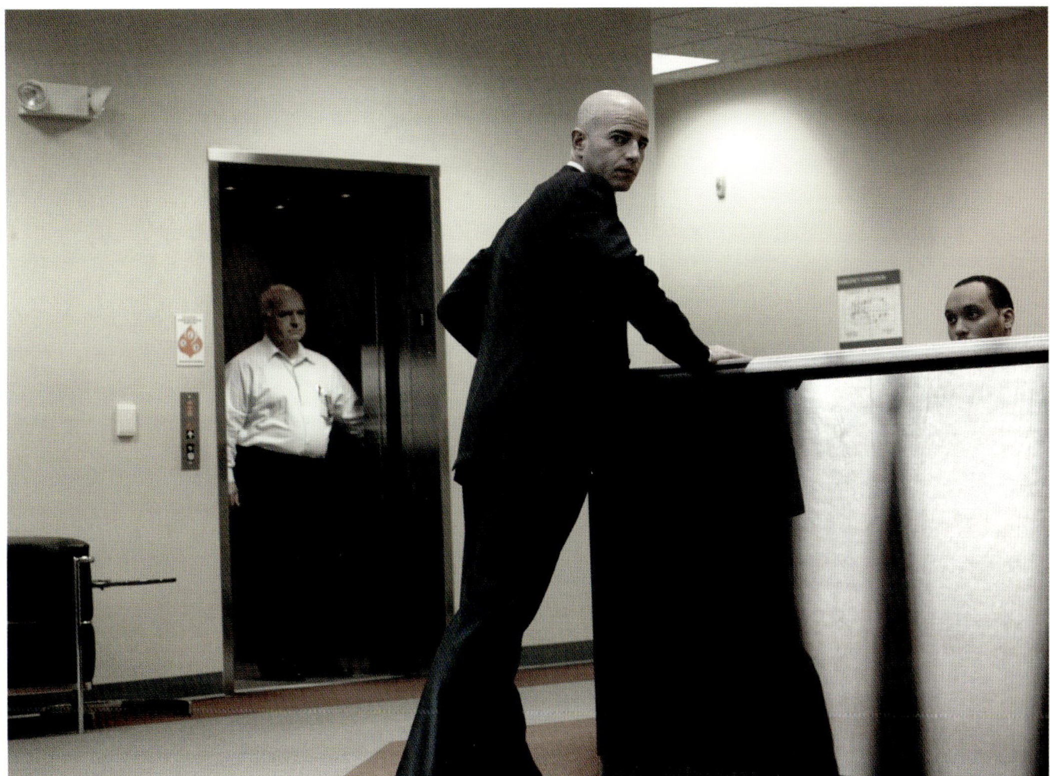

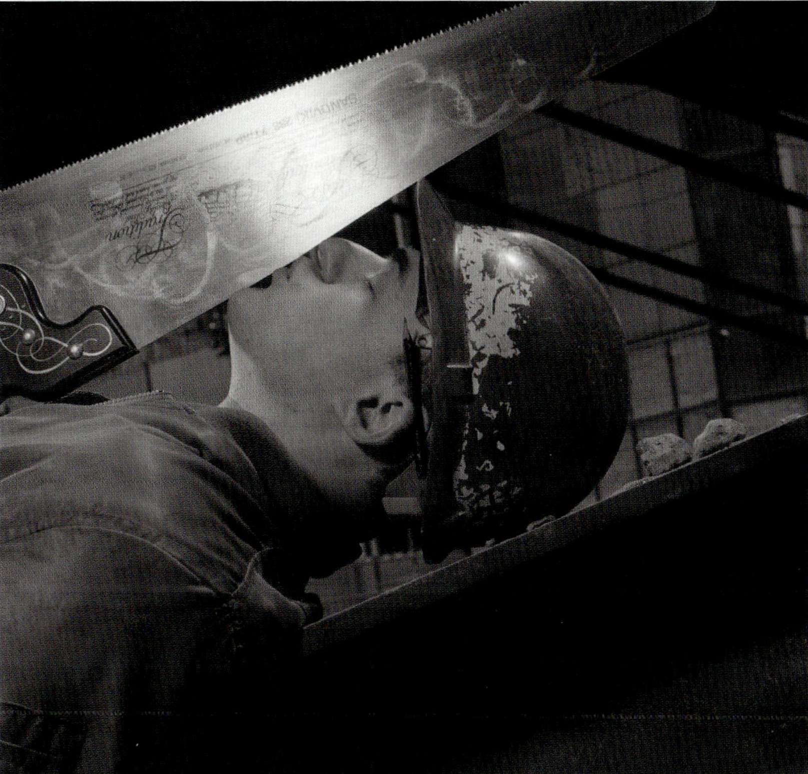

LEFT TO RIGHT
Brian Griffin photographing Team Stadium
Alastair Cathcart, Contract Manager, RLE from *Team*
Carpenter, from *Workers*

order to compress perspectives and bring the subjects closer together, meticulously marking their positions on the ground with tape before arranging them within the frame. Although the brief required him to shoot in relevant locations, the stadia and offices are usually relegated to minor roles. 'I always feel that if you use a really powerful background it tends to overshadow the subject,' he reasons.

With the exception of Olympics minister Tessa Jowell, who resisted Griffin's initial suggestion that she be photographed reclining on the floor of her office, all of the sitters willingly adopted his highly controlled poses. In some portraits, such as that of Denise Lewis and Jonathan Edwards, and that of Ken Livingstone and his consultant Tony Winterbottom, Griffin took this finely detailed precision to new lengths, and he likens the results to the bronze and fibreglass human sculptures created by American artist Duane Hanson.

'After leaving school I was a trainee draughtsman and I think that comes through. Extreme clarity is important to me – that's why I use very high resolution. *Road to 2012* has encouraged me to develop the sculptural aspects of my work even further. I want the people in my portraits to look like they live and breathe.'

EMMA HARDY

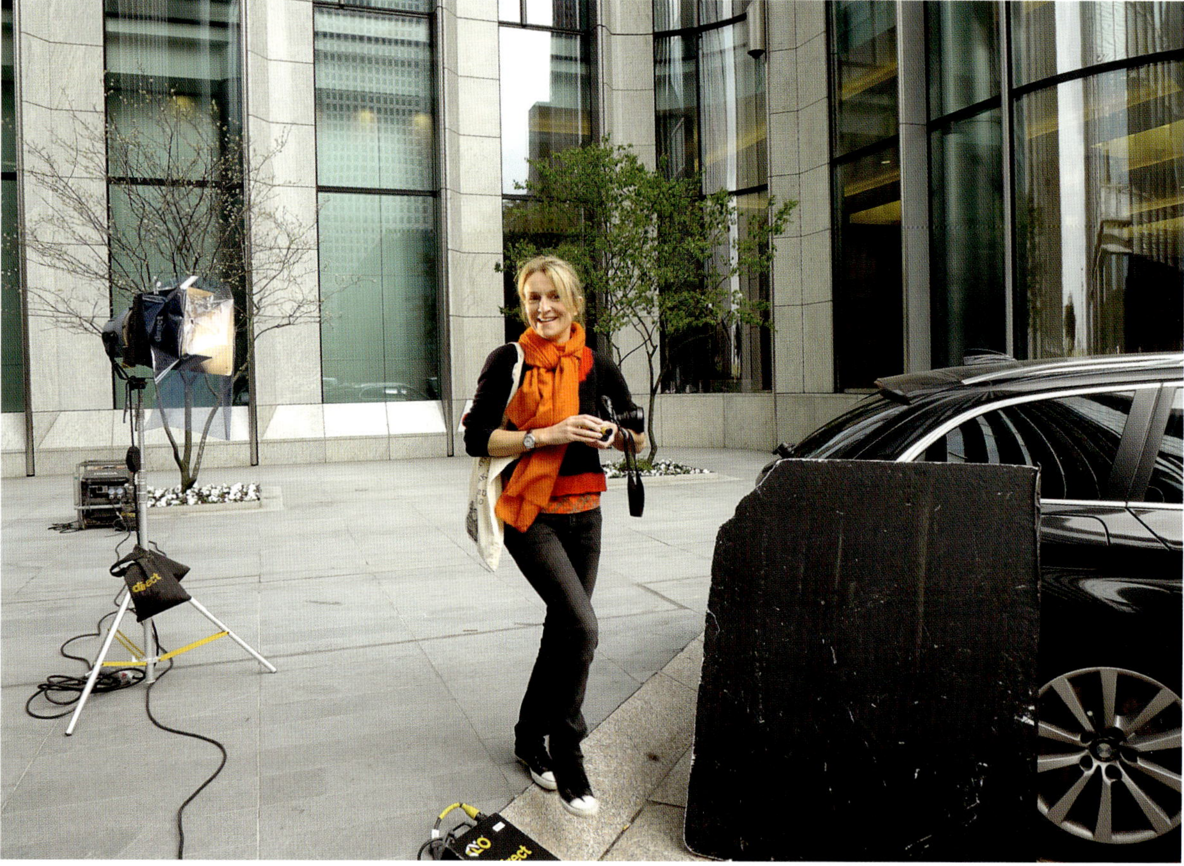

Born: London, 1963
Education: Bristol University
Recent projects: Commissions for *Vogue*, the *New York Times* and *Vanity Fair*; *Exceptional Youth*, National Portrait Gallery, London (2006)
Publications: *C International Photo Magazine*

There is an intimacy and informality that runs throughout Emma Hardy's portraits of the men and women responsible for the preparations and staging of the London 2012 Games: Sebastian Coe stops for a breather during his daily run through Greenwich Park; Michael Morpurgo shoots the breeze with his colleague Greg Nugent over a leisurely pint in a sun-dappled pub; police chief Chris Allison takes a break from coordinating the country's largest peacetime security operation to relax with a train set and table tennis.

By depicting her subjects removed from their everyday workplaces, Hardy wanted to evoke the inspirational thinking that they brought to their highly pressured roles. 'You don't necessarily find inspiration in your prescribed place of work, so I chose to set my subjects in locations which stimulate them or where they find head space,' she explains. 'I love it when a particular place or landscape enriches the portrait or brings a new dimension to someone whose work may be office-bound or screen-based.'

As part of her working process, Hardy spoke to most of her sitters in advance to break the ice and agree an appropriate location. In the case of Ruth Mackenzie, director of the 2012 Cultural Olympiad, the pair spent an hour together in Tate Modern's Rothko room, Mackenzie's favourite place of contemplation, before setting up in the Turbine Hall as the gallery opened. By contrast, Sebastian Coe's hectic schedule meant that photographer and subject didn't meet until a few minutes before the session. 'Coe is only pictured in a suit and tie these days, but to me he will always be an athlete, a national hero,' says Hardy. 'I wanted him back in a tracksuit. Running is a meditative state for him. That's when he does a lot of his thinking.'

Largely self-taught, Hardy was an actress before turning to photography in her late twenties, since when her portraiture and fashion editorials have featured in British *Vogue* and *Vanity Fair*, while her portfolio of talented British teens, *Exceptional Youth*, was

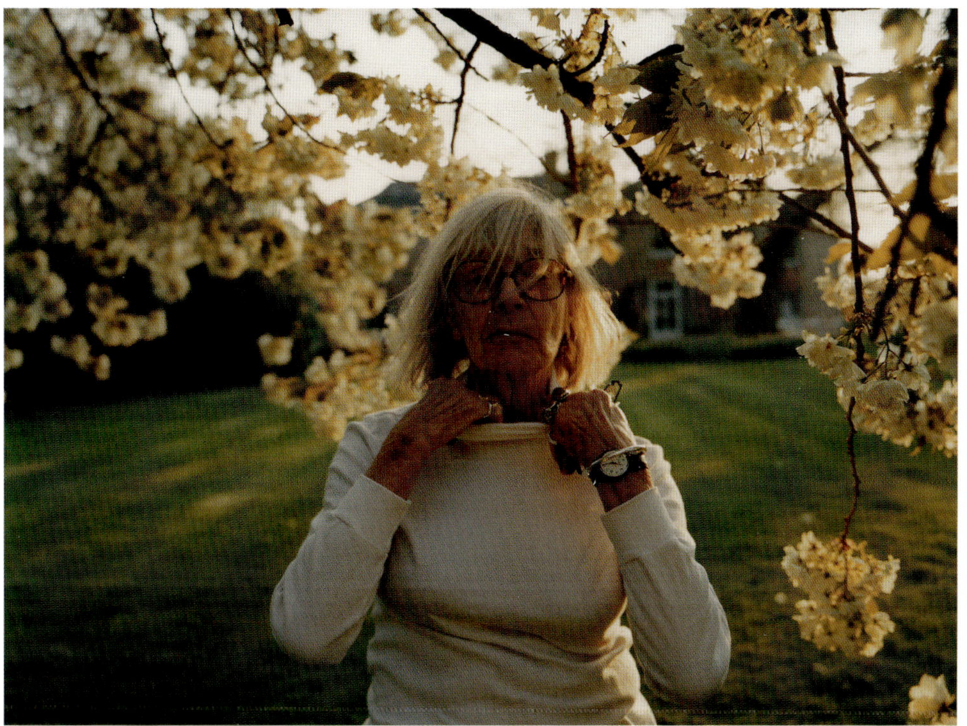

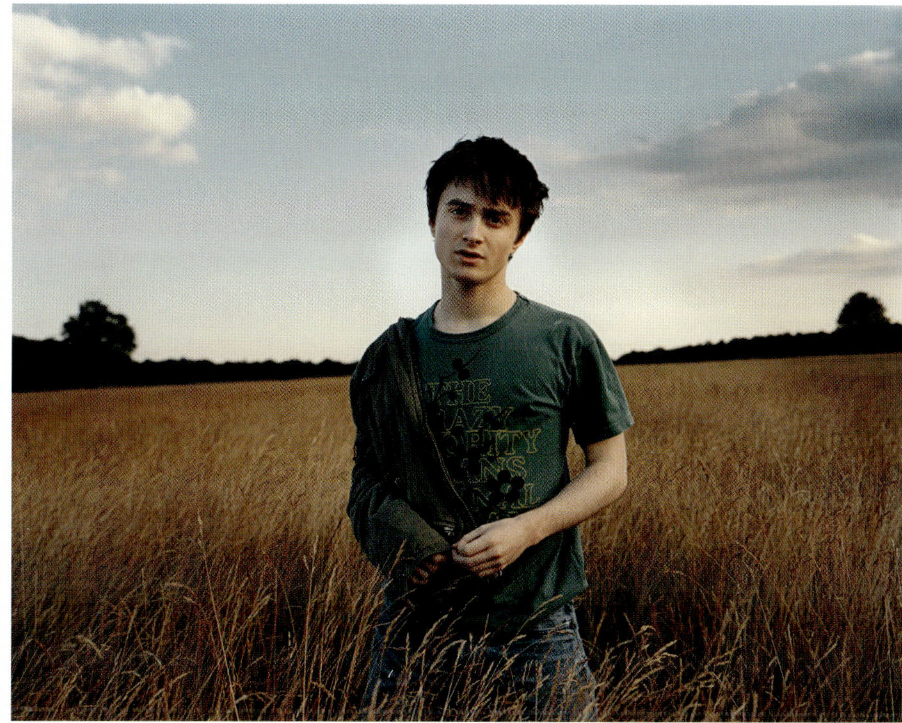

displayed at the National Portrait Gallery in 2006. She believes her acting background has benefited her work. 'It means I can empathise with anybody in front of my camera. I know what it's like to feel self-conscious; that's what held my acting back. So I can help my subjects get beyond that barrier to authenticity.'

She describes her brief to record the Games' behind-the-scenes facilitators as akin to photographing a swan on a river. 'My task wasn't to document the graceful creature you see on the surface, but to see how fast its feet were paddling and against which currents. It was like taking my camera underwater.'

She surfaced with some memorable images, all of them shaped by her desire to work as simply as she can, using only film, natural light whenever possible, and her 'veteran, clunky' Pentax 67 camera. 'I'm not so interested in using complicated devices just to get an arresting image, and I try not to impose technique or too much of myself on my subjects,' she states. 'I don't have much of a set plan. If I could turn up with a camera in a lunchbox I would.'

LEFT TO RIGHT

Emma Hardy photographing Charlie Wijeratna and Chris Townsend

White blossom, with barely disguised fury

Daniel Radcliffe, from *Exceptional Youth*

NADAV KANDER

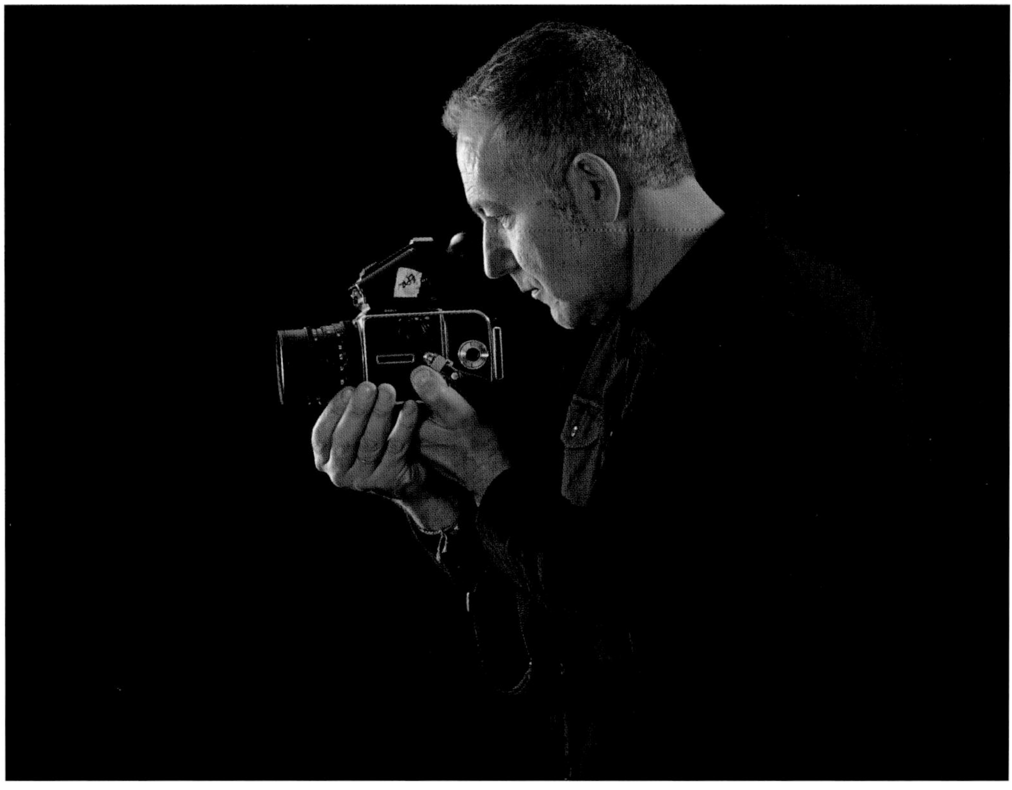

Born: Tel Aviv, 1961
Recent projects: *Obama's People*, Flowers Galleries, London (2009), *The Kennedys*, Berlin and Herzliya Museum of Contemporary Art, Israel (2010); *Yangtze – The Long River*, Flowers East Gallery (2010) and Museum of Photographic Arts, San Diego (2011); *Nadav Kander: Selected Portraits, 1999–2011*, The Lowry (2011)
Publications: *Beauty's Nothing* (2001); *Night* (2001); *Obama's People* (2009); *Yangtze – The Long River* (2010)

As the culminating commission of the *Road to 2012* project, Nadav Kander, widely regarded as one of our most original and versatile photographers, was invited to photograph several of Britain's most promising young sportsmen and women, as well as portraying the members of the public chosen to be Torchbearers as the Olympic flame journeyed around the UK ahead of the opening ceremony.

He opted to tackle these two series in very different ways, firstly by creating a series of 'simple and striking' black and white portraits of the teenage athletes. In his youth, Kander was influenced by Leni Riefenstahl's 'singular, lushly beautiful' pictures of the 1936 Olympics in Berlin, in spite of her political resonances, though he draws a distinction between their two bodies of work. 'My Olympic portraits are wholly different: harder, blacker, with more edge and soul, and the athletes are not elevated in any way,' he says. 'I could easily have been seduced by their great bodies, but I didn't want any Herb Ritts-style pictures of glistening muscles.'

Instead, when Jodie Williams arrived at his studio, accompanied by her mother, Kander was struck by the sprinter's vulnerability, which he sought to capture through his lens. Although he was aware of Williams' growing reputation on the track, he avoids researching his subjects and keeps conversation to a minimum before the shoot, preferring to connect non-verbally with his sitters.

'I try not to speak to the subjects too much, but respond to what I am seeing and feeling. There can be an incredibly potent communication between two human beings without talking. I want it to be like meeting someone for the first time. It doesn't help the picture by me knowing them too well; I prefer not to socialise with a person before the session.'

Having moved away from his earlier preference for shooting large-format 5x4 negatives with a tripod, Kander made the series with a medium-format digital camera. It was a technique he also used for his portraits of Barack Obama's inaugural administration in 2009, the first time in the history of the *New York Times Magazine* that an entire issue was devoted to one photographer. 'What I lose in terms of print quality, I gain in greater mobility,' he notes.

As with all his work, Kander planned the concept for the Rising Stars and Torchbearers in advance. 'The portraits of the Torchbearers are quite ordinary, almost like photocopies, but I wanted them to be beautiful objects,' he says. 'The figures are raised slightly from the ground to show the transforming experience of running with the flame.'

The breadth of Kander's work was underlined in 2011 when his study of David Cameron graced the cover of *Time* magazine, and The Lowry in Salford staged a retrospective of his arts-based portraits, including those of Michael Stipe and David Lynch. 'My portraits are about how I respond to an individual and how I express my perception of a person,' he concludes. 'I am in these portraits enormously. When you look at a Picasso or a Matisse, you really feel the artist, probably more than the subject. My photography is no different.'

CLOCKWISE FROM LEFT
Nadav Kander photographing Jodie Williams
Barack Obama, from *Obama's People*
Chongqing IV (Sunday Picnic), Chongqing Municipality, from *Yangtze – The Long River*

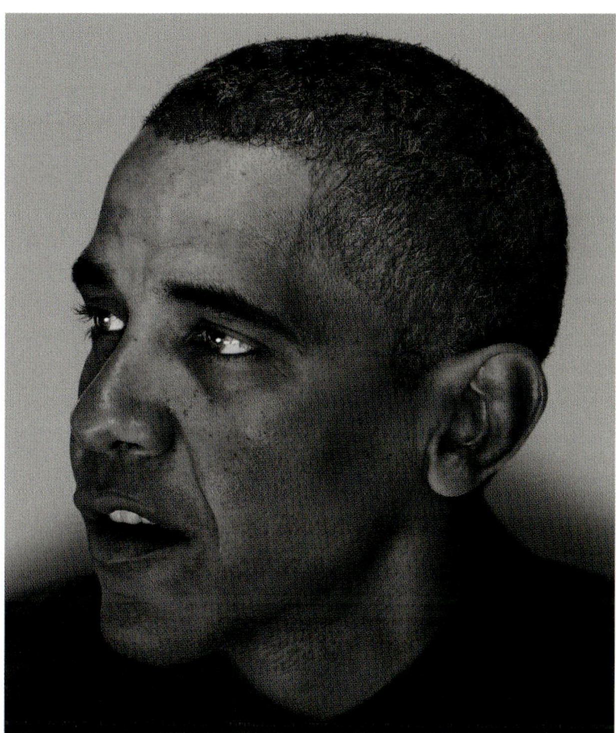

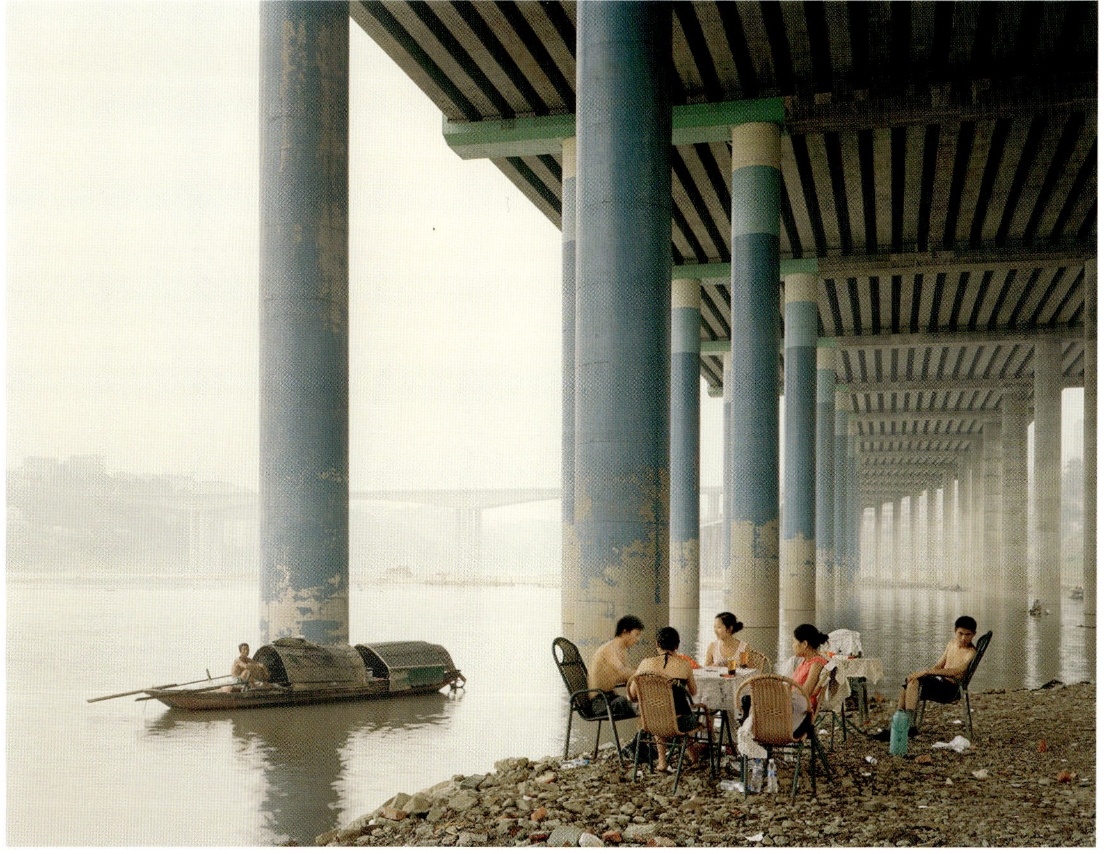

FINLAY MACKAY

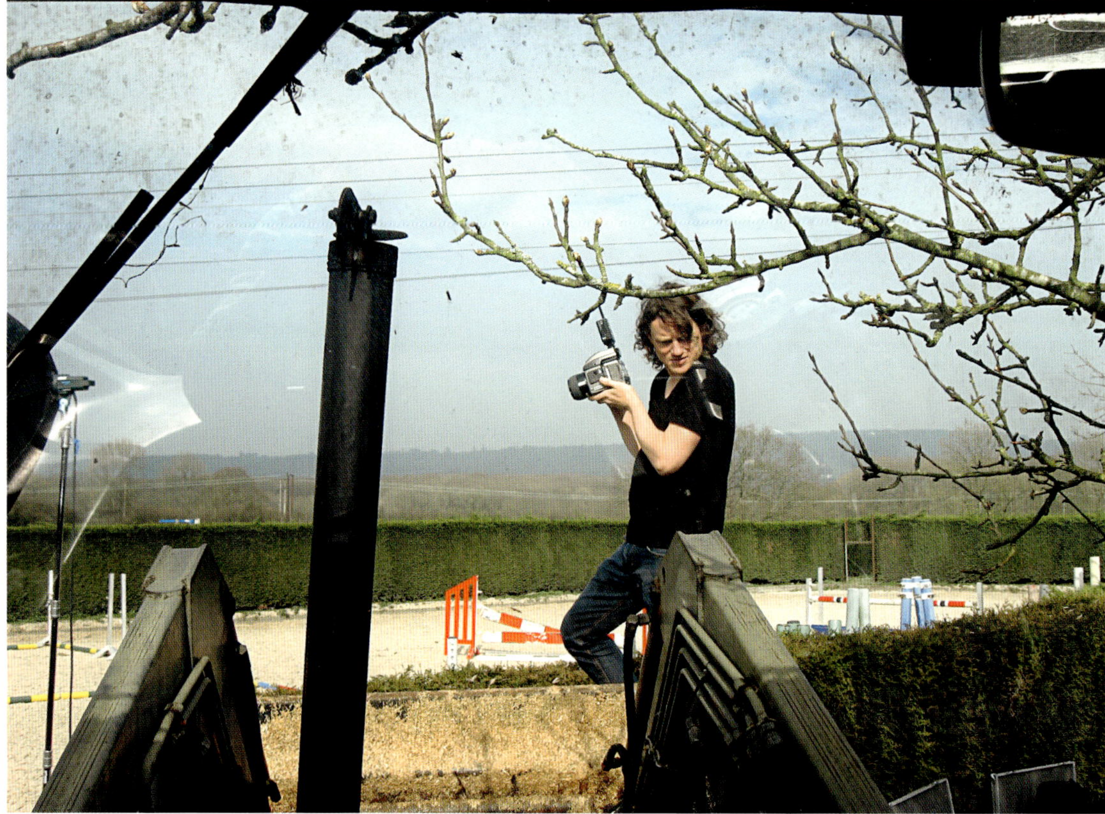

Born: Scotland, 1972
Education: Glasgow School of Art
Recent projects: Commissions for the *New York Times*, *Wired* and *GQ*; advertising clients include Absolut, Puma, Polartec, Bacardi, Umbro, Nike, adidas, Olympus, British Telecom, the Scottish Ballet, Channel 4, the English National Opera and Harrods

Scottish photographer Finlay MacKay's brief was to record Olympic and Paralympic medal prospects with the trainers, coaches or family members who they nominated as being pivotal to their success. It saw him largely move away from the high-action sport shots he has produced for the *New York Times Magazine* and advertising campaigns for Nike, adidas and Umbro. Instead, he deliberately pulled back from his subjects, giving equal emphasis to the athletes' surroundings or equipment.

'I had got to a point in my career where I felt I had done these very close-up, high-action shots to death, and I didn't want to repeat myself,' explains MacKay. 'The new images are more about the environment, and what it adds to the narrative. It wasn't just about getting the athlete to perform his or her sport. It was about getting them into a landscape that tells you who they are and what they do. It made a nice change not to shove my camera into people's faces.'

MacKay displayed an Olympian-like fortitude when handed the assignment of photographing oarsmen Pete Reed and Andrew Triggs Hodge as they rowed on the Team GB training lake in Berkshire one cold March day, and was congratulated on his focus and drive by coach Jürgen Grobler. After his companion boat proved too unstable for him to get the picture, the Scottish photographer pulled on some waders and braved the icy waters. 'I was in there for about half an hour, with the waders overflowing, trying not to drop a £20,000 camera,' he recalls. 'I went from freezing cold to burning hot; it felt like I was getting hypothermia.'

In the portrait of triple jumper Phillips Idowu and his coach Aston Moore at the High Performance Centre in Birmingham, it is the textured sandpit ('reminiscent of a Zen garden') that dominates. In the diptych of pommel specialist Louis Smith and trainer Paul Hall at their Huntingdon gym, the human figures compete for space with the apparatus and kit crowded about them.

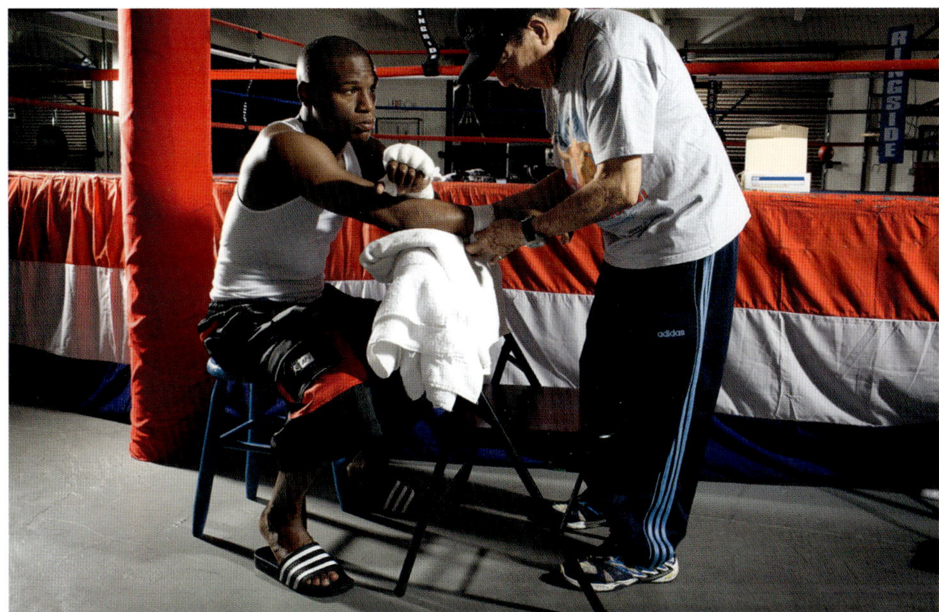

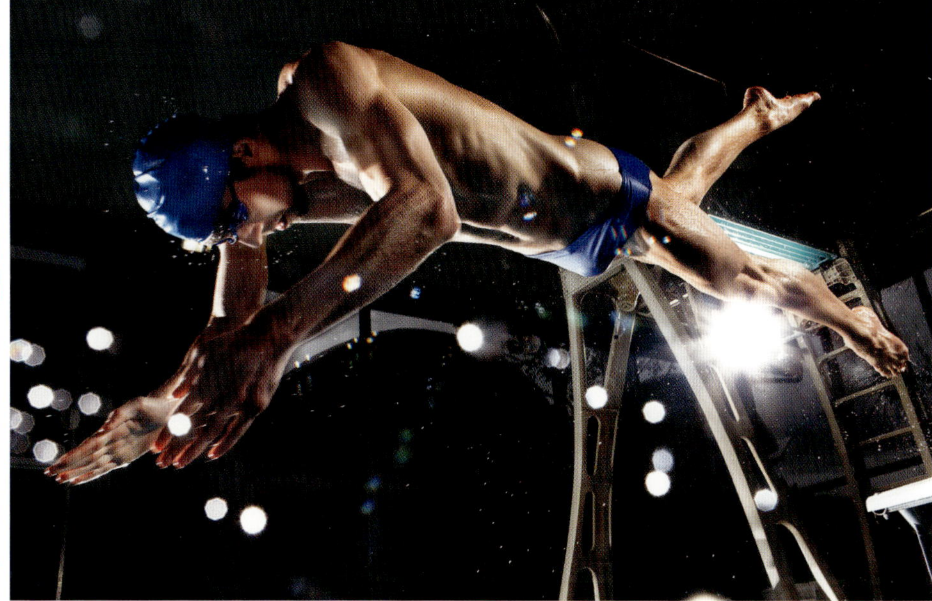

LEFT TO RIGHT
Finlay MacKay photographing Pippa Funnell
Floyd Mayweather
Michael Phelps

Rather than force the image, MacKay simply framed the shot and allowed his subjects to go about their routine. 'I didn't want to overthink things. It's best to let people do what they do, then steer them subtly.'

Most of the portraits are composites of multiple photographs. Typically, he used a Phase One P65 digital camera to shoot a grid pattern of between six and nine separate images which were later 'stitched' together using computer software. This post-production work is a crucial part of his creative thinking. 'With the Phase One, you get big prints and it looks beautiful. You can lose yourself in the detail.'

The project also reined in MacKay's self-confessed addiction to artificial lighting. Previously, he had sometimes used more than 30 different flash units and studio strobes for his advertising campaigns. For *Road to 2012*, he never went above six. 'It used to be like an obsessive-compulsive disorder,' he laughs. 'In the past I went overboard, often using lighting to the point where the image looked computer-generated because of the amount of flash on it. I still love lighting, but right now I am exploring things that are a little more real.'

BETTINA VON ZWEHL

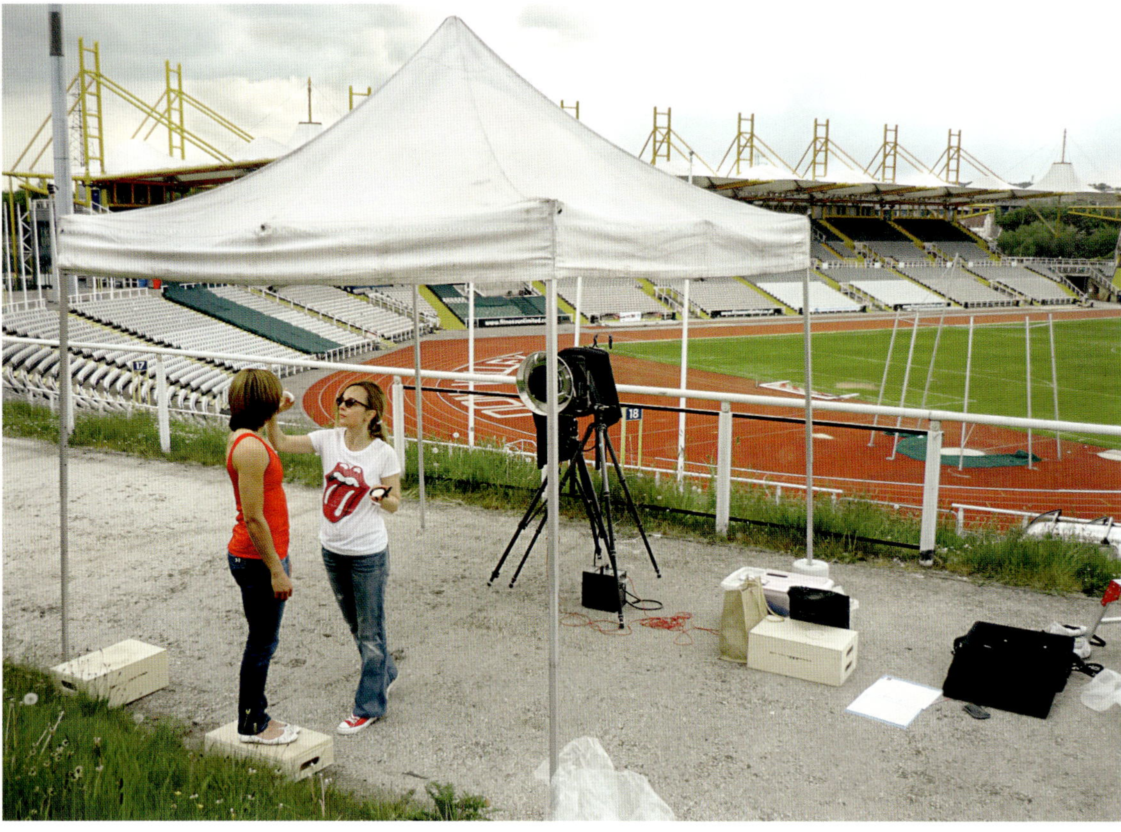

Born: Germany, 1971
Education: Royal College of Art (1997–99)
Recent projects: *Alina*, The Photographers' Gallery (2005); *Profiles III*, V&A Museum of Childhood (2009); Artist in Residence at the Victoria and Albert Museum (2011); *Made up love song*, Purdy Hicks Gallery (2011); *Seduced by Art: Photography Past and Present*, the National Gallery, London (2012)
Publications: *Bettina von Zwehl – A Steidl/Photoworks Monograph* (2007)

Bettina von Zwehl was presented with a number of challenges when she accepted the commission to record Team GB athletes in outdoor settings where they either live or train. The German-born conceptual artist has built an international reputation on her carefully orchestrated photographic portrait series, but she had never before made portraits of public figures, had zero interest in sport, and rarely worked outside her studio.

'I always photograph ordinary people; I haven't worked with celebrities before,' explains von Zwehl. 'Many of these people are already over-represented in the press, so it's not something I have ever pursued. But I was keen to work out of my comfort zone.'

The portraits were shot on 10x8 film with von Zwehl's favoured large-plate, nineteenth-century-style camera, which she uses to bring a 'beauty of detail and clarity' to her work. Transporting the cumbersome equipment across the country required the help of her assistant and husband David Robinson, though the novel experience of scouting for locations was somewhat soured by the vagaries of the British weather, not least a monsoon-like downpour as she photographed track cyclist Victoria Pendleton in Macclesfield Forest.

'Victoria turned up with her two crazy dogs and was completely distracted. In all that chaos, I had to focus and concentrate. I have a very calm and controlled environment in my studio and I was a bit scared to be working outdoors. But I got used to blocking out environmental noises and grew to like it more and more; it brings challenges that enrich the work.'

To avoid both the visual noise of sportswear logos and the risk of falling foul of the strict Olympic branding rules, she dressed the athletes in a selection of clothes loaned from a boutique near her studio in London's East End, even

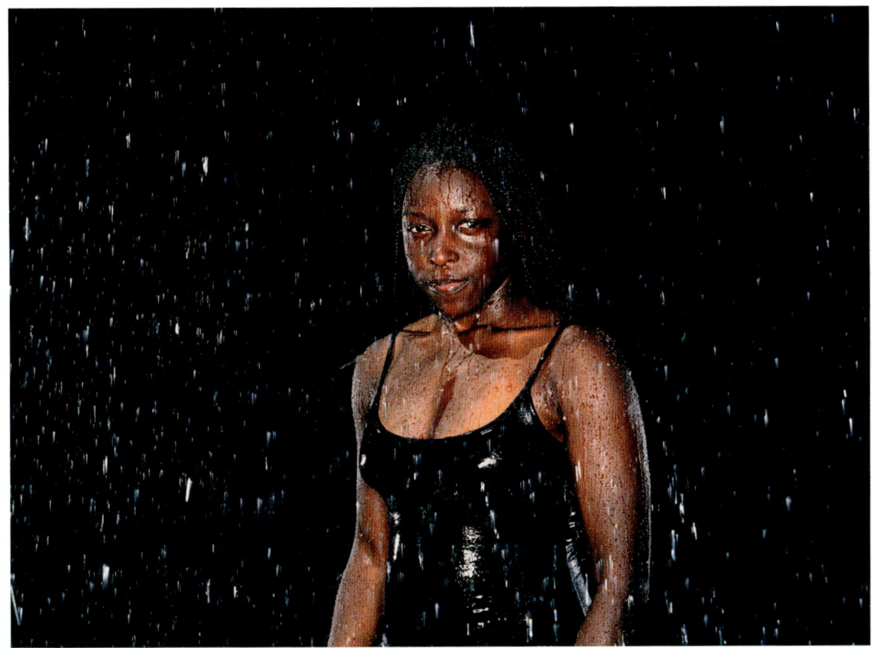

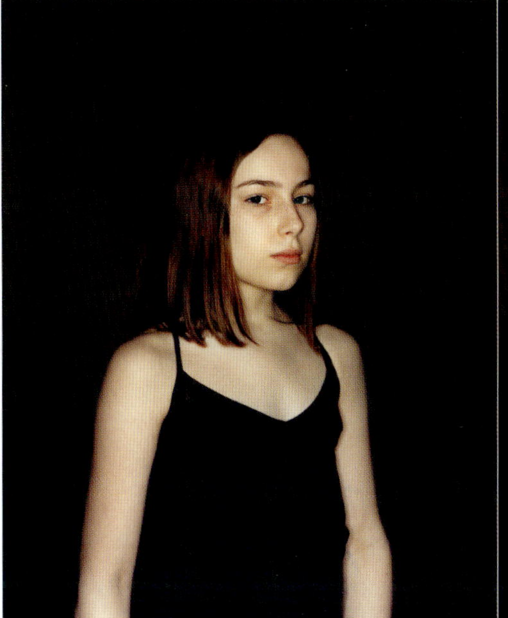

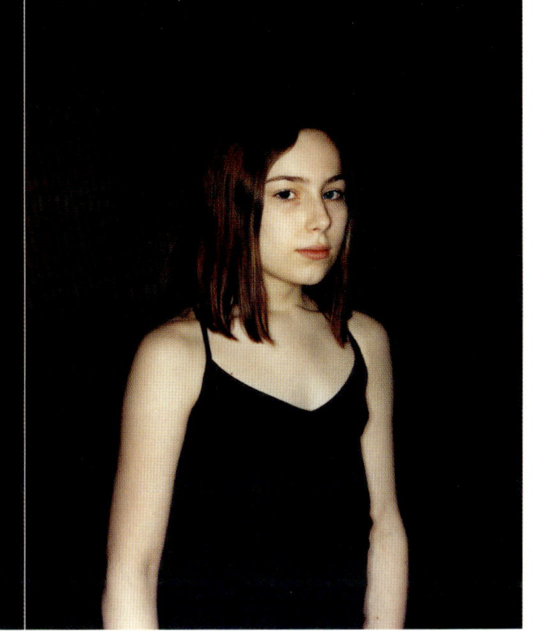

persuading a doubtful Katherine Grainger out of her Lycra and into a dress. However, when Jessica Ennis arrived for her shoot at Sheffield's Don Valley Stadium, von Zwehl asked the heptathlete to remove most of her make-up. 'I wanted to effect a transformation, but not turn it into a fashion shoot,' she says. 'People look more interesting without make-up. There is a rawness and a purity.'

While the meditative nature of her *Road to 2012* portraits may perhaps seem at odds with the explosive exertion usually associated with competitive sport, von Zwehl points to the quiet strength of her subjects. 'Stillness is an element that we don't necessarily think about in sport,' she notes. 'But the concentration and focus displayed by Tom Daley before a dive is the ultimate stillness.'

The portrait of Daley is among the photographer's favourites from the series, in part because of the rapport she established with the teenage diver. 'If there is a chemistry or connection it helps you produce better work,' she says. 'Tom has an openness, sweetness and youthfulness. I need my subjects to give me something. If they are holding back, there is no picture.'

LEFT TO RIGHT
Bettina von Zwehl photographing Jessica Ennis
Rain No6
Inhalation Exhalation No4

LOCAL HEROES

As a major part of *Road to 2012*, the National Portrait Gallery set out to connect with people in east London, documenting their stories of achievement and inspiration as well as their aspirations and hopes at this time of extraordinary investment and momentous change in their local area.

With photographer Katherine Green, the Gallery interviewed and created portraits of members of sporting and social clubs across the five Olympic host boroughs of Hackney, Tower Hamlets, Waltham Forest, Newham and Greenwich. This is the first time the Gallery has undertaken a participation project at the heart of a major commission, and the initiative echoes the inclusive spirit of the London 2012 Games.

East London is rich in sporting heritage. Sport, both amateur and professional, has flourished there, with much of it linked to the distinctive economic and social history of the area. Boxing has always been a working-class East End sport, and this part of the city also has several high-profile football clubs whose origins are linked to local industries: Millwall F.C. was formed in 1885 by workers at Morton's Jam Factory on the Isle of Dogs, and West Ham United was founded as the works side Thames Ironworks F.C. in 1895. By connecting with east London sporting organisations and individuals, the National Portrait Gallery aimed to encourage participants to share their thoughts, hopes and aspirations during one of the most ambitious programmes of investment and rebuilding that east London has seen since the period following the Second World War. These fascinating interviews and photographs tell stories of outstanding commitment and drive, often in exceptionally difficult circumstances. What emerges is a story of talent and achievement, and a determination to maximise the opportunities that London 2012 and its legacy aim to bring to east London.

'Talent can be built upon or it can just be there. Anyone can do it if they believe in it.'

DEBORAH, EAST LONDON WHEELCHAIR ATHLETICS CLUB

Through these local stories, another perspective on the impact of the London 2012 Games is revealed alongside the body of more formal photographic portraits commissioned for the project. Parallels become evident between the high-profile athletes at the pinnacle of their professions and those participating in sport at a grass-roots level who share the same determination to achieve their personal best. The project was also an opportunity to highlight and celebrate the dedication of these participants along with the trainers, family members and mentors whose hours of hard work help young people reach their potential.

East London-based photographer Katherine Green was commissioned to document the community project in a series of portraits at sports clubs and groups. Katherine's practice and body of work reflects the identity of the people and places in her local area, and her expertise in capturing local stories and their effect on communities has brought an additional dimension to the project.

The portraits featured here show participants at Repton Boxing Club in Bethnal Green, Docklands Sailing and Watersport Centre in the Isle of Dogs, Youngs Table Tennis Club in Abbey Wood, the East London Wheelchair Athletics Club in Mile End, Blackheath Fencing Club in Greenwich, London Fields Lido in Hackney and Lee Valley Riding Centre in Waltham Forest.

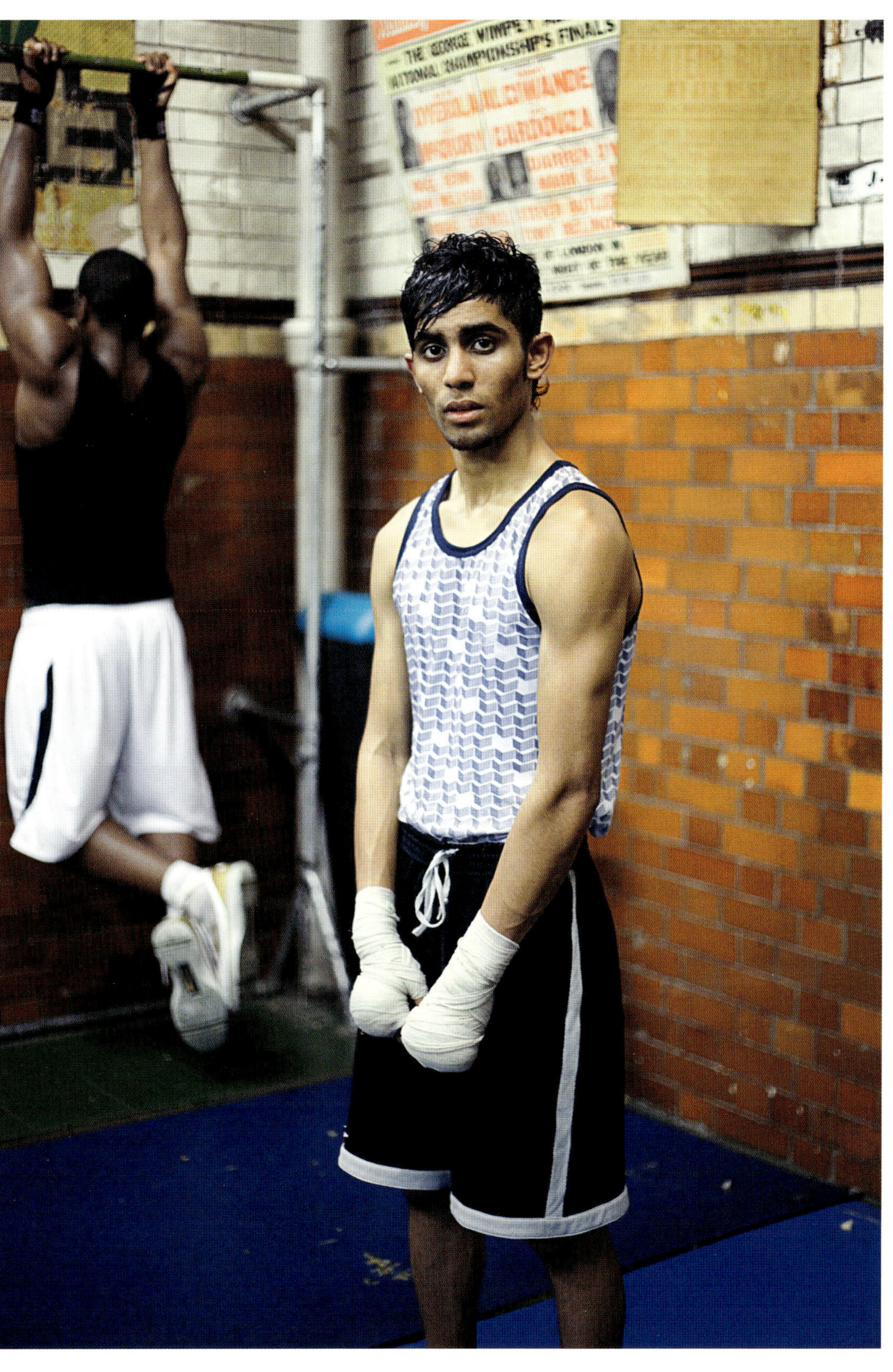

RIGHT
Luqmaan, Repton Boxing Club

'You have to be dedicated. It's not just showing up to the session: it's putting everything you've got into every session.'

JESSICA, EAST LONDON DISABILITY SWIMMING GROUP

'I started riding when I was four … and twenty-odd years down the line I'm still doing it.'

MANDY, LEE VALLEY RIDING CENTRE

'I'm looking forward to the Games, and hopefully seeing some world-class athletes.'

FAHINE, YOUNGS TABLE TENNIS CLUB

'This area has changed so much in the last ten years.'

MALGOSIA, BLACKHEATH FENCING CLUB

'I hope when the Olympics finish there will be a legacy … that local people in the boroughs can benefit.'

MATT, DOCKLANDS SAILING AND WATERSPORTS CENTRE

'I think kids are born with talent.'

TONY, REPTON BOXING CLUB

Repton Boxing Club has a unique heritage and continues to fulfil its nineteenth-century founding mission of encouraging and supporting young men from all backgrounds to achieve their potential through the discipline and art of boxing.

Docklands Sailing and Watersports Centre, based in Canary Wharf, provides opportunities for those from all backgrounds to try out a new sport. The centre has an all-inclusive approach to encourage new participants into the sport.

Youngs Table Tennis Club works with young people and adults to encourage participation in table tennis, and the club has teams playing in the local leagues. Club members ranging in age from sixteen to seventy meet regularly to practise their skills at St Michael's Church Hall in Abbey Wood.

The East London Wheelchair Athletics Club, based in Mile End, enables young people to try out and progress in wheelchair athletics, providing an environment for participants to push boundaries and reach new milestones. The dedication and determination of the participants, coaches and parents is inspiring.

Blackheath Fencing Club is one of the top fencing clubs in Kent, with a wealth of competitive experience and county titles amongst its members. The club is based at Blackheath High School and provides weekly training sessions for children, young people and adults.

The East London Disability Swimming Group delivers intensive training sessions twice a week for young people who want to excel in swimming and have an ambition to compete in the Paralympics. The group trains at London Fields Lido and Mile End Leisure Centre.

Set in the heart of east London, in the surroundings of the Lee Valley Regional Park, Lee Valley Riding Centre provides accessible riding classes for children, young people and adults. The centre has horses and ponies suitable for riders of all abilities, as well as an indoor arena, two floodlit outdoor arenas and jumping facilities.

OPPOSITE PAGE, CLOCKWISE FROM TOP LEFT: Cameron, Lee Valley Riding Centre; Lauren, East London Disability Swimming Group; Corsini, Blackheath Fencing Club; Megan, Lee Valley Riding Centre; Rebecca and Danny, East London Wheelchair Athletics Club; Phoebe, Blackheath Fencing Club; James, East London Wheelchair Athletics Club; Zaki, Docklands Sailing and Watersports Centre; Levi, Repton Boxing Club; Michael, Repton Boxing Club; Dervis, East London Disability Swimming Group; Richoux, Youngs Table Tennis Club; Michael, Youngs Table Tennis Club; Kirsty, Docklands Sailing and Watersports Centre. All photographed by Katherine Green in London, 2010–11.

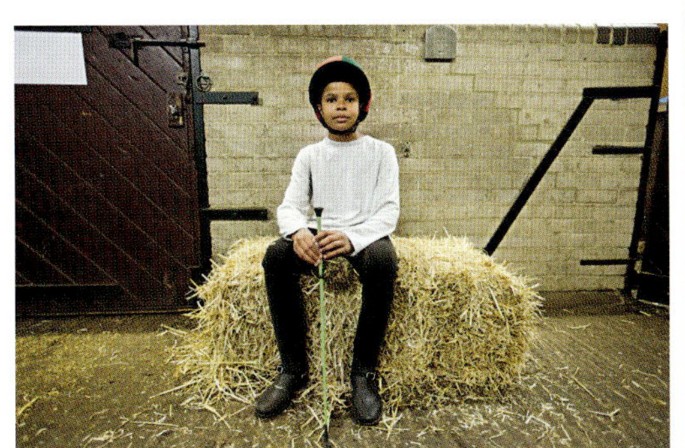
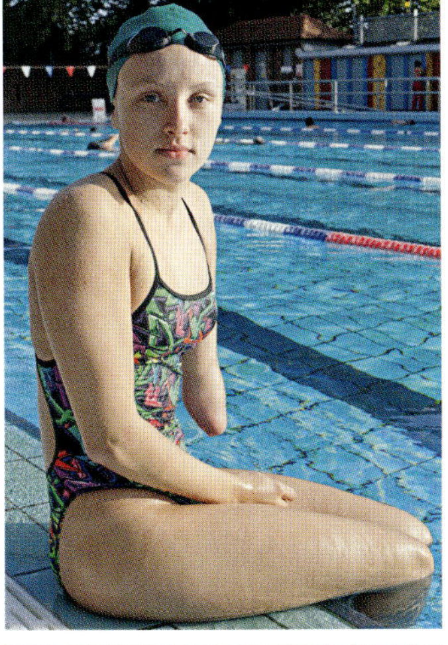
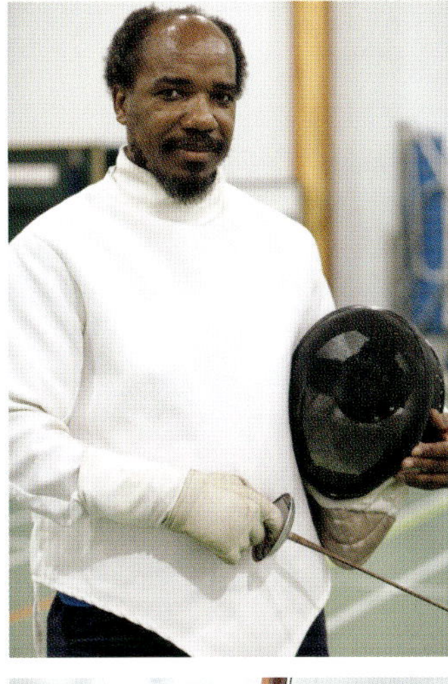
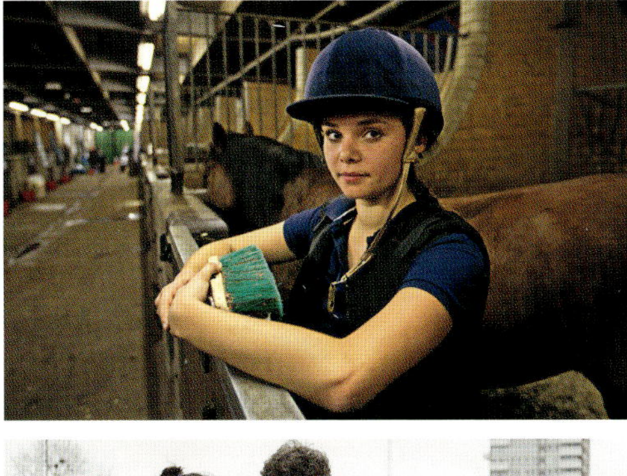
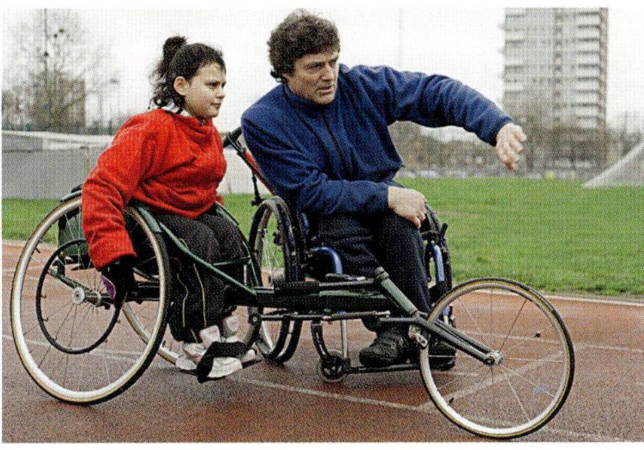
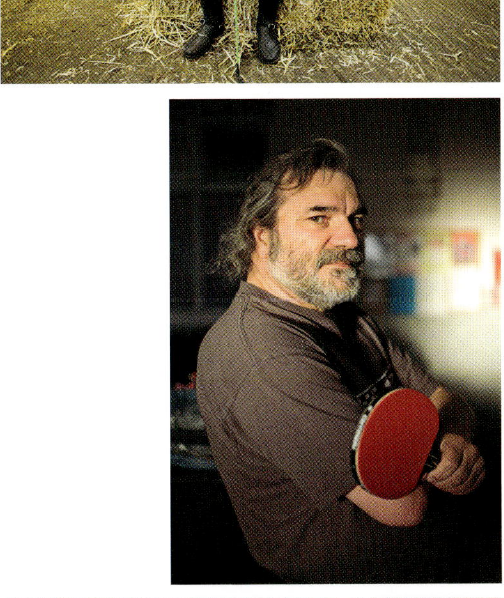
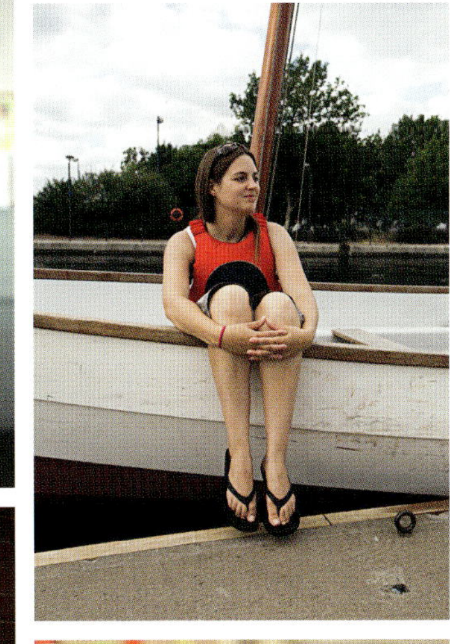
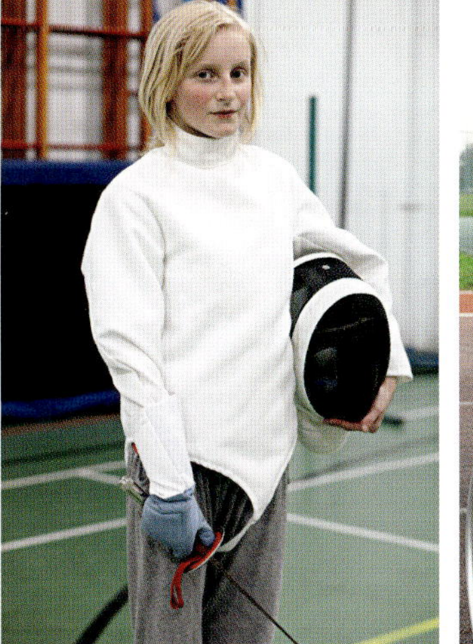
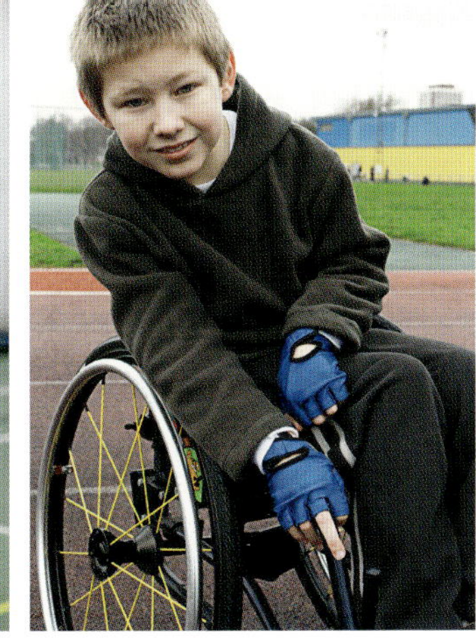
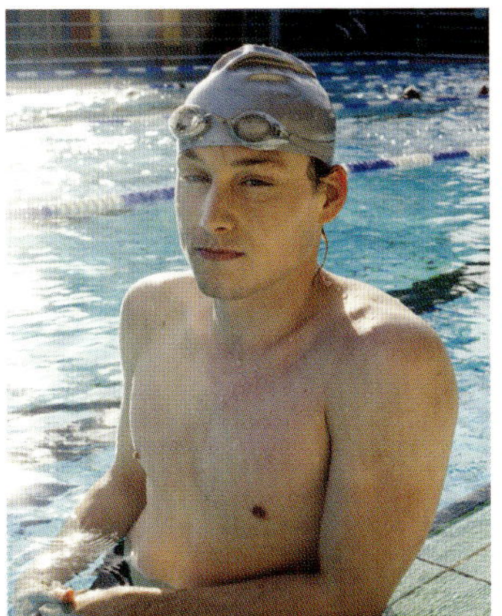
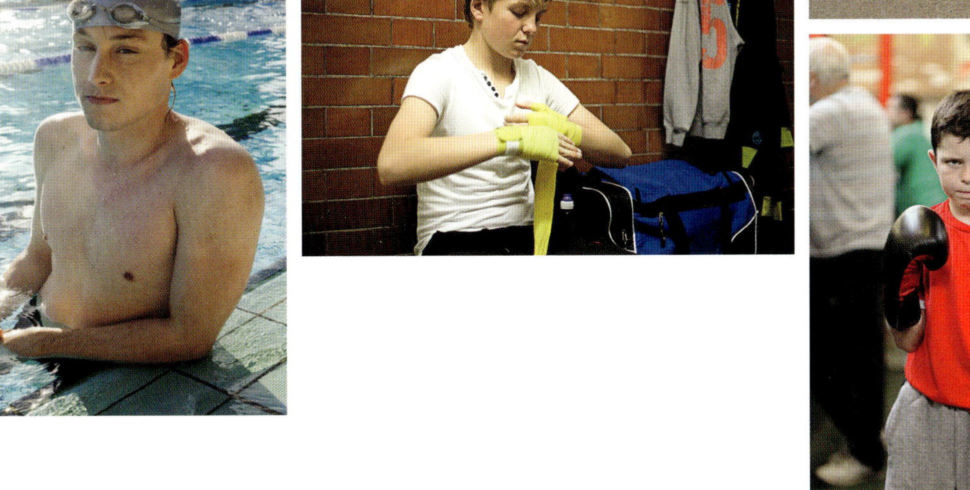
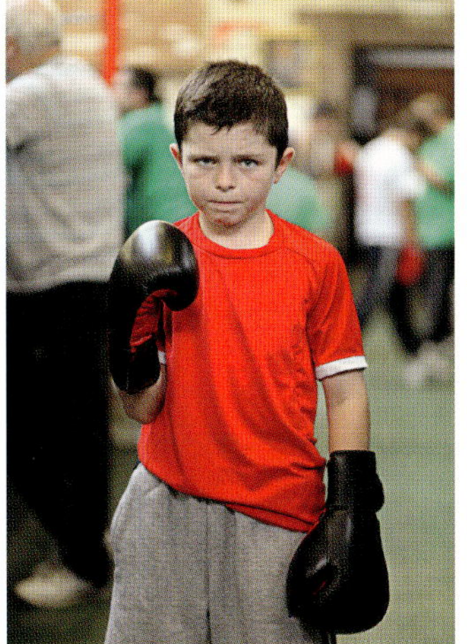
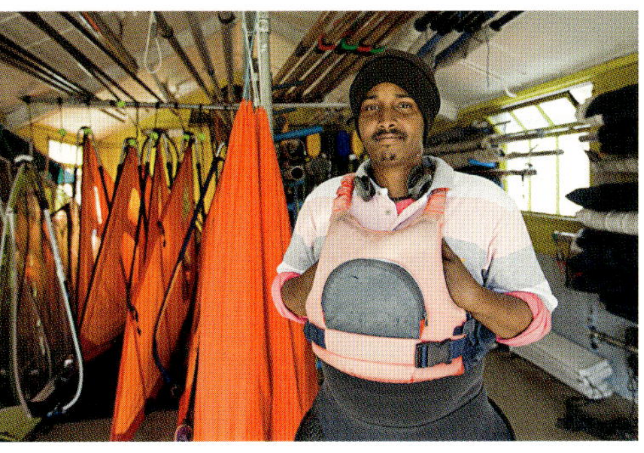

INDEX OF SITTERS

Page numbers in **bold** refer to a portrait

ACKNOWLEDGEMENTS

The National Portrait Gallery would like to thank the following people for their valuable contributions to the broad and ambitious *Road to 2012* project over the past three years, in addition to those thanked in the Director's Foreword (p.10).

Naomi Conway, Head of Development, was involved in developing the initial concept (within a framework for 2012 created by Diana Spiegelberg) and in securing the sponsorship from BT and leading the setting-up of the three-way partnership between the National Portrait Gallery, the sponsor and colleagues at LOCOG. Together with Jane Chambers, Naomi has been instrumental in continuing to manage these relationships.

Liz Smith, Director of Participation and Learning, has overseen the project with immense verve from the outset, providing invaluable guidance and leadership. Anne Braybon's remarkable vision and tenacity have extended beyond the commission to every aspect of the project, which is all the stronger for her input and collaboration.

Leigh Amor, Esther Collins, Matt Lewis, Lucy Ribeiro and Helen Whiteoak have brought the *Road to 2012* project to life beyond the Gallery through online, film and audio material as well as creative participation projects across east London.

Thanks also to Faisal Abdu'Allah, Peter Cobb and Ralph Hall at the University of East London, Julian Henriquez at Goldsmiths, University of London, and Martyn Ware, producer and sound artist, for the important parts they have played in shaping the creative programmes.

Curator of photographs Terence Pepper brought thirty-seven years of wisdom, as well as some inspired thinking, to the project's unexpected challenges. His team – Clare Freestone, Helen Trompeteler, Georgia Atienza, Constantia Nicolaides, Inga Fraser and Magda Keaney – were constant in their support and interest.

The branding of *Road to 2012* has been led by Denise Vogelsang (working closely in the first year with NB Studio), and the press campaign has been led by Neil Evans – both of whom have regularly collaborated with colleagues at BT and LOCOG.

Laura Down has energetically led the creation of the *Road to 2012* national tour, made possible with the management of Alastair Pickard.

Sarah Ruddick, Editor, has tirelessly led the process to create this wonderful record of the project, with support from her colleagues Rob Carr-Archer and Christopher Tinker.

The Gallery would like to thank the former CEO of the British Olympic Association, Simon Clegg, for introducing the commission team to Olympic sports with such passion. BBC London Olympics correspondent Adrian Warner has been a lively and knowledgeable source of information since the start of the project, as has sports journalist Mike Rowbottom.

At LOCOG, Martin Green, head of the Ceremonies Team, with his colleagues Jenny Hutt and Anna Rodgers, were generous with their time even when under enormous pressure themselves. Film executive Paul Jennings and his colleague Anthony Palmer, previously at the ODA, played a crucial part in helping with access to the Olympic Park and escorting the team on shoots. Shahab Udin, lawyer with the BOA, led the project team through the complexities of athletes' sponsorship and LOCOG branding directives, and his input has been critical in planning the commissions.

The photographers and sitters are the stars of this project, and their collaboration, creative thinking, patience and endurance have resulted in a powerful series of portraits that will make an important contribution to the legacy of London 2012.

PICTURE CREDITS

Unless otherwise stated, all images are copyright © the artist – National Portrait Gallery/BT *Road to 2012* project.

Anderson & Low: 26 (E, F, I – see top right), 51, 63, 69, 70, 72, 73, 125, 126

Jillian Edelstein: 26 (P, L, S – see top right), 39, 41, 45, 49, 55, 68, 95, 97, 100

Katherine Green: 18, 153, 155

Brian Griffin: 2, 8, 26 (K, O, R – see top right), 36, 40, 52, 53, 54, 57, 59, 60, 65, 71, 76, 77, 81, 84, 91, 107, 109, 121, 124

Emma Hardy: 4, 12, 26 (A, N, Q – see top right), 29, 32, 37, 46, 47, 56, 61, 66, 93, 94, 99, 101, 103, 116, 117, 127, 160

Nadav Kander: 26 (G, D – see top right), 33, 105, 113

Finlay MacKay: 6–7, 26 (C, J, M – see top right), 30–1, 34, 35, 42, 43, 74, 75, 79, 82, 83, 85, 86, 87, 88, 89, 123, 128–9, 132, 133

Bettina von Zwehl: 9, 26 (B, H, T – see top right), 38, 67, 106, 111, 112, 114, 115, 119, 120, 130, 131

14, 142 © David Bentley

17, 134 (B – see bottom right) © Rich Hendry

18, 141, 153, 155 © Katherine Green

19l © The National Gallery 2012

19r, 134 (J – see bottom right) © Anna Stübbe

20, 134 (M – see bottom right), 150 © David Robinson

21, 22l, 23t, 24, 25, 134 (A, C, D, E, F, G, H, I, K, L – see bottom right), 144, 148 © Anne Braybon

22r, 145 © Emma Hardy

23b © Figge Art Museum, successors to the Estate of Nan Wood Graham/ Licensed by VAGA, New York, NY. Photo © The Art Institute of Chicago.

136–7 © Anderson & Low

138 © Pierre Maelzer

139 © Jillian Edelstein

140 © Nicola Tree

143 © Brian Griffin

146 © Felicity McCabe

147 © Nadav Kander

149 © Finlay MacKay

151 © Bettina von Zwehl

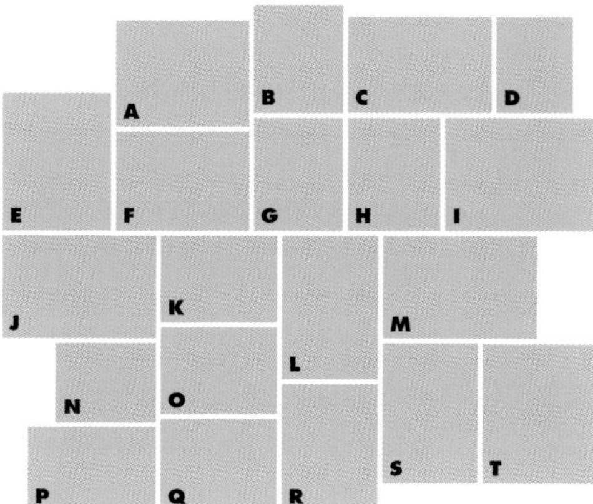

Page 26

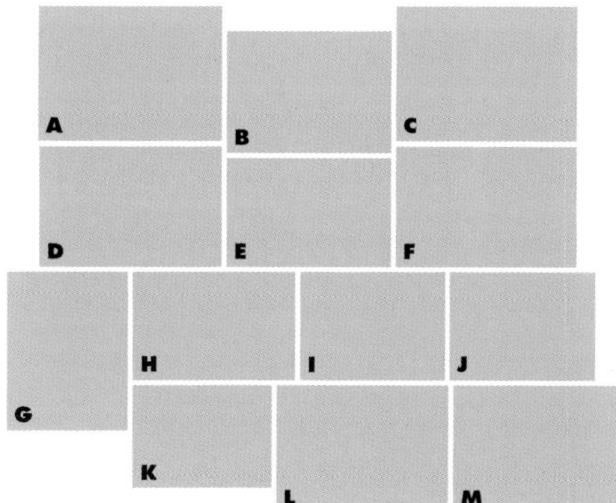

Page 134

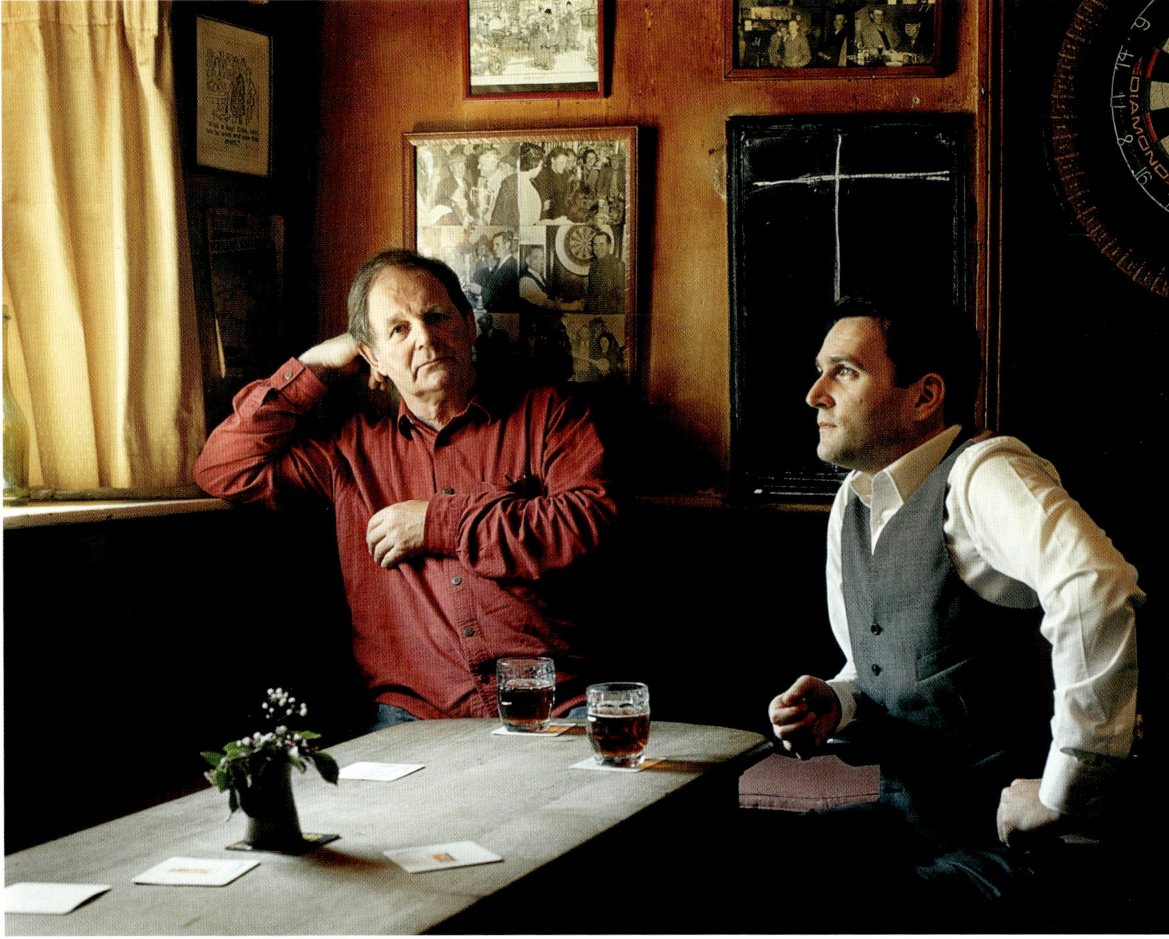

Michael Morpurgo and Greg Nugent, by Emma Hardy

Published in Great Britain by
National Portrait Gallery Publications,
St Martin's Place, London WC2H 0HE

Published to accompany the National Portrait Gallery displays:
Road to 2012: Setting Out (20 July–26 September 2010)
Road to 2012: Changing Pace (25 July–25 September 2011)
Road to 2012: Aiming High (19 July–23 September 2012)

For a complete catalogue of current publications, please write to the National Portrait Gallery at the address above, or visit our website at www.npg.org.uk/publications

'The Project' by Richard McClure with Anne Braybon
Photographers' profiles by Richard McClure
'Local Heroes' by Liz Smith

ISBN 978 1 85514 434 7

10 9 8 7 6 5 4 3 2 1

Managing Editor: Christopher Tinker
Editor: Sarah Ruddick
Assistant Editor: Kate Tolley
Production Manager: Ruth Müller-Wirth
Design: Smith & Gilmour

Front cover: David Weir, by Finlay MacKay (detail)
Back cover: GB Women's Hockey Team, by Anderson & Low
Page 2: David Higgins, Ian Galloway and Sir John Armitt, by Brian Griffin
Page 4: Chris Holmes, by Emma Hardy
Pages 6–7: Andy Triggs Hodge and Pete Reed, by Finlay MacKay
Page 8: Mike Kenny, Jason Kenny and Mick Fee, by Brian Griffin
Page 9: Jessica Ennis, by Bettina von Zwehl

Printed in Italy.

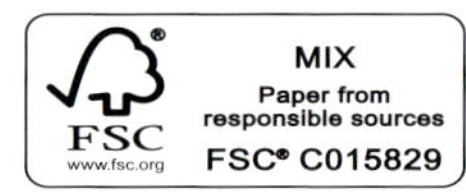